Great Britain. Committee on Homosexual Offences and Prostitution.

Report
of the Committee on
Homosexual Offences
and
Prostitution

Presented to Parliament by the Secretary of State for the Home Department
and the Secretary of State for Scotland
by Command of Her Majesty
September 1957

HQ
76.2
.G7
G74
1976

GREENWOOD PRESS, PUBLISHERS
WESTPORT, CONNECTICUT

207996

Library of Congress Cataloging in Publication Data

Great Britain. Committee on Homosexual Offences and
   Prostitution.
   Report.

   Reprint of the 1957 ed. published by H. M. Stationery
Office, London as cmnd. 247 of Papers by command.
   1. Homosexuality--Great Britain. 2. Prostitution--
Great Britain. I. Series: Great Britain. Parliament.
Papers by command ; cmnd. 247.
HQ76.G7 1976   392.6   76-24924
ISBN 0-8371-8839-3

British Crown copyright. First published by Her Majesty's Stationery Office London 1957. Reprinted by permission of the Controller of Her Britannic Majesty's Stationery Office.

Reprinted in 1976 by Greenwood Press,
a division of Williamhouse-Regency Inc.

Library of Congress Catalog Card Number 76-24924

ISBN 0-8371-8839-3

Printed in the United States of America

MEMBERS OF THE COMMITTEE

SIR JOHN WOLFENDEN, C.B.E. (*Chairman*)
MR. JAMES ADAIR, O.B.E.,
MRS. MARY G. COHEN, O.B.E.,
DR. DESMOND CURRAN,
THE REVD. CANON V. A. DEMANT,
THE HON. MR. JUSTICE DIPLOCK,
SIR HUGH LINSTEAD, O.B.E., M.P.,
THE MARQUESS OF LOTHIAN,
MRS. KATHLEEN LOVIBOND, C.B.E., J.P.,
MR. VICTOR MISHCON, D.L.,
*MR. GORONWY REES,
†THE REVD. R. F. V. SCOTT,
LADY STOPFORD,
MR. WILLIAM T. WELLS, Q.C., M.P.,
DR. JOSEPH WHITBY.

* Resigned, April 1956.
† Resigned, March 1956.

Secretary: MR. W. C. ROBERTS (*Home Office*)

Assistant Secretary: MR. E. J. FREEMAN (*Scottish Home Dept.*)

NOTE.—The estimated cost of preparing this Report is £8,046 of which £735 represents the estimated cost of printing and publication.

CONTENTS

PART ONE.—INTRODUCTORY

Chapter		Paragraphs	Page
I	PROCEDURAL AND GENERAL		
	Terms of Reference	1	7
	Meetings	2–3	7
	Acknowledgments	4–6	7
	Consolidation of the Law	7–8	8
	Scottish Aspects	9–11	8
II	OUR APPROACH TO THE PROBLEM		
	The Function of the Criminal Law	12–15	9
	The Relationship between Law and Public Opinion	16	10

PART TWO.—HOMOSEXUAL OFFENCES

		Paragraphs	Page
III	GENERAL		
	Homosexuality; the Distinction between Propensity and Behaviour	17–24	11
	The Conception of Homosexuality as a "Disease"	25–30	13
	Implications of this conception	31–34	15
	"Invert" and "Pervert"	35	16
	Homosexuality not Peculiar to Particular Professions or Social Classes	36	17
IV	THE EXTENT OF THE PROBLEM		
	Inadequacy of Statistical Information	37–40	17
	The Drawbacks of Quantitative Estimates based on Subjective Evidence	41	18
	Prevalence of Homosexuality in Great Britain at the Present Time	42–47	19
V	THE PRESENT LAW AND PRACTICE		
	(i) *General review*		
	The Function of the Law in this Field	48–49	20
	Homosexual Behaviour between Consenting Adults in Private	50–52	21
	Arguments in Favour of the Present Law Considered and Rejected	53–62	21
	"Consent"	63	25
	"In Private"	64	25
	"Adult"	65–71	25
	Offences by Minors	72–74	27
	The Defence of "Reasonable Cause to Believe"	75	28
	Limits of the Proposed Changes in the Law	76	28
	(ii) *Detailed consideration*		
	Tabular Statement of the Present Law	77	29
	Buggery (Sodomy)	78–94	31
	Indecent Assault	95–103	36
	Gross Indecency between Males	104–114	38
	Blackmail	109–113	39
	Procuring or Attempting to Procure Acts of Gross Indecency	115	42

3

51824   B 2

Chapter		Paragraphs	Page
V	Importuning by Males	116–124	42
(continued)	Bye-law Offences	125–126	45
	Application of General Criminal Law to Homosexual Offences	127	45
	Police Procedures	128–134	46
	Differences between English and Scottish Criminal Procedures	136–143	50
	Offences in Disciplined Services and Establishments	144	53
	Offences by Inmates of Approved Schools	145–147	53
VI	THE TREATMENT OF OFFENDERS		
	The Meaning of "Treatment"	148	54
	The Alternatives to Imprisonment	149–168	54
	Absolute and Conditional Discharge	151	55
	Binding Over	152	55
	Probation	153–157	55
	Fines	158	56
	Borstal Training	159	56
	Detention in a Detention Centre	160	57
	Committal to an Approved School	161	57
	Committal to the Care of a "Fit Person"	162	57
	Attendance at an Attendance Centre	163	58
	Persistent Offenders	164–166	58
	Alternatives in Scotland	167–168	59
	Selection of the Appropriate Method of Disposal	169–172	60
	Disparity in Sentencing	173–177	60
	Committal to Prison "For Treatment"	178–179	61
	The Prison Medical Service	180	62
	Medical Reports	181–189	62
	Therapeutic Measures	190–200	65
	Prison as a Form of Treatment	201–208	69
	Oestrogens	209–211	71
	Castration	212	72
	Note by Medical Members of the Committee—following	212	
VII	PREVENTIVE MEASURES AND RESEARCH		
	Proposals for Research	213–216	77
	Preventive Measures	217–221	77

PART THREE.—PROSTITUTION

		Paragraphs	Page
VIII	GENERAL CONSIDERATIONS		
	Prostitution, the Prostitute and the Law	222–228	79
IX	STREET OFFENCES		
	The Extent of the Problem	229–232	81
	The Present Law	233–248	82
	Defects of the Present Law	249–250	85
	The Requirement to Establish "Annoyance"	251–256	86
	The Prostitute as the Subject of Express Legislation	257–265	87
	Non-urban Areas	266	90
	"Kerb-Crawling"	267	90
	Police Procedures	268–272	90
	Women Police	273	92

Chapter		Paragraphs	Page
IX	Penalties	274–284	92
(*continued*)	Possible Consequences of Amending the Law	285–290	95
	Licensed Brothels	291–296	97
	Research	297	98
X	LIVING ON THE EARNINGS OF PROSTITUTION		
	The Law Stated	298–299	98
	Statistics	300	98
	The Law Considered	301–307	99
XI	PREMISES USED FOR THE PURPOSES OF PROSTITUTION		
	The Law Stated	308–314	101
	The Legal Distinction between Brothels and other Premises used for Prostitution	315–317	103
	Proposals for Amendment of the Law	318–332	104
	Prosecutions by Local Authorities	333–335	108
	Statistics	336	109
XII	PROCURATION		
	The Law Stated	337–341	109
	The Law Considered	342–346	111
	MISCELLANEOUS PROVISIONS		
	Refreshment Houses, &c.	347–351	112
	Aliens	352–353	113
	The Punishment of Offences	354	114

PART FOUR

SUMMARY OF RECOMMENDATIONS	355	115
RESERVATIONS	...	117

APPENDICES

Appendix		Page
I	Statistics relating to Homosexual Offences	130
II	Statistics relating to Prostitution Offences	143
III	Note on the Law relating to Homosexual Offences in European Countries	149
IV	List of Witnesses	152

To:
> The Secretary of State for the Home Department.
> The Secretary of State for Scotland.

REPORT OF THE DEPARTMENTAL COMMITTEE ON HOMOSEXUAL OFFENCES AND PROSTITUTION

PART ONE.—INTRODUCTORY

CHAPTER I
PROCEDURAL AND GENERAL

Terms of Reference
  1. We were appointed on 24th August, 1954, to consider:
  (*a*) the law and practice relating to homosexual offences and the treatment of persons convicted of such offences by the courts; and
  (*b*) the law and practice relating to offences against the criminal law in connection with prostitution and solicitation for immoral purposes,

and to report what changes, if any, are in our opinion desirable.

Meetings
  2. We have met on 62 days, of which 32 were devoted to the oral examination of our witnesses.

  3. Our meetings have been held throughout in private. We were aware of the general kind of criticism directed against the present laws, and we realised that any proposals for changing or retaining any of them would raise issues on which opinion was liable to be swayed by unbalanced or sensational use of what might transpire at our meetings. Further, only in genuinely private session could our witnesses, giving evidence on these delicate and controversial matters, speak to us with the full frankness which the subjects of our enquiry demanded. We decided, therefore, at the outset, that only by meeting in private could we properly conduct the dispassionate and impartial examination of the present law and practice which was required of us.

Acknowledgments
  4. We wish to record our gratitude and appreciation for the help we have received from our many witnesses. A representative list of these will be found in Appendix IV. In addition to those named in that list, there are others, too numerous to be mentioned by name, who have helped us by tendering evidence, either written or oral, on various aspects of the matters with which we were charged to deal. We realise that some of our witnesses put themselves in a position of delicacy in order to assist us in our enquiry, and to them we are especially grateful. We have not invited for oral hearing all those who submitted written evidence, because many of them set out facts or views which had already been presented to us. We were not thereby

attaching any less importance to what they had written to us, but saving them the trouble and ourselves the time which would have been involved if we had asked them to supplement orally their written evidence.

5. We have also had the advantage of access to data collected by the Cambridge University Department of Criminal Science in connection with a survey of sexual offences committed during the year 1947; and by the Oxford University Department of Criminology in connection with a survey of cases in which, during the year 1953, the offender was placed on probation with a requirement to submit to medical treatment. We are grateful to Dr. Leon Radzinowicz, Dr. Max Grünhut and their colleagues for making this material available to us.

6. We also wish to place on record our gratitude to our Secretary, Mr. W. C. Roberts of the Home Office, and our Assistant Secretary, Mr. E. J. Freeman of the Scottish Home Department, for the industry and patience with which they have shown throughout a long and arduous task. Mr. Roberts has been tireless in the help he has given to us, both at our meetings and in the many enquiries he has made, and we are greatly indebted to him for his thoroughness and for the pains he has taken on our behalf. Mr. Freeman has kept valuable notes of our meetings and has supplied us with much necessary information about the law and practice in Scotland. We wish, too, to record our admiration of the skill and accuracy with which the shorthand writers recorded our conversations with witnesses who submitted oral evidence.

Consolidation of the Law

7. Since the date of our appointment, the law dealing with much of the matter under review has, so far as it relates to England and Wales, been consolidated in the Sexual Offences Act, 1956. Accordingly we have, where appropriate, stated the law by reference to this Act rather than by reference to the enactments in force at the time when we were appointed.

8. In the body of the report we have, so far as we have been able to do so consistently with accuracy, stated the law in general terms instead of interrupting the narrative with extracts from the relevant statutes. We have, however, included references to the statutes where this seemed desirable.

Scottish Aspects

9. Throughout our enquiry, we have been conscious that our terms of reference extend to Scotland as well as to England and Wales. We therefore invited and received evidence from Scottish sources and visited Scotland for the purpose of taking evidence.

10. So far as they may be applicable there, our recommendations are intended to apply to Scotland as well as to England and Wales. There are, however, some matters in which Scots law differs from the English, and there are some respects in which the criminal procedure in Scotland differs fundamentally from that which operates in England and Wales.

For example, where homosexual offences are concerned, the law is substantially similar on both sides of the border; but the Scottish system, under which criminal proceedings are in practice instituted only by a public prosecutor, acting in the public interest and subject to the control of the Lord Advocate, makes for a uniformity of practice in regard to the prosecution of these offences that is absent in England and Wales. And the fact that all but the most serious of these offences may be dealt with summarily in the Sheriff courts, with a limited maximum penalty, makes for greater uniformity of sentence than is apparent in England and Wales.

As regards prostitution, the laws relating to loitering or importuning for the purposes of prostitution which are in force in the Scottish burghs differ fundamentally from those in force in the English towns in that it is not necessary to establish, for the purposes of a conviction, that annoyance was caused to residents or passers-by.

Accordingly, some of our recommendations apply only to England and Wales; and some of our criticisms have less force, and some of our other recommendations less application, in relation to Scotland than they have in relation to England and Wales.

11. In several places in the report we have quoted decisions of the courts on the interpretation of the statutory or common law. Not all the points decided by the English courts have been decided by the Scottish courts; and while the courts on either side of the border always pay great attention to the decisions of those on the other, they do not necessarily follow them. If, therefore, a particular statute applies to both England and Scotland, or a statute which applies to England is paralleled by a similar provision applicable to Scotland, the courts will not necessarily interpret the law in the same way in the two countries. Where, however, the statutes relating to the matters with which we are concerned are similarly framed in regard both to England and to Scotland, it seems unlikely that the Scottish courts would differ substantially from the English courts in their interpretation of them.

CHAPTER II

Our Approach to the Problem

12. It will be apparent from our terms of reference that we are concerned throughout with the law and offences against it. We clearly recognise that the laws of any society must be acceptable to the general moral sense of the community if they are to be respected and enforced. But we are not charged to enter into matters of private moral conduct except in so far as they directly affect the public good; nor does our commission extend to assessing the teaching of theology, sociology or psychology on these matters, though on many points we have found their conclusions very relevant to our thinking.

13. Further, we do not consider it to be within our province or competence to make a full examination of the moral, social, psychological and biological causes of homosexuality or prostitution, or of the many theories advanced about these causes. Our primary duty has been to consider the extent to which homosexual behaviour and female prostitution should come under the condemnation of the criminal law, and this has presented us with the difficulty of deciding what are the essential elements of a criminal offence. There appears to be no unquestioned definition of what constitutes or ought to constitute a crime. To define it as " an act which is punished by the State " does not answer the question: What acts ought to be punished by the State? We have therefore worked with our own formulation of the function of the criminal law so far as it concerns the subjects of this enquiry. In this field, its function, as we see it, is to preserve public order and decency, to protect the citizen from what is offensive or injurious, and to provide sufficient

safeguards against exploitation and corruption of others, particularly those who are specially vulnerable because they are young, weak in body or mind, inexperienced, or in a state of special physical, official or economic dependence.

14. It is not, in our view, the function of the law to intervene in the private lives of citizens, or to seek to enforce any particular pattern of behaviour, further than is necessary to carry out the purposes we have outlined. It follows that we do not believe it to be a function of the law to attempt to cover all the fields of sexual behaviour. Certain forms of sexual behaviour are regarded by many as sinful, morally wrong, or objectionable for reasons of conscience, or of religious or cultural tradition; and such actions may be reprobated on these grounds. But the criminal law does not cover all such actions at the present time; for instance, adultery and fornication are not offences for which a person can be punished by the criminal law. Nor indeed is prostitution as such.

15. We appreciate that opinions will differ as to what is offensive, injurious or inimical to the common good, and also as to what constitutes exploitation or corruption; and that these opinions will be based on moral, social or cultural standards. We have been guided by our estimate of the standards of the community in general, recognising that they will not be accepted by all citizens, and that our estimate of them may be mistaken.

16. We have had to consider the relationship between the law and public opinion. It seems to us that there are two over-definite views about this. On the one hand, it is held that the law ought to follow behind public opinion, so that the law can count on the support of the community as a whole. On the other hand, it is held that a necessary purpose of the law is to lead or fortify public opinion. Certainly it is clear that if any legal enactment is markedly out of tune with public opinion it will quickly fall into disrepute. Beyond this we should not wish to dogmatise, for on the matters with which we are called upon to deal we have not succeeded in discovering an unequivocal "public opinion," and we have felt bound to try to reach conclusions for ourselves rather than to base them on what is often transient and seldom precisely ascertainable.

PART TWO.—HOMOSEXUAL OFFENCES

CHAPTER III

Homosexuality

17. We are concerned, in this part of our enquiry, with homosexual offences. Any lengthy or detailed study of the nature or origins of homosexuality would, in our view, have fallen outside our terms of reference, even if we had felt ourselves qualified to embark upon it. Nevertheless, since we are concerned also with the treatment of those who have been convicted of homosexual offences we have found it necessary to acquaint ourselves with at least the elements of the subject in general, and the following paragraphs set out some of the points and problems which have been raised in our discussions. We owe much to the evidence of our medical witnesses and, in the interpretation and assessment of that evidence, to our own medical colleagues, to whom the non-medical members of the Committee are greatly indebted.

18. It is important to make a clear distinction between "homosexual offences" and "homosexuality." The former are enumerated in paragraph 77 below. For the latter, we are content to rely on the dictionary definition that homosexuality is a sexual propensity for persons of one's own sex. Homosexuality, then, is a state or condition, and as such does not, and cannot, come within the purview of the criminal law.

19. This definition of homosexuality involves the adoption of some criteria for its recognition. As in other psychological fields, an inference that the propensity exists may be derived from either subjective or objective data, that is, either from what is felt or from what is done by the persons concerned. Either method may lead to fallacious results. In the first place, introspection is neither exhaustive nor infallible; an individual may quite genuinely not be aware of either the existence or the strength of his motivations and propensities, and there is a natural reluctance to acknowledge, even to oneself, a preference which is socially condemned, or to admit to acts that are illegal and liable to a heavy penalty. Rationalisation and self-deception can be carried to great lengths, and in certain circumstances lying is also to be expected. Secondly, some of those whose main sexual propensity is for persons of the opposite sex indulge, for a variety of reasons, in homosexual acts. It is known, for example, that some men who are placed in special circumstances that prohibit contact with the opposite sex (for instance, in prisoner-of-war camps or prisons) indulge in homosexual acts, though they revert to heterosexual behaviour when opportunity affords; and it is clear from our evidence that some men who are not predominantly homosexual lend themselves to homosexual practices for financial or other gain. Conversely, many homosexual persons have heterosexual intercourse with or without homosexual fantasies. Furthermore, a homosexual tendency may not be manifested exclusively, or even at all, in sexual fields of behaviour, as we explain in paragraph 23 below.

20. There is the further problem how widely the description "homosexual" should be applied. According to the psycho-analytic school, a homosexual component (sometimes conscious, often not) exists in everybody; and if this is correct homosexuality in this sense is universal. Without going so far as to accept this view *in toto*, it is possible to realise that the issue of latent homosexuality, which we discuss more fully in paragraph 24 below, is relevant to any assessment of the frequency of occurrence of the condition of homosexuality. However, for the purposes of the main body of our report,

and in connection with our recommendations, we are strictly speaking concerned only with those who, for whatever reason, commit homosexual offences.

21. In spite of difficulties such as those we have mentioned in the preceding paragraphs, there is a general measure of agreement on two propositions: (i) that there exists in certain persons a homosexual propensity which varies quantitatively in different individuals and can also vary quantitatively in the same individual at different epochs of life; (ii) that this propensity can affect behaviour in a variety of ways, some of which are not obviously sexual; although exactly how much and in what ways may be matters for disagreement and dispute.

22. The first of these propositions means that homosexuality as a propensity is not an "all or none" condition, and this view has been abundantly confirmed by the evidence submitted to us. All gradations can exist from apparently exclusive homosexuality without any conscious capacity for arousal by heterosexual stimuli to apparently exclusive heterosexuality, though in the latter case there may be transient and minor homosexual inclinations, for instance in adolescence. According to the psycho-analytic school, all individuals pass through a homosexual phase. Be this as it may, we would agree that a transient homosexual phase in development is very common and should usually cause neither surprise nor concern.

It is interesting that the late Dr. Kinsey, in his study entitled "The Sexual Behaviour of the Human Male," formulated this homosexual-heterosexual continuum on a 7-point scale, with a rating of 6 for sexual arousal and activity with other males only, 3 for arousals and acts equally with either sex, 0 for exclusive heterosexuality, and intermediate ratings accordingly. The recognition of the existence of this continuum is, in our opinion, important for two reasons. First, it leads to the conclusion that homosexuals cannot reasonably be regarded as quite separate from the rest of mankind. Secondly, as will be discussed later, it has some relevance in connection with claims made for the success of various forms of treatment.

23. As regards the second proposition, we have already pointed out that a distinction should be drawn between the condition of homosexuality (which relates to the direction of sexual preference) and the acts or behaviour resulting from this preference. It is possible to draw a further distinction between behaviour which is overtly sexual and behaviour, not overtly sexual, from which a latent homosexuality can be inferred.

It must not be thought that the existence of the homosexual propensity necessarily leads to homosexual behaviour of an overtly sexual kind. Even where it does, this behaviour does not necessarily amount to a homosexual offence; for instance, solitary masturbation with homosexual fantasies is probably the most common homosexual act. Many persons, though they are aware of the existence within themselves of the propensity, and though they may be conscious of sexual arousal in the presence of homosexual stimuli, successfully control their urges towards overtly homosexual acts with others, either because of their ethical standards or from fear of social or penal consequences, so that their homosexual condition never manifests itself in overtly sexual behaviour. There are others who, though aware of the existence within themselves of the propensity, are helped by a happy family life, a satisfying vocation, or a well-balanced social life to live happily without any urge to indulge in homosexual acts. Our evidence suggests however that complete continence in the homosexual is relatively uncommon—as, indeed, it is in the heterosexual—and that even where the individual is by disposition continent, self-control may break down temporarily under the influence of factors like alcohol, emotional, distress or mental or physical disorder or disease.

24. Moreover, it is clear that homosexuals differ one from another in the extent to which they are aware of the existence within themselves of the propensity. Some are, indeed, quite unaware of it, and where this is so the homosexuality is technically described as latent, its existence being inferred from the individual's behaviour in spheres not obviously sexual. Although there is room for dispute as to the extent and variety of behaviour of this kind which may legitimately be included in the making of this inference, there is general agreement that the existence of a latent homosexuality is an inference validly to be drawn in certain cases. Sometimes, for example, a doctor can infer a homosexual component which accounts for the condition of a patient who has consulted him because of some symptom, discomfort or difficulty, though the patient himself is completely unaware of the existence within himself of any homosexual inclinations. There are other cases in which the existence of a latent homosexuality may be inferred from an individual's outlook or judgment; for instance, a persistent and indignant preoccupation with the subject of homosexuality has been taken to suggest in some cases the existence of repressed homosexuality. Thirdly, among those who work with notable success in occupations which call for service to others, there are some in whom a latent homosexuality provides the motivation for activities of the greatest value to society. Examples of this are to be found among teachers, clergy, nurses and those who are interested in youth movements and the care of the aged.

25. We believe that there would be a wide measure of agreement on the general account of homosexuality and its manifestations that we have given above. On the other hand, the general position which we have tried to summarise permits the drawing of many different inferences, not all of them in our opinion justified. Especially is this so in connection with the concept of "disease." There is a tendency, noticeably increasing in strength over recent years, to label homosexuality as a "disease" or "illness." This may be no more than a particular manifestation of a general tendency discernible in modern society by which, as one leading sociologist puts it, "the concept of illness expands continually at the expense of the concept of moral failure."[1] There are two important practical consequences which are often thought to follow from regarding homosexuality as an illness. The first is that those in whom the condition exists are sick persons and should therefore be regarded as medical problems and consequently as primarily a medical responsibility. The second is that sickness implies irresponsibility, or at least diminished responsibility. Hence it becomes important in this connection to examine the criteria of "disease," and also to examine the claim that these consequences follow.

26. We are informed that there is no legal definition of "disease" or "disease of the mind"; that there is no precise medical definition of disease which covers all its varieties; that health and ill-health are relative terms which merge into each other, the "abnormal" being often a matter of degree or of what is accepted as the permissible range of normal variation; and that doctors are often called upon to deal not only with recognisable diseases, but also with problems of attitude and with anomalies of character and instinct.

The traditional view seems to be that for a condition to be recognised as a disease, three criteria must be satisfied, namely (i) the presence of

---

[1] Barbara Wootton: "Sickness or Sin." The Twentieth Century, May 1956.

abnormal symptoms, which are caused by (ii) a demonstrable pathological condition, in turn caused by (iii) some factor called "the cause," each link in this causal chain being understood as something necessarily antecedent to the next. An example would be the invasion of the body by diphtheria bacilli, leading to pathological changes, leading to the symptoms of diphtheria.

While we have found this traditional view a convenient basis for our consideration of the question whether or not homosexuality is a disease, it must be recognised that the three criteria, as formulated above, are over-simplified, and that each needs some modification. Moreover, there are conditions now recognised as diseases though they do not satisfy all three criteria. Our evidence suggests, however, that homosexuality does not satisfy any of them unless the terms in which they are defined are expanded beyond what could reasonably be regarded as legitimate.

27. In relation, first, to the presence of abnormal symptoms, it is nowadays recognised that many people behave in an unusual, extraordinary or socially unacceptable way, but it seems to us that it would be rash to assume that unorthodox or aberrant behaviour is necessarily symptomatic of disease if it is the only symptom that can be demonstrated. To make this assumption would be to underestimate the very wide range of "normal" human behaviour, and abundant evidence is available that what is socially acceptable or ethically permissible has varied and still varies considerably in different cultures. From the medical standpoint, the existence of significant abnormality can seldom be diagnosed from the mere exhibition of unusual behaviour, be this criminal or not, the diagnosis depending on the presence of associated symptoms. Further, a particular form of behaviour, taken by itself, can seem to be within the range of the normal but may nevertheless be symptomatic of abnormality, the abnormality consisting in (i) the intensity and duration of the symptoms, (ii) their combination together, and (iii) the circumstances in which they arise. Certain mental diseases, for example, can be diagnosed by the mere association of symptoms to form a recognised psychiatric syndrome, an example of this being schizophrenia, which has no known or generally accepted physical pathology. On the criterion of symptoms, however, homosexuality cannot legitimately be regarded as a disease, because in many cases it is the only symptom and is compatible with full mental health in other respects. In some cases, associated psychiatric abnormalities do occur, and it seems to us that if, as has been suggested, they occur with greater frequency in the homosexual, this may be because they are products of the strain and conflict brought about by the homosexual condition and not because they are causal factors. It has been suggested to us that associated psychiatric abnormalities are less prominent, or even absent, in countries where the homosexual is regarded with more tolerance.

28. As regards the second criterion, namely, the presence of a demonstrable pathological condition, some, though not all, cases of mental illness are accompanied by a demonstrable physical pathology. We have heard no convincing evidence that this has yet been demonstrated in relation to homosexuality. Biochemical and endocrine studies so far carried out in this field have, it appears, proved negative, and investigations of body-build and the like have also so far proved inconclusive. We are aware that studies carried out on sets of twins suggest that certain genes lay down a potentiality which will lead to homosexuality in the person who possesses them, but even if this were established (and the results of these studies have not commanded universal acceptance), a genetic predisposition would not necessarily amount to a pathological condition, since it may be no more than a natural biological variation comparable with variations in stature, hair pigmentation, handedness and so on.

In the absence of a physical pathology, psychopathological theories have been constructed to explain the symptoms of various forms of abnormal behaviour or mental illness. These theories range from rather primitive formulations like a repressed complex or a mental " abscess " to elaborate systems. They are theoretical constructions to explain observed facts, not the facts themselves, and similar theories have been constructed to explain " normal " behaviour. These theoretical constructions differ from school to school. The alleged psychopathological causes adduced for homosexuality have, however, also been found to occur in others besides the homosexual.

29. As regards the third criterion, that is, the " cause," there is never a single cause for normal behaviour, abnormal behaviour or mental illness. The causes are always multiple. Even the invasion of the body by diphtheria bacilli does not of itself lead to the disease of diphtheria, as is shown by the existence of " carriers " of live diphtheria bacilli. To speak, as some do, of some single factor such as seduction in youth as the " cause " of homosexuality is unrealistic unless other factors are taken into account. Besides genetic predisposition, a number of such factors have been suggested, for instance, unbalanced family relationships, faulty sex education, or lack of opportunity for heterosexual contacts in youth. In the present state of our knowledge, none of these can be held to bear a specific causal relationship to any recognised psychopathology or physical pathology; and to assert a direct and specific causal relationship between these factors and the homosexual condition is to ignore the fact that they have all, including seduction, been observed to occur in persons who become entirely heterosexual in their disposition.

30. Besides the notion of homosexuality as a disease, there have been alternative hypotheses offered by others of our expert witnesses. Some have preferred to regard it as a state of arrested development. Some, particularly among the biologists, regard it as simply a natural deviation. Others, again, regard it as a universal potentiality which can develop in response to a variety of factors.

We do not consider ourselves qualified to pronounce on controversial and scientific problems of this kind, but we feel bound to say that the evidence put before us has not established to our satisfaction the proposition that homosexuality is a disease. Medical witnesses have, however, stressed the point, and it is an important one, that in some cases homosexual offences do occur as symptoms in the course of recognised mental or physical illness, for example, senile dementia. We have the impression, too, that those whose homosexual offences stem from some mental illness or defect behave in a way which increases their chances of being caught.

31. Even if it could be established that homosexuality were a disease, it is clear that many individuals, however their state is reached, present social rather than medical problems and must be dealt with by social, including penological, methods. This is especially relevant when the claim that homosexuality is an illness is taken to imply that its treatment should be a medical responsibility. Much more important than the academic question whether homosexuality is a disease is the practical question whether a doctor should carry out any part or all of the treatment. Psychiatrists deal regularly with problems of personality which are not regarded as diseases, and conversely the treatment of cases of recognised psychiatric illness may not be strictly medical but may best be carried out by non-medical supervision or environmental change. Examples would be certain cases of senile dementia or chronic schizophrenia which can best be managed at home. In fact, the treatment of behaviour disorders, even when medically supervised, is rarely

confined to psychotherapy or to treatment of a strictly medical kind. This is not to deny that expert advice should be sought in very many homosexual cases. We shall have something more to say on these matters in connection with the treatment of offenders.

32. The claim that homosexuality is an illness carries the further implication that the sufferer cannot help it and therefore carries a diminished responsibility for his actions. Even if it were accepted that homosexuality could properly be described as a "disease," we should not accept this corollary. There are no *prima facie* grounds for supposing that because a particular person's sexual propensity happens to lie in the direction of persons of his or her own sex it is any less controllable than that of those whose propensity is for persons of the opposite sex. We are informed that patients in mental hospitals, with few exceptions, show clearly by their behaviour that they can and do exercise a high degree of responsibility and self-control; for example, only a small minority need to be kept in locked wards. The existence of varying degrees of self-control is a matter of daily experience— the extent to which coughing can be controlled is an example—and the capacity for self-control can vary with the personality structure or with temporary physical or emotional conditions. The question which is important for us here is whether the individual suffers from a condition which causes diminished responsibility. This is a different question from the question whether he was responsible in the past for the causes or origins of his present condition. That is an interesting enquiry and may be of relevance in other connections; but our concern is with the behaviour which flows from the individual's present condition and with the extent to which he is responsible for that behaviour, whatever may have been the causes of the condition from which it springs. Just as expert opinion can give valuable assistance in deciding on the appropriate ways of dealing with a convicted person, so can it help in assessing the additional factors that may affect his present responsibility.

33. Some psychiatrists have made the point that homosexual behaviour in some cases may be "compulsive," that is, irresistible, but there seems to be no good reason to suppose that at least in the majority of cases homosexual acts are any more or any less resistible than heterosexual acts, and other evidence would be required to sustain such a view in any individual case. Even if immunity from penal sanctions on such grounds were claimed or granted, nevertheless preventive measures would have to be taken for the sake of society at large, in much the same way as it is necessary to withhold a driving licence from a person who is subject to epileptic fits. This is particularly true of the offender who is a very bad risk for recurrence, but is not certifiable either as insane or as a mental defective.

34. When questions of treatment or disposal of offenders are being considered, the assessment of prognosis is very important, and expert advice may need to be sought on such questions as whether the factors that in view of the doctors lead to diminished control, that is, diminished "responsibility," are capable of modification, or what environmental changes should be advocated or ordered to reduce the chances of a recurrence. Thus it is just as reasonable for a doctor to recommend that a paedophiliac should give up schoolmastering as it would be to recommend to another patient never to return to a hot climate.

35. Some writers on the subject, and some of our witnesses, have drawn a distinction between the "invert" and the "pervert." We have not found this distinction very useful. It suggests that it is possible to distinguish between two men who commit the same offence, the one as the result of his

constitution, the other from a perverse and deliberate choice, with the further suggestion that the former is in some sense less culpable than the latter. To make this distinction as a matter of definition seems to prejudge a very difficult question.

Similarly, we have avoided the use of the terms "natural" and "unnatural" in relation to sexual behaviour, for they depend for their force upon certain explicit theological or philosophical interpretations, and without these interpretations their use imports an approving or a condemnatory note into a discussion where dispassionate thought and statement should not be hindered by adherence to particular preconceptions.

36. Homosexuality is not, in spite of widely held belief to the contrary, peculiar to members of particular professions or social classes; nor, as is sometimes supposed, is it peculiar to the *intelligentsia*. Our evidence shows that it exists among all callings and at all levels of society; and that among homosexuals will be found not only those possessing a high degree of intelligence, but also the dullest oafs.

Some homosexuals, it is true, choose to follow occupations which afford opportunities for contact with those of their own sex, and it is not unnatural that those who feel themselves to be "misfits" in society should gravitate towards occupations offering an atmosphere of tolerance or understanding, with the result that some occupations may appear to attract more homosexuals than do others. Again, the arrest of a prominent national or local figure has greater news value than the arrest of (say) a labourer for a similar offence, and in consequence the Press naturally finds room for a report of the one where it might not find room for a report of the other. Factors such as these may well account to some extent for the prevalent misconceptions.

CHAPTER IV

The Extent of the Problem

37. Our consideration of the problems we have had to face would have been made much easier if it had been possible to arrive at some reasonably firm estimate of the prevalence either of the condition of homosexuality or of the commission of homosexual acts. So far as we have been able to discover, there is no precise information about the number of men in Great Britain who either have a homosexual disposition or engage in homosexual behaviour.

38. No enquiries have been made in this country comparable to those which the late Dr. Kinsey conducted in the United States of America. Dr. Kinsey concluded that in the United States, 4 per cent. of adult white males are exclusively homosexual throughout their lives after the onset of adolescence. He also found evidence to suggest that 10 per cent. of the white male population are more or less exclusively homosexual for at least three years between the ages of sixteen and sixty-five, and that 37 per cent. of the total male population have at least some overt homosexual experience, to the point of orgasm, between adolescence and old age. Dr. Kinsey's findings have aroused opposition and scepticism. But it was noteworthy that some of our medical witnesses expressed the view that something very like these figures would be established in this country if similar enquiries were made. The majority, while stating quite frankly that they did not really know, indicated that their impression was that his figures would be on the high side for Great Britain.

39. A recent enquiry in Sweden suggested that 1 per cent. of all men were exclusively homosexual and 4 per cent. had both homosexual and heterosexual impulses, and we were interested to learn from official sources in Sweden that other information available seemed to indicate that these figures were too low. But here again, there is no evidence that similar enquiries in this country would yield similar results.

40. Such statistical information as we have been able to obtain about incidence in this country has been extracted almost entirely from criminal and medical records. It is obvious that only a minority of homosexuals, or, for that matter, of those who indulge in homosexual acts, fall into the hands of the police, and it is likely also that only a minority of such persons find their way to the doctor's consulting room. But it is impossible to determine what proportion of the persons concerned these minorities represent; still less, on this evidence, what proportion of the total population falls within the description " homosexual." These figures, therefore, cannot be relied on as an indication of the extent of homosexuality or homosexual behaviour among the community as a whole. The only figures relating to the systematic examination of anything like a " normal " sample in this country were provided by one of our witnesses, a psychologist, who had examined 100 male undergraduates and found that 30 of them had had homosexual trends and fantasies at some time in their lives and that five of these still retained them at the age of 20-plus. Our witness, while certainly not prepared to say that none of the five would outgrow their condition, felt that such a change was unlikely. This sample is, however, neither sufficiently large nor sufficiently representative of the population as a whole to enable any valid conclusions to be drawn.

41. It is tempting to construct hypotheses, on the basis of one or other of the sets of figures we have mentioned, about the prevalence of homosexuality or homosexual behaviour. But it is very dangerous to do so because, as we have said earlier, there can be no guarantee either that the individuals selected for study have told the whole truth or that when they have tried to do so their introspection has been accurate or complete. Moreover, the capacity for self-expression varies considerably as between one individual and another; dull and inarticulate persons are often unable to give more than the crudest account of their psychosexual reactions, and an accurate assessment of propensities or of the significance of behaviour is correspondingly difficult. Quantitative estimates based on subjective evidence of this sort are therefore in themselves liable to a considerable degree of error; and when applied to the population as a whole the final result may be dangerously misleading.[1]

---

[1] At a meeting of the Psychiatric Section of the Royal Society of Medicine held on 9th April, 1957, the subject for discussion was " Homosexuality." Dr. Denis Parr concluded his opening paper with the following words, which he has kindly allowed us to quote:—

"Having begun by deprecating the surfeit of speculation in the literature on homosexuality, I should like to end with some highly speculative arithmetic.

If the incidence of homosexuality in different age groups in the male population of England and Wales was the same as in the groups of in-patients we have studied, and if the average figure of 15 criminal acts a year each applied to all these homosexuals, then the ratio of criminal acts to known indictable homosexual crime would be of the order of 2,500 to 1. To take another series of assumptions, if the Kinsey findings were true of England and Wales, then within the age group 21 to 30 only, this ratio would be 30,000 to 1.

Such fanciful figures may be of little more than journalistic value. Their exact validity, however, is less important than the fact that there is an almost astronomical disparity between the numbers of illicit sexual acts that occur, and those that are detected and prosecuted by the guardians of the law. Perhaps on this point—if on no other—we can all agree."

42. It is widely believed that the prevalence of homosexuality in this country has greatly increased during the past fifty years and that homosexual behaviour is much more frequent than used to be the case. It is certainly true that the whole subject of homosexuality is much more freely discussed to-day than it was formerly; but this is not in itself evidence that homosexuality is to-day more prevalent, or homosexual behaviour more widespread, than it was when mention of it was less common. Sexual matters in general are more openly talked about to-day than they were in the days of our parents and grandparents; and it is not surprising that homosexuality should take its place, among other sexual topics, in this wider range of permissible subjects of conversation. Public interest in the subject has undoubtedly increased, with the consequences that court cases are more frequently reported and that responsible papers and magazines give considerable space to its discussion. In general literature, too, there is a growing number of works dealing incidentally or entirely with the subject. All this has no doubt led to a much greater public awareness of the phenomenon and its manifestations. But it does not necessarily follow that the behaviour which is so discussed is more widespread than it was before.

43. It is certainly true also, as will be seen from Table I in Appendix I of this report, that the number of homosexual offences known to the police has increased considerably. It does not, however, necessarily follow from these figures that there has been an increase either in homosexuality or in homosexual behaviour; still less can these figures be regarded as an infallible measure of any increase which may have occurred during that period. Unlike some offences (*e.g.*, housebreaking) which, by their nature, tend to be reported to the police as they occur, many sexual offences, particularly those taking place between consenting parties, become " known to the police " only when they are detected by the police or happen to be reported to them. Any figures relating to homosexual offences known to the police will therefore be conditioned to a large extent both by the efficiency of the police methods of detecting and recording, and by the intensity of police activity. These factors vary from time to time and from place to place.

Clearly, the more efficient the police methods of detection, the higher the proportion of offences detected. It was to be expected that the more intensive training given to police officers in recent years, particularly in methods of detection, would result in the discovery of a higher proportion of offences; but this does not necessarily indicate that more offences have occurred. We understand, too, that efforts have been made in recent years to improve the methods by which offences known to the police are recorded, and these may have been reflected in higher figures without any necessary implication of a higher number of offences. Lastly, the extent to which the police follow up suspicions of homosexual behaviour varies considerably as between one police force and another according to the outlook of the senior officers; and sometimes even within a given police force the intensity of action varies from time to time along with the ups and downs of public indignation aroused, or public annoyance caused, by the behaviour of the offenders.

In brief, therefore, it would be dangerous to argue from the police statistics alone either that there was an overall increase or that homosexual behaviour was most prevalent in those areas where the number of cases recorded as known to the police was the highest.

44. Some of us have a definite impression, derived from what we have observed or read, and by inference from the tenor of evidence submitted to us, that there has been an increase in the amount of homosexual behaviour. Others of us prefer, in the absence of conclusive evidence, not to commit themselves to expressing even a general impression.

45. Those who have the impression of a growth in homosexual practices find it supported by at least three wider considerations. First, in the general loosening of former moral standards, it would not be surprising to find that leniency towards sexual irregularities in general included also an increased tolerance of homosexual behaviour and that greater tolerance had encouraged the practice. Secondly, the conditions of war time, with broken families and prolonged separation of the sexes, may well have occasioned homosexual behaviour which in some cases has been carried over into peace time. Thirdly, it is likely that the emotional insecurity, community instability and weakening of the family, inherent in the social changes of our civilisation, have been factors contributing to an increase in homosexual behaviour.

Most of us think it improbable that the increase in the number of offences recorded as known to the police can be explained entirely by greater police activity, though we all think it very unlikely that homosexual behaviour has increased proportionately to the dramatic rise in the number of offences recorded as known to the police.

46. Our medical evidence seems to show three things: first, that in general practice male homosexuals form a very small fraction of the doctor's patients; secondly, that in psychiatric practice male homosexuality is a primary problem in a very small proportion of the cases seen; and thirdly, that only a very small percentage of homosexuals consult doctors about their condition. It is almost impossible to compare the incidence of homosexual behaviour with the incidence of other forms of sexual irregularity, most of which are outside the purview of the criminal law and are therefore not recorded in criminal statistics; our impression is that of the total amount of irregular sexual conduct, homosexual behaviour provides only a very small proportion. It cannot, however, be ignored. The male population of Great Britain over the age of fifteen numbers nearly eighteen million, and even if the Swedish figures quoted in paragraph 39 above, which are the lowest figures relating to incidence that have come to our notice, are at all applicable to this country, the incidence of homosexuality and homosexual behaviour must be large enough to present a serious problem.

47. Our conclusion is that homosexual behaviour is practised by a small minority of the population, and should be seen in proper perspective, neither ignored nor given a disproportionate amount of public attention. Especially are we concerned that the principles we have enunciated above on the function of the law should apply to those involved in homosexual behaviour no more and no less than to other persons.

CHAPTER V

The Present Law and Practice

(i) General Review

48. It is against the foregoing background that we have reviewed the existing provisions of the law in relation to homosexual behaviour between male persons. We have found that with the great majority of these provisions we are in complete agreement. We believe that it is part of the function of the law to safeguard those who need protection by reason of their youth or some mental defect, and we do not wish to see any change in the law that would weaken this protection. Men who commit offences against such persons should be treated as criminal offenders. Whatever may be the causes

of their disposition or the proper treatment for it, the law must assume that the responsibility for the overt acts remains theirs, except where there are circumstances which it accepts as exempting from accountability. Offences of this kind are particularly reprehensible when the men who commit them are in positions of special responsibility or trust. We have been made aware that where a man is involved in an offence with a boy or youth the invitation to the commission of the act sometimes comes from him rather than from the man. But we believe that even when this is so that fact does not serve to exculpate the man.

49. It is also part of the function of the law to preserve public order and decency. We therefore hold that when homosexual behaviour between males takes place in public it should continue to be dealt with by the criminal law. Not all the elements in the apprehension of offenders, or in their trial, seem to us to be satisfactory, and on these points we comment later. But so far as the law itself is concerned we should not wish to see any major change in relation to this type of offence.

50. Besides the two categories of offence we have just mentioned, namely, offences committed by adults with juveniles and offences committed in public places, there is a third class of offence to which we have had to give long and careful consideration. It is that of homosexual acts committed between adults in private.

51. In England and Wales, during the three years ended March 1956, 480 men aged twenty-one or over were convicted of offences committed in private with consenting partners also aged twenty-one or over. Of these, however, 121 were also convicted of, or admitted, offences in public places (parks, open spaces, lavatories, &c.), and 59 were also convicted of, or admitted, offences with partners under twenty-one. In Scotland, during the same period, 9 men over twenty-one were convicted of offences committed in private with consenting adult partners. Of these, one also admitted offences in public places and one admitted offences with a partner under twenty-one. Thus 307 men (300 in England and Wales and 7 in Scotland), guilty as far as is known only of offences committed in private with consenting adult partners, were convicted by the courts during this period. Tables VI and XI in Appendix I show how the 307 offenders were dealt with by the courts.

52. We have indicated (in Chapter II above) our opinion as to the province of the law and its sanctions, and how far it properly applies to the sexual behaviour of the individual citizen. On the basis of the considerations there advanced we have reached the conclusion that legislation which covers acts in the third category we have mentioned goes beyond the proper sphere of the law's concern. We do not think that it is proper for the law to concern itself with what a man does in private unless it can be shown to be so contrary to the public good that the law ought to intervene in its function as the guardian of that public good.

53. In considering whether homosexual acts between consenting adults in private should cease to be criminal offences we have examined the more serious arguments in favour of retaining them as such. We now set out these arguments and our reasons for disagreement with them. In favour of retaining the present law, it has been contended that homosexual behaviour between adult males, in private no less than in public, is contrary to the public good on the grounds that—

(i) it menaces the health of society;

(ii) it has damaging effects on family life;

(iii) a man who indulges in these practices with another man may turn his attention to boys.

54. As regards the first of these arguments, it is held that conduct of this kind is a cause of the demoralisation and decay of civilisations, and that therefore, unless we wish to see our nation degenerate and decay, such conduct must be stopped, by every possible means. We have found no evidence to support this view, and we cannot feel it right to frame the laws which should govern this country in the present age by reference to hypothetical explanations of the history of other peoples in ages distant in time and different in circumstances from our own. In so far as the basis of this argument can be precisely formulated, it is often no more than the expression of revulsion against what is regarded as unnatural, sinful or disgusting. Many people feel this revulsion, for one or more of these reasons. But moral conviction or instinctive feeling, however strong, is not a valid basis for overriding the individual's privacy and for bringing within the ambit of the criminal law private sexual behaviour of this kind. It is held also that if such men are employed in certain professions or certain branches of the public service their private habits may render them liable to threats of blackmail or to other pressures which may make them "bad security risks." If this is true, it is true also of some other categories of person: for example, drunkards, gamblers and those who become involved in compromising situations of a heterosexual kind; and while it may be a valid ground for excluding from certain forms of employment men who indulge in homosexual behaviour, it does not, in our view, constitute a sufficient reason for making their private sexual behaviour an offence in itself.

55. The second contention, that homosexual behaviour between males has a damaging effect on family life, may well be true. Indeed, we have had evidence that it often is; cases in which homosexual behaviour on the part of the husband has broken up a marriage are by no means rare, and there are also cases in which a man in whom the homosexual component is relatively weak nevertheless derives such satisfaction from homosexual outlets that he does not enter upon a marriage which might have been successfully and happily consummated. We deplore this damage to what we regard as the basic unit of society; but cases are also frequently encountered in which a marriage has been broken up by homosexual behaviour on the part of the wife, and no doubt some women, too, derive sufficient satisfaction from homosexual outlets to prevent their marrying. We have had no reasons shown to us which would lead us to believe that homosexual behaviour between males inflicts any greater damage on family life than adultery, fornication or lesbian behaviour. These practices are all reprehensible from the point of view of harm to the family, but it is difficult to see why on this ground male homosexual behaviour alone among them should be a criminal offence. This argument is not to be taken as saying that society should condone or approve male homosexual behaviour. But where adultery, fornication and lesbian behaviour are not criminal offences there seems to us to be no valid ground, on the basis of damage to the family, for so regarding homosexual behaviour between men. Moreover, it has to be recognised that the mere existence of the condition of homosexuality in one of the partners can result in an unsatisfactory marriage, so that for a homosexual to marry simply for the sake of conformity with the accepted structure of society or in the hope of curing his condition may result in disaster.

56. We have given anxious consideration to the third argument, that an adult male who has sought as his partner another adult male may turn from such a relationship and seek as his partner a boy or succession of boys. We should certainly not wish to countenance any proposal which might tend to increase offences against minors. Indeed, if we thought that any recommendation for a change in the law would increase the danger to minors

we should not make it. But in this matter we have been much influenced by our expert witnesses. They are in no doubt that whatever may be the origins of the homosexual condition, there are two recognisably different categories among adult male homosexuals. There are those who seek as partners other adult males, and there are paedophiliacs, that is to say men who seek as partners boys who have not reached puberty.([1])

57. We are authoritatively informed that a man who has homosexual relations with an adult partner seldom turns to boys, and *vice-versa*, though it is apparent from the police reports we have seen and from other evidence submitted to us that such cases do happen. A survey of 155 prisoners diagnosed as being homosexuals on reception into Brixton prison during the period 1st January, 1954, to 31st May, 1955, indicated that 107 (69 per cent.) were attracted to adults, 43 (27·7 per cent.) were attracted to boys, and 5 (3·3 per cent.) were attracted to both boys and adults. This last figure of 3·3 per cent. is strikingly confirmed by another investigation of 200 patients outside prison. But paedophiliacs, together with the comparatively few who are indiscriminate, will continue to be liable to the sanctions of criminal law, exactly as they are now. And the others would be very unlikely to change their practices and turn to boys simply because their present practices were made legal. It would be paradoxical if the making legal of an act at present illegal were to turn men towards another kind of act which is, and would remain, contrary to the law. Indeed, it has been put to us that to remove homosexual behaviour between adult males from the listed crimes may serve to protect minors; with the law as it is there may be some men who would prefer an adult partner but who at present turn their attention to boys because they consider that this course is less likely to lay them open to prosecution or to blackmail than if they sought other adults as their partners. If the law were changed in the way we suggest, it is at least possible that such men would prefer to seek relations with older persons which would not render them liable to prosecution. In this connection, information we have received from the police authorities in the Netherlands suggests that practising homosexuals in that country are to some extent turning from those practices which are punishable under the criminal law to other practices which are not. Our evidence, in short, indicates that the fear that the legalisation of homosexual acts between adults will lead to similar acts with boys has not enough substance to justify the treatment of adult homosexual behaviour in private as a criminal offence, and suggests that it would be more likely that such a change in the law would protect boys rather than endanger them.

58. In addition, an argument of a more general character in favour of retaining the present law has been put to us by some of our witnesses. It is that to change the law in such a way that homosexual acts between consenting adults in private ceased to be criminal offences must suggest to the average citizen a degree of toleration by the Legislature of homosexual behaviour, and that such a change would "open the floodgates" and result in unbridled licence. It is true that a change of this sort would amount to a limited degree of such toleration, but we do not share the fears of our witnesses that the change would have the effect they expect. This expectation seems to us to exaggerate the effect of the law on human behaviour. It may well be true that the present law deters from homosexual acts some who would otherwise

---

[1] There are reasons for supposing that paedophilia differs from other manifestations of homosexuality. For example, it would seem that in some cases the propensity is for partners of a particular age rather than for partners of a particular sex. An examination of the records of the offences covered by the Cambridge survey reveals that 8 per cent. of the men convicted of sexual offences against children had previous convictions for both heterosexual and homosexual offences.

commit them, and to that extent an increase in homosexual behaviour can be expected. But it is no less true that if the amount of homosexual behaviour has, in fact, increased in recent years, then the law has failed to act as an effective deterrent. It seems to us that the law itself probably makes little difference to the amount of homosexual behaviour which actually occurs; whatever the law may be there will always be strong social forces opposed to homosexual behaviour. It is highly improbable that the man to whom homosexual behaviour is repugnant would find it any less repugnant because the law permitted it in certain circumstances; so that even if, as has been suggested to us, homosexuals tend to proselytise, there is no valid reason for supposing that any considerable number of conversions would follow the change in the law.

59. As will be observed from Appendix III, in only very few European countries does the criminal law now take cognisance of homosexual behaviour between consenting parties in private. It is not possible to make any useful statistical comparison between the situation in countries where the law tolerates such behaviour and that in countries where all male homosexuals acts are punishable, if only because in the former the acts do not reflect themselves in criminal statistics. We have, however, caused enquiry to be made in Sweden, where homosexual acts between consenting adults in private ceased to be criminal offences in consequence of an amendment of the law in 1944. We asked particularly whether the amendment of the law had had any discernible effect on the prevalence of homosexual practices, and on this point the authorities were able to say no more than that very little was known about the prevalence of such practices either before or after the change in the law. We think it reasonable to assume that if the change in the law had produced any appreciable increase in homosexual behaviour or any large-scale proselytising, these would have become apparent to the authorities.

60. We recognise that a proposal to change a law which has operated for many years so as to make legally permissible acts which were formerly unlawful, is open to criticisms which might not be made in relation to a proposal to omit, from a code of laws being formulated *de novo,* any provision making these acts illegal. To reverse a long-standing tradition is a serious matter and not to be suggested lightly. But the task entrusted to us, as we conceive it, is to state what we regard as a just and equitable law. We therefore do not think it appropriate that consideration of this question should be unduly influenced by a regard for the present law, much of which derives from traditions whose origins are obscure.

61. Further, we feel bound to say this. We have outlined the arguments against a change in the law, and we recognise their weight. We believe, however, that they have been met by the counter-arguments we have already advanced. There remains one additional counter-argument which we believe to be decisive, namely, the importance which society and the law ought to give to individual freedom of choice and action in matters of private morality. Unless a deliberate attempt is to be made by society, acting through the agency of the law, to equate the sphere of crime with that of sin, there must remain a realm of private morality and immorality which is, in brief and crude terms, not the law's business. To say this is not to condone or encourage private immorality. On the contrary, to emphasise the personal and private nature of moral or immoral conduct is to emphasise the personal and private responsibility of the individual for his own actions, and that is a responsibilty which a mature agent can properly be expected to carry for himself without the threat of punishment from the law.

62.(¹) We accordingly recommend that homosexual behaviour between consenting adults in private should no longer be a criminal offence.

63. This proposal immediately raises three questions: What is meant by "consenting"; What is meant by "in private"; What is meant by "adult"?

So far as concerns the first of these, we should expect that the question whether or not there has been "consent" in a particular case would be decided by the same criteria as apply to heterosexual acts between adults. We should expect, for example, that a "consent" which had been obtained by fraud or threats of violence would be no defence to a criminal charge; and that a criminal charge would also lie where drugs had been used to render the partner incapable of giving or withholding consent, or where the partner was incapable for some other reason (for example, mental defect) of giving a valid consent.

We are aware that the quality of the consent may vary; consent may amount to anything from an eager response to a grudging submission. We are aware, too, that money, gifts or hospitality are sometimes used to induce consent. But these considerations apply equally to heterosexual relationships, and we find in them no ground for differentiating, so far as the behaviour of adults is concerned, between homosexual and heterosexual relationships.

64.(²) Our words "in private" are not intended to provide a legal definition. Many heterosexual acts are not criminal if committed in private but are punishable if committed in circumstances which outrage public decency, and we should expect the same criteria to apply to homosexual acts. It is our intention that the law should continue to regard as criminal any indecent act committed in a place where members of the public may be likely to see and be offended by it, but where there is no possibility of public offence of this nature it becomes a matter of the private responsibility of the persons concerned and as such, in our opinion, is outside the proper purview of the criminal law. It will be for the courts to decide, in cases of doubt, whether or not public decency has been outraged, and we cannot see that there would be any greater difficulty about establishing this in the case of homosexual acts than there is at present in the case of heterosexual acts.

65. The question of the age at which a man is to be regarded as "adult" is much more difficult. A wide range of ages has been covered by proposals made in the evidence which has been offered to us by our witnesses. On the analogy of heterosexual behaviour there is a case for making the age sixteen, for heterosexual acts committed by consenting partners over that age in private are not criminal. At the other end of the scale an age as high as thirty was suggested. Within these two extremes, the ages most frequently suggested to us have been eighteen and twenty-one.

66. It seems to us that there are four sets of considerations which should govern the decision on this point. The first is connected with the need to protect young and immature persons; the second is connected with the age at which the pattern of a man's sexual development can be said to be fixed; the third is connected with the meaning of the word "adult" in the sense of "responsible for his own actions"; and the fourth is connected with the consequences which would follow from the fixing of any particular age. Unfortunately, these various considerations may not all lead to the same answer.

(¹) See Reservation I (a), page 117.
(²) See Reservation I (b), page 121.

67. So far as concerns the first set of considerations, we have made it clear throughout our report that we recognise the need for protecting the young and immature. But this argument can be pressed too far; there comes a time when a young man can properly be expected to " stand on his own feet " in this as in other matters, and we find it hard to believe that he needs to be protected from would-be seducers more carefully than a girl does. It could indeed be argued that in a simply physical sense he is better able to look after himself than she is. On this view, there would be some ground for making sixteen the age of " adulthood," since sexual intercourse with a willing girl of this age is not unlawful.

68. We have given special attention to the evidence which has been given to us in connection with the second set of considerations—those which relate the notion of " adulthood " to a recognisable age in the fixation of a young man's sexual pattern—for we should not wish to see legalised any forms of behaviour which would swing towards a permanent habit of homosexual behaviour a young man who without such encouragement would still be capable of developing a normal habit of heterosexual adult life. On this point we have been offered many and conflicting opinions which agree however in admitting the difficulty of equating stabilisation of sexual pattern with a precise chronological age. Our medical witnesses were unanimously of the view that the main sexual pattern is laid down in the early years of life, and the majority of them held that it was usually fixed, in main outline, by the age of sixteen. Many held that it was fixed much earlier. On this ground again, then, it would seem that sixteen would be an appropriate age.

69. We now turn to the third set of considerations, that is, the age at which a person may be regarded as sufficiently adult to take decisions about his private conduct and to carry the responsibility for their consequences. In other fields of behaviour the law recognises the age of twenty-one as being appropriate for decisions of this kind; for example, this is the age at which a man is deemed to be capable of entering into legal contracts, including (in England and Wales) the contract of marriage, on his own responsibility. Apart altogether from legal or medical technicalities, we believe that it would be generally accepted, as a matter of ordinary usage, that " adult " means, broadly speaking, " of the age of twenty-one or more "; and we believe that it is, as a matter of common sense, reasonable to accept this as designating the age at which a man is regarded as being maturely responsible for his actions.

70. To suggest that the age of adulthood for the purposes we have in mind should be twenty-one leads us to the fourth set of considerations we have mentioned, namely, the consequences which would follow from the decision about any particular age. To fix the age at twenty-one (or indeed at any age above seventeen) raises particular difficulties in this connection, for it involves leaving liable to prosecution a young man of almost twenty-one for actions which in a few days' time he could perform without breaking the law. This difficulty would admittedly arise whatever age was decided upon, for it would always be the case that an action would be illegal a few days below that age and legal above it. But this difficulty would present itself in a less acute form if the age were fixed at eighteen, which is the other age most frequently suggested to us. For whereas it would be difficult to regard a young man of nearly twenty-one charged with a homosexual offence as a suitable subject for " care or protection " under the provisions of the Children and Young Persons Acts, it would not be entirely inappropriate so to regard a youth under eighteen. If the age of adulthood for the purposes of our amendment were fixed at eighteen, and if the " care or protection " provisions

were extended to cover young persons up to that age, there would be a means of dealing with homosexual behaviour by those under that age without invoking the penal sanctions of the criminal law.

71. There must obviously be an element of arbitrariness in any decision on this point; but all things considered the legal age of contractual responsibility seems to us to afford the best criterion for the definition of adulthood in this respect. While there are some grounds for fixing the age as low as sixteen, it is obvious that however " mature " a boy of that age may be as regards physical development or psycho-sexual make-up, and whatever analogies may be drawn from the law relating to offences against young girls, a boy is incapable, at the age of sixteen, of forming a mature judgment about actions of a kind which might have the effect of setting him apart from the rest of society. The young man between eighteen and twenty-one may be expected to be rather more mature in this respect. We have, however, encountered several cases in which young men have been induced by means of gifts of money or hospitality to indulge in homosexual behaviour with older men, and we have felt obliged to have regard to the large numbers of young men who leave their homes at or about the age of eighteen and, either for their employment or their education or to fulfil their national service obligations, are then for the first time launched into the world in circumstances which render them particularly vulnerable to advances of this sort. It is arguable that such men should be expected, as one of the conditions of their being considered sufficiently grown-up to leave home, to be able to look after themselves in this respect also, the more so if they are being trained for responsibility in the services or in civil life. Some of us feel, on various grounds, that the age of adulthood should be fixed at eighteen. Nevertheless, most of us would prefer to see the age fixed at twenty-one, not because we think that to fix the age at eighteen would result in any greater readiness on the part of young men between eighteen and twenty-one to lend themselves to homosexual practices than exists at present, but because to fix it at eighteen would lay them open to attentions and pressures of an undesirable kind from which the adoption of the later age would help to protect them, and from which they ought, in view of their special vulnerability, to be protected. We therefore recommend that for the purpose of the amendment of the law which we have proposed, the age at which a man is deemed to be an adult should be twenty-one.

72. If our recommendation is accepted, any indecent homosexual act committed by a male person under twenty-one will continue to be an offence, wherever and with whomsoever it is committed. It is not, however, our intention to suggest that criminal proceedings ought to be taken in respect of any and every detected homosexual offence committed by a person under that age. Where the offender violates public decency or otherwise causes a public nuisance, for example by persistent importuning, proceedings should continue to be taken as they are at present. And where his behaviour is such as to constitute an indecent assault, that is to say where a homosexual act is carried out against the consent of the partner, or with a partner who is incapable by reason of age or mental defect of giving consent, then clearly the law should continue to deal with it. But, short of this, it is our view that no proceedings should be taken unless the behaviour has been accompanied by conduct of a patently criminal or vicious nature, as for instance " bullying " at a school or institution, the abuse of his position by a superior in one of the Services, or an element of prostitution or blackmail. We hope that the responsible authorities, as well as parents or others under whose care the young man concerned might be living, would be ready to distinguish

between conduct of this kind and behaviour which is often no more than the physical expression of a transient phase. Cases of the latter sort ought, in our view, seldom to reach the courts, though there may occasionally be cases where the offender would benefit from being placed on probation with a view either to treatment or to supervision of a more general kind.

In order to ensure uniformity of practice, we recommend that the law be so amended as to provide that except for prosecutions instituted by the Director of Public Prosecutions, no prosecution for a homosexual offence committed in private, other than in indecent assault, should be commenced in England and Wales against a person under the age of twenty-one without the sanction of the Attorney-General.([1]) As regards Scotland, we are satisfied that the necessary uniformity of practice is ensured by the fact that prosecutions can be commenced only by the Procurator-Fiscal, acting in the public interest (see paragraph 137 below).

73. As regards offences by young persons under the age of seventeen, the provisions of the Children and Young Persons Acts are sufficient to ensure that in deciding how to deal with an offence the welfare of the young person concerned will be the overriding consideration. We have no doubt that where there has been no vicious or criminal intent the appropriate authorities would deal with the offender, if it were necessary to bring him to court at all, under the " care or protection " provisions of the Acts rather than by charging him with a criminal offence.

74. We have discussed the possibility of trying to adapt the " care or protection " provisions of these Acts in such a way as to cover persons between the ages of seventeen and twenty-one, but we have come to the conclusion that this would be impracticable and that it would be more appropriate to leave such persons to be dealt with as we have suggested above where they cannot be dealt with by persons under whose authority they may be living. If the recommendations of the Committee (the Children and Young Persons Committee) at present considering the powers of the courts in relation to juvenile offenders result in the raising of the age for care or protection, the higher age limit would automatically apply to those we are here considering.

75. Since it is a defence to a first charge of sexual intercourse with a girl under sixteen that the man, if he is under the age of twenty-four, had reasonable cause for believing that the girl was over sixteen, we have considered whether a similar defence should be available to a man, up to an age to be specified, who had committed a homosexual act with a young man under twenty-one in the belief that he was above that age. We do not believe that it should. This defence applies only in the special case we have mentioned; it applies only to offenders within an age-range specified on no very clear grounds, and we see no valid reason for importing into the homosexual field a provision designed to deal with a particular heterosexual offence.

76. We wish to make it perfectly clear that our recommendation that the law should no longer regard as criminal offences homosexual acts between consenting adults in private is not intended to countenance any forms of behaviour approximating to the objectionable activities associated with female prostitution with which we deal elsewhere in this report. In accordance with our conception of the functions of the criminal law as expressed in paragraph 13 above, we should expect that the law would continue to make provision for the preservation of public order and decency, the protection

---

([1]) *Cf.* Punishment of Incest Act, 1908, Section 6.

of the citizen from what is offensive or injurious and the suppression of the exploitation of the weaker members of society. The question of solicitation by males is dealt with in paragraph 116 below. Conduct approximating to "living on the earnings of prostitution" will be covered to some extent by our recommendation (paragraph 115) that procuring or attempting to procure the commission of homosexual acts by third parties should continue to be an offence; but as an added safeguard, we recommend that the law relating to living on the earnings of prostitution should be made to apply, so far as may be practicable, to the earnings of male prostitution as it does to the earnings of female prostitution. Finally, we recommend that, if necessary, the law should be amended so as to make it explicit that the word "brothel" includes premises used for homosexual practices as well as those used for heterosexual lewdness.

(ii) Detailed Consideration

77. We now proceed to a more detailed consideration of the present law and practice. The expression "homosexual offences" is not defined in our terms of reference, but we have regarded the following criminal offences as "homosexual offences" for the purposes of our enquiry:—

(a) England and Wales

Offence	Statute, &c.	Where triable	Maximum punishment
Buggery (see note (a))	Sexual Offences Act, 1956, Section 12	Assizes only	Imprisonment for life
Attempted buggery	Common law (see paragraph 127 below)	Assizes or Quarter Sessions	Ten years' imprisonment
Indecent assault on a male by a male	Sexual Offences Act, 1956, Section 15 (i)	Ditto (but see note (b))	Ditto (but see note (b))
Indecent assault on a female by a female	Sexual Offences Act, 1956, Section 14 (i)	Ditto (but see note (b))	Two years' imprisonment (but see note (b))
Acts of gross indecency between males	Sexual Offences Act, 1956, Section 13	Assizes: and Quarter Sessions if the Chairman is legally qualified	Two years' imprisonment
Procuring acts of gross indecency between males	Ditto	Ditto	Ditto
Attempting to procure acts of gross indecency between males	Common law (see paragraph 127 below).	Ditto	Ditto
Assaults with intent to commit buggery	Sexual Offences Act, 1956, Section 16 (i)	Assizes or Quarter Sessions	Ten years' imprisonment
Persistent soliciting or importuning of males by males for immoral purposes (where the "immoral purposes" involve homosexual behaviour)	Sexual Offences Act, 1956, Section 32	(i) Magistrates' Court (ii) Assizes or Quarter Sessions	(i) Six months' imprisonment (ii) Two years' imprisonment

(a) England and Wales (continued)

Offence	Statute, &c.	Where triable	Maximum punishment
Offences against bye-laws (where the offences involve acts of indecency between persons of the same sex)	See paragraph 125 below	Magistrates' Court	£5 fine

NOTES.—
(a) The offence of buggery consists of sexual intercourse (a) *per anum* between man and man; or (b) in the same manner between man and woman; or (c) in any manner between man or woman and beast. Only in the first of these forms does the act constitute a "homosexual offence", and the act in its other forms is outside our terms of reference. Both parties to the act, if consenting, are equally guilty unless one of them is under the age of fourteen, in which case he is deemed in law to be incapable of committing the offence. For the purpose of the law, intercourse is deemed to be complete on proof of penetration.

(b) Where the victim of an indecent assault is under the age of sixteen, the case may be tried by a magistrates' court with the consent of the accused (and of the Director of Public Prosecutions where he is conducting the prosecution), and the maximum penalty is then six months' imprisonment and/or a fine of £100.

(b) Scotland

Offence	Statute, &c.	Where triable (see note (b))	Maximum punishment (see note (b))
Sodomy (see note (a))	Common law	High Court of Justiciary	Imprisonment for life
Attempted sodomy	Common law (see paragraph 102)	(i) High Court of Justiciary	(i) Imprisonment for life
Indecent assault on a male by a male		(ii) Sheriff Court (with jury)	(ii) Two years' imprisonment
Indecent assault on a female by a female		(iii) Sheriff Court (without jury)	(iii) Three months' imprisonment
Lewd and libidinous practices and behaviour (between male persons)			
Acts of gross indecency between males	Criminal law Amendment Act, 1885, Section 11 (as applied by Section 15)	(i) Sheriff Court (with jury)	(i) Two years' imprisonment
Procuring acts of gross indecency between males		(ii) Sheriff Court (without jury)	(ii) Three months' imprisonment
Attempting to procure acts of gross indecency between males			

(b) Scotland (*continued*)

Offence	Statute, &c.	Where triable (see note (*b*))	Maximum punishment (see note (*b*))
Persistent soliciting or importuning of males by males for immoral purposes (where the "immoral purposes" involve homosexual behaviour)	Immoral Traffic (Scotland) Act, 1902, Section 1; Criminal Law Amendment Act, 1912, Section 7 (2) and (5)	(i) Sheriff Court (with jury) (ii) Any court of summary jurisdiction	(i) Two years' imprisonment (ii) Six months' imprisonment
Offences against bye-laws (where the offences involve acts of indecency between persons of the same sex)	See paragraph 125	Any court of summary jurisdiction	Fine of £5

Notes—
(*a*) The offence known to English law as buggery is, when committed between human beings, known to Scots law as sodomy.

(*b*) In Scotland, the maximum penalty for a common law offence depends on the manner in which it is prosecuted. If summary proceedings are taken, the term of imprisonment may not exceed three months, except that where a person is convicted summarily in the Sheriff Court of an offence involving personal violence aggravated by at least two previous convictions of any such offence, the maximum sentence is six months. If proceedings are on indictment in the Sheriff Court, the maximum term is two years' imprisonment; and if the charge is brought in the High Court of Justiciary, or the offender is remitted there for sentence, any term of imprisonment may be imposed. The decision as to the manner of prosecution and the court in which the proceedings shall be taken rests with the prosecuting authorities, who in all serious cases are the Lord Advocate or his officers. Sodomy is always prosecuted in the High Court. Charges of indecent assault or lewd or libidinous practices or behaviour are brought on indictment or summarily according to the gravity of the offence or offences.

Offences against the Criminal Law Amendment Act, 1885, and the Immoral Traffic (Scotland) Act, 1902, are "crimes and offences" at Scots law, and as such may be tried in the Sheriff Court either on indictment or summarily. If the case is dealt with summarily, the court may not impose imprisonment for more than three months except where wider power is conferred by statute in relation to the particular offence. As in the case of common law offences, the decision as to the manner of prosecution and the court in which the proceedings shall be taken rests with the prosecuting authorities.

Buggery (Sodomy)

78. As the law at present stands, it singles out buggery from other homosexual offences and prescribes a maximum penalty of life imprisonment. From the figures in Table VI in Appendix I it will be apparent that the offence of buggery is, in practice, punished more severely than other forms of homosexual behaviour even when committed in similar circumstances, and we have accordingly considered whether any justification exists, from the point of view either of the offender or the offence itself, for the imposition of heavier penalties in respect of this particular form of behaviour.

79. As regards the offender, some of our witnesses, more particularly our judicial and police witnesses, have suggested to us that those who commit buggery possess poorer personalities and tend to be more generally anti-social than those whose homosexual behaviour takes other forms. It was also

suggested to us that they are more inclined to repeat their offences; and a few of our medical witnesses held that those who indulged in buggery responded less satisfactorily to treatment than other homosexual offenders.

80. We have found no convincing evidence to support these suggestions. It has to be borne in mind that there are many homosexuals whose behaviour never comes to the notice of the police or the courts, and it is probable that the police and the courts see only the worst cases; the more anti-social type of person is more likely to attract the attention of the police than the discreet person with a well-developed social sense. Moreover, those of our medical witnesses who thought that those who indulged in buggery responded less well to treatment than other homosexual offenders were doctors who saw a high proportion of persons on a criminal charge, so that here again the sample would tend to be representative of the more anti-social types.

81. From information supplied to us by the Prison Commissioners it would appear that there is no significant difference in social, occupational or educational level as between those who had been convicted of buggery and those whose offences took other forms. This was confirmed by the evidence of our medical witnesses who, almost unanimously, found no significant difference from other practising homosexuals in personality, social or economic success, stability or social worth. The information supplied by the Prison Commissioners also indicates that the proportion of male prostitutes is no higher among those convicted of buggery than among those convicted of other homosexual offences. Moreover, medical evidence, while granting that individuals did differ in their preferences, suggested that the majority of practising homosexuals indulged at some time or other in all types of homosexual acts, both actively and passively, and the police reports we have seen tend to confirm this.

82. The suggestion that those who indulge in buggery are more inclined to repeat their offences is not borne out by our statistical evidence. Table VIII in Appendix I shows that offenders convicted of buggery are in a similar category, as regards the numbers of their previous offences, homosexual or otherwise, to those convicted of other homosexual offences, and include a larger proportion of first offenders than some other classes of offenders. In so far, therefore, as the frequency of conviction can be taken as an index of persistence in crime, these figures suggest that persons who commit buggery are no more prone to repeat their offences than those convicted of other homosexual offences. They also show that they are less prone to repeat them than some other classes of offenders.

83. On the question of treatability, the evidence submitted to us by the Prison Commissioners indicated that there was no significant difference, as between those convicted of buggery and those convicted of other homosexual offences, in the proportions found suitable for treatment, accepted for treatment or benefiting from treatment, and our medical evidence on the whole confirms this view.

84. If, therefore, the question of the maximum penalty were to be considered simply in relation to its deterrent effect on the particular offender or to the possibility of successful treatment, there would be no clear case for attaching to buggery a penalty heavier than that applicable to other homosexual offences.

85. As regards the offence itself, the risk of physical injury to the passive partner, especially if young, has been mentioned to us as a justification for attaching a specially heavy penalty to buggery. Our evidence suggests that cases in which physical injury results from the act of buggery are very

rare. Moreover, there are other forms of homosexual behaviour which are no less likely to result in physical damage; and since the general law provides for the punishment of acts causing bodily harm, there is no apparent justification for attaching a special penalty to buggery on the ground that it might cause physical injury. It seems probable, too, that a homosexual act which caused bodily harm would amount in most cases to an "indecent assault," and the present maximum penalty of ten years' imprisonment for indecent assault allows sufficiently for any case in which physical injury is caused.

86. There remains the possibility of emotional or psychological damage, whether in the sense of producing homosexual deviation or in the sense of producing more general damage of an emotional or moral kind. In the first sense, this possibility arises only in relation to offences with boys or youths, since the direction of sexual preference is usually fixed at an early age. Homosexual behaviour between adults is not likely to affect the direction of the sexual preference of the participants, so that the question does not arise in relation to homosexual behaviour between adults even in those cases where we propose that this should remain amenable to the criminal law. As regards offences with young persons, it will be apparent from what we say elsewhere that we are not convinced that homosexual behaviour is a decisive factor in the production of the homosexual condition; and even in those cases where seduction in youth can legitimately be regarded as one of the factors in producing the condition, our medical evidence suggests that this result is dependent more on the make-up of the individual boy or youth than on the nature of the physical act to which he was subjected. On the question of more general emotional or moral damage, our medical witnesses regarded this as depending more on the surrounding circumstances, including the kind of approach made and the emotional relationships between the partners, than on the specific nature of the homosexual act committed.

87. There is therefore no convincing case for attaching a heavier penalty to buggery on the ground that it may result in greater physical, emotional or moral harm to the victim than other forms of homosexual behaviour.

88. Other arguments of a more general kind have, however, been adduced in favour of the retention of buggery as a separate offence. It is urged that there is a long and weighty tradition in our law that this, the "abominable crime" (as earlier statutes call it), is in its nature distinct from other forms of indecent assault or gross indecency; that there is in the minds of many people a stronger instinctive revulsion from this particular form of behaviour than from any other; that it is particularly objectionable because it involves coition and thus simulates more nearly than any other homosexual act the normal act of heterosexual intercourse; that it may sometimes approximate in the homosexual field to rape in the heterosexual; and that it therefore ought to remain a distinct offence with a maximum penalty equivalent to that for rape.

89.([1]) We believe that there is some case for retaining buggery as a separate offence; and there may even be a case for retaining the present maximum penalty of life imprisonment for really serious cases (for example, those in which repeated convictions have failed to deter a man from committing offences against young boys, or cases in which serious physical injury is caused in circumstances approximating to rape), though cases of this sort would fall into the category of indecent assault, and we think that the maximum penalty of ten years' imprisonment which we propose for indecent assault should normally suffice for even the most serious cases. But it is ludicrous that two

---

([1]) See Reservation II, page 123.

consenting parties should be liable to imprisonment for life simply because the act of indecency takes a particular form, while they would be liable to only two years' imprisonment if the act took some other form which may be no less repulsive to ordinary people; and if the law were to be changed in the sense we propose in paragraph 62 above, it would be even more ludicrous that two young men just under twenty-one should be liable to imprisonment for life for an act they could perform with impunity a little later on, or that two men over twenty-one should be liable to imprisonment for life because they happened to be found committing in public an act which, if committed in private, would not be criminal at all.

90. We appreciate that in determining the appropriate sentence the courts have regard to the circumstances of the particular case, and in practice it is most unlikely that the courts would ever contemplate imposing life imprisonment for offences committed between consenting parties, whether in private or in public. But it is apparent from the figures in Table VI in Appendix I that the courts inflict heavier sentences for buggery than they do for gross indecency even where the offences are committed between consenting parties; and as long as the law provides the maximum penalty of life imprisonment for buggery without any regard to the circumstances in which the offence is committed, this is likely to be the case. We feel, therefore, that although it may be appropriate that the law should distinguish in some way between buggery and other homosexual acts, and although there may be a case for retaining the present maximum penalty for buggery in certain circumstances, the law ought, in defining the offences, and in prescribing the penalties to be attached thereto, to have regard to their gravity as measured by the circumstances surrounding their commission, and not merely to the nature of the physical act. An offence by a man with a boy or youth, for example, is a more serious matter than a similar offence with a partner of comparable age; and an act committed with an unwilling partner is more serious than one carried out by mutual consent. There is no new principle involved here: sexual intercourse with a girl under 13 is punishable with life imprisonment, while sexual intercourse with a girl over 13 but under 16 carries only two years' imprisonment; breaking and entering a dwelling house with intent to commit a felony is punishable with life imprisonment if committed by night, but with seven years' imprisonment if committed in the day time; and so on.

91.([1]) We recognise that it would not be practicable to provide in this way for every conceivable set of circumstances in which a homosexual act could take place, but it is possible to devise a few broad categories, each carrying a maximum penalty within which the courts would be able to pass sentences commensurate with the gravity of the particular offence. We accordingly recommend that the following offences should be recognised, and we suggest the maximum penalties for them:

Offence	Suggested maximum penalty
(a) Buggery with a boy under the age of sixteen	Life imprisonment (as at present)
(b) Indecent assault. (This would embrace all acts of buggery or gross indecency committed against the will of the partner, whatever his age; it would also cover, except for the special case mentioned in the footnote to paragraph 114 below, all acts of gross indecency committed with boys under sixteen.)	Ten years' imprisonment (as at present in England and Wales)

([1]) See Reservations III and IV (a), pages 125 and 126.

Offence	Suggested maximum penalty
(c) Buggery or gross indecency committed by a man over twenty-one with a person of or above the age of sixteen but below the age of twenty-one, in circumstances not amounting to an indecent assault.	Five years' imprisonment
(d) Buggery or gross indecency committed in any other circumstances (that is, by a person under twenty-one with a consenting partner of or above the age of sixteen; or by any persons in public in circumstances which do not attract the higher penalties; or the special case mentioned in the footnote to paragraph 114).	Two years' imprisonment

92. It will be observed that the scale of penalties proposed in the preceding paragraph increases the maximum penalty that can at present be imposed for acts of gross indecency other than buggery committed by a man over twenty-one with a consenting partner below that age. This is because the danger of emotional or psychological damage is, as we have explained earlier, dependent more on the surrounding circumstances than on the specific nature of the act committed. We have in mind particularly the sort of corruption to which we refer in paragraph 97 below, and we feel that the amendment we have proposed might serve, in some measure, as a further protection of the young from the undesirable attentions of older men. It is not, however, our intention that the courts should assume that every offence with a person under twenty-one should automatically be visited with a heavier sentence than would have been the case if the law were not changed. In prescribing maximum penalties, the law must necessarily have regard to the worst case that could arise, and the penalties we have suggested are intended to be maximum penalties applicable to the worst cases that could arise in each of the categories. Such cases would include, for example, those offences committed against minors by their parents or foster-parents or others having a direct responsibility for their upbringing; those involving the use of violence towards youthful victims; those involving the systematic abuse of authority by men holding superior rank in a disciplined service; those committed against inmates of homes, hospitals or other institutions by members of the staffs of such establishments; and those in which the offender had deliberately corrupted a number of minors.

93. It has not escaped us that the offence of buggery as known to the present law comprises some acts which are not homosexual offences and which are accordingly outside our terms of reference.[1] We assume, however, that if our recommendations are adopted, the Legislature will make corresponding adjustments, if it deems them necessary, in the penalties attaching to buggery in its other forms.

94. In English law, buggery is classified as a felony. A person who knows that a felony has been committed himself commits a criminal offence, known as misprision of felony, if he fails to reveal it to the proper authorities. In practice, prosecutions for misprision of felony are extremely rare; there is, indeed, now some doubt about what the ingredients of the offence are. But it has been suggested to us that a doctor who fails to report to the

---

[1] See Note (a) to the table of offences (England and Wales) in paragraph 77 above.

proper authorities an act of buggery disclosed to him by a patient is technically liable to such prosecution, and that this fact may make some homosexuals reluctant to confide in a doctor. We think that anything which tends to discourage a homosexual from seeking medical advice is to be deprecated. Further, it is important that doctors called upon to furnish medical reports for the information of the courts should enjoy the full confidence of the person under examination if an accurate prognosis is to be made. This is not likely to be the case if the person being examined feels, rightly or wrongly, that the doctor is under an obligation to reveal to the court every act of buggery disclosed in the course of the examination. We accordingly recommend that buggery, if it is retained as a separate offence, should be re-classified as a misdemeanour.

Indecent Assaults

95. An indecent assault has been defined by the courts as " an assault accompanied by circumstances of indecency on the part of the person assaulting towards the person alleged to have been assaulted."[1] The law applies irrespective of the person by whom the assault was committed, but our terms of reference apply only to assaults by persons of the same sex as the victim. It is a defence to a charge of indecent assault that the person alleged to have been assaulted consented to what was done to him,[2] but a child under sixteen cannot, in law, give any such consent, nor can a mental defective.[3] Where, therefore, the victim is under sixteen, or is mentally defective, an act which could not in the ordinary sense of the word be regarded as an assault becomes one in law simply by reason of the victim's incapacity to give " consent " to what is done to him. Accordingly, an act amounting in law to an indecent assault does not necessarily involve any violence towards the " victim "; indeed, we have evidence that offenders frequently approach their victims with gentleness, and there is no doubt, too, that in many cases the child is a willing party to, and in some cases even the instigator of, the act which takes place. For example, only 43 per cent. of the 524 boys under sixteen involved in the sexual offences covered by the Cambridge survey showed any resentment or offered any objection to the misconduct of the offenders.

96. In many cases, too, the misbehaviour which constitutes the " assault " is of a relatively minor character; frequently it amounts to no more than placing the hands on or under the clothing of the victim and handling, or attempting to handle, the private parts; in some cases it may amount to nothing more than horse-play. The Cambridge survey shows that of 624 male victims of sexual offences only 21 (3·4 per cent.) received any physical injury. Seventeen of these received slight injuries only, and four received considerable bodily injury requiring medical attention. Unfortunately we have no figures distinguishing between cases in which the offender was charged with indecent assault and those in which he was charged with another offence, for example, buggery or gross indecency. If, as is likely, the cases in which the victim received some physical injury were cases in which the act of buggery had been perpetrated, it follows that the proportion of cases in which injury is caused by indecent assaults not involving buggery is even smaller.

---

[1] *Beal* v. *Kelley*. 35 Cr. App. R. 128.
[2] *R.* v. *Wollaston* (1872), 12 Cox 180.
[3] Sexual Offences Act, 1956, Sections 14 and 15.

97. One consequence of homosexual behaviour with young persons can, however, be serious and detrimental. Even where no resistance is offered or no physical harm ensues, there may be considerable damage to the moral and emotional development of the victim. For example, a boy or youth who is induced by means of gifts, whether in money or in kind, to participate in homosexual behaviour, may come to regard such behaviour as a source of easy money or as a means of enjoying material comforts or other pleasures beyond those which he could expect by decent behaviour, and we have encountered cases where this has happened. Indeed, it is our opinion that this sort of corruption is a more likely consequence than the possible conversion of the victim to a condition of homosexuality.

98. It is a view widely held, and one which found favour among our police and legal witnesses, that seduction in youth is the decisive factor in the production of homosexuality as a condition, and we are aware that this view has done much to alarm parents and teachers. We have found no convincing evidence in support of this contention. Our medical witnesses unanimously hold that seduction has little effect in inducing a settled pattern of homosexual behaviour, and we have been given no grounds from other sources which contradict their judgment. Moreover, it has been suggested to us that the fact of being seduced often does less harm to the victim than the publicity which attends the criminal proceedings against the offender and the distress which undue alarm sometimes leads parents to show.

99. We have, it is true, found that men charged with homosexual offences frequently plead that they were seduced in their youth, but we think that this plea is a rationalisation or an excuse, and that the offender was predisposed to homosexual behaviour before the " seduction " took place. We have little doubt that the fact that this account of the origin of their condition is so frequently given by homosexual offenders has led the police and the courts to form the impression we have mentioned. It has to be said, on the other hand, that in the case of an individual so predisposed, acts of seduction at a susceptible age may have a profound effect in precipitating a course of behaviour which might otherwise have been avoided, especially if such acts are skilfully managed over a fairly prolonged period. This danger is even greater where the seduction is carried out by a member of the family or some other person with whom there is a close emotional tie.

100. It has been suggested to us that there is no justification for the disparity in the maximum periods of imprisonment which may be imposed in England and Wales in respect of indecent assaults on males (ten years) and females (two years) respectively. We are inclined to agree; but we feel that any step which might be interpreted as minimising the seriousness of assaults on young persons is to be deprecated, and if the maximum sentences are to be assimilated this should, from the point of view of public expediency, be done by raising the maximum in respect of assaults on females rather than by reducing the maximum in respect of assaults on males.

101. In practice, where homosexual offences are concerned, most cases of indecent assault relate to offences against boys under sixteen, and the majority of such cases are dealt with under Section 19 of the Magistrates' Courts Act, 1952, by magistrates' courts, where the maximum sentence that can be imposed is one of six months' imprisonment, or twelve months if the offender is convicted of more than one offence. Of such offenders as are dealt with by the higher courts, only a minority receive sentences exceeding two years' imprisonment; for instance, in 1955, only 54 of the 274 offenders convicted by the higher courts received sentences in excess of two years, and of these, 25 had previous convictions for similar offences.

Scotland

102. In Scotland, "indecent assault" is more narrowly interpreted. In practice, indecent acts committed by adult males with boys who have not reached puberty are prosecuted as "lewd and libidinous practices and behaviour"; and if both parties are over the age of puberty, attempted sodomy or indecent assault are usually charged as an act of gross indecency unless there is an element of "attack," that is, the use or attempted use of force.

Indecent Assaults by Females on Females

103. Since an indecent assault by one female on another could take the form of a homosexual act, we have included indecent assaults on females by females in the lists of homosexual offences in paragraph 77 above. We have, however, found no case in which a female has been convicted of an act with another female which exhibits the libidinous features that characterise sexual acts between males. We are aware that the criminal statistics occasionally show females as having been convicted of indecent assaults on females; but on enquiry we find that this is due in the main to the practice of including in the figures relating to any particular offence not only those convicted of the offence itself, but also those convicted of aiding and abetting the commission of the offence. Thus, a woman convicted of aiding and abetting a man to commit an indecent assault on a female would be shown in the statistics as having herself committed such an assault.

Gross Indecency between Males

104. It is an offence for a male person (*a*) to commit an act of gross indecency with another male person, whether in public or in private; or (*b*) to be a party to the commission of such an act; or (*c*) to procure the commission of such an act. "Gross indecency" is not defined by statute. It appears, however, to cover any act involving sexual indecency between two male persons. If two male persons acting in concert behave in an indecent manner the offence is committed even though there has been no actual physical contact.([1])

105. From the police reports we have seen and the other evidence we have received it appears that the offence usually takes one of three forms; either there is mutual masturbation; or there is some form of intercrural contact; or oral-genital contact (with or without emission) takes place. Occasionally the offence may take a more recondite form; techniques in heterosexual relations vary considerably, and the same is true of homosexual relations.

106. Buggery and attempted buggery have long been criminal offences, wherever and with whomsoever committed; but, in England and Wales at least, other acts of gross indecency committed in private between consenting parties first became criminal offences in 1885. Section 11 of the Criminal Law Amendment Act of that year contained the provisions now re-enacted in Section 13 of the Sexual Offences Act, 1956.

These provisions have been criticised by various witnesses on three grounds: (*a*) that they introduced an entirely new principle into English law in that they took cognizance of the private acts of consentient parties, (*b*) that they were inserted into a Bill introduced for totally different purposes without adequate consideration by Parliament; and (*c*) that they created a particularly fruitful field for blackmail.

([1]) *R.* v. *Hunt;* 34 Cr. App. R., 135.

107. The first of these criticisms is without foundation. The Act of 1885 merely extended to homosexual indecencies other than buggery the law which previously applied to buggery. Buggery had for over three hundred years been a criminal offence whether committed in public or in private, and whether by consenting parties or not.

108. The second criticism is valid. The section was introduced in the late stages of " a Bill to make further provision for the protection of women and girls, the suppression of brothels and other purposes." It was, in fact, introduced in the House of Commons on the report stage of the Bill (which had previously been passed by the Lords, where it was introduced, without any reference to indecency between males) by Mr. Henry Labouchère, who explained that its purpose was

> "that at present any person on whom an assault of the kind here dealt with was committed must be under the age of 13, and the object with which he had brought forward this clause was to make the law applicable to any person whether under the age of 13 or over that age."[1]

The Clause was passed by the House without any discussion on its substance, the only question raised being whether it was in order to move an amendment which dealt with a class of offence totally different from those contemplated by the Bill to which the House had given a second reading. On this, the Speaker ruled that anything could be introduced by leave of the House, and the amendment was adopted. The clause certainly went much wider than Mr. Labouchère's apparent intention, and it seems probable that Parliament let it pass without the detailed consideration which such an amendment would almost certainly receive to-day. However that may be, the amendment became and has since remained law.

Blackmail

109. The third criticism was one that found more frequent expression among our witnesses, and we were more than once reminded that the Labouchère amendment has frequently been referred to as " the Blackmailer's Charter." This amendment certainly provided greater opportunities for the blackmailer. Nevertheless, the fact that buggery, attempted buggery and indecent assault were already criminal offences offered ample scope for the blackmailer and would have continued to do so even if the amendment had not passed into law. Indeed, English law has recognised the special danger of blackmail in relation to buggery and attempted buggery in Section 29 of the Larceny Act, 1916.[2]

110. We know that blackmail takes place in connection with homosexual acts. There is no doubt also that a good many instances occur where from fear of exposure men lay themselves open to repeated small demands for money or other benefit, which their previous conduct makes it difficult for them to resist; these often do not amount to blackmail in the strict sense, but they arise out of the same situation as gives rise to blackmail itself. Most victims of the blackmailer are naturally hesitant about reporting their

---

[1] Daily Debates, 6th August, 1885. Col. 1397.

[2] Under Section 29 of the Larceny Act, 1916, it is a felony, punishable with life imprisonment, to accuse or threaten to accuse a person of a crime to which the section applies with intent to extort or gain any property or valuable thing. The section applies to any crime punishable with death or with life imprisonment, and also applies expressly to " . . . . any solicitation, persuasion, promise, or threat offered or made to any person, whereby to move or induce such person to commit or permit the abominable crime of buggery . . . ."

misfortunes to the police, so that figures relating to prosecutions do not afford a reliable measure of the amount of blackmail that actually goes on. However, of 71 cases of blackmail reported to the police in England and Wales in the years 1950 to 1953 inclusive, 32 were connected with homosexual activities. These figures represent an average of eight cases a year, and even allowing for the reluctance of the victim to approach the police, they suggest that the amount of blackmail which takes place has been considerably exaggerated in the popular mind.

111. We would certainly not go so far as some of our witnesses have done and suggest that the opportunities for blackmail inherent in the present law would be sufficient ground for changing it. We have found it hard to decide whether the blackmailer's primary weapon is the threat of disclosure to the police, with the attendant legal consequences, or the threat of disclosure to the victim's relatives, employer or friends, with the attendant social consequences. It may well be that the latter is the more effective weapon; but it may yet be true that it would lose much of its edge if the social consequences were not associated with (or, indeed, dependent upon) the present legal position. At the least, it is clear that even if this is no more than one among other fields of blackmailing activity, the present law does afford to the blackmailer opportunities which the law might well be expected to diminish.

112. There is the further point that men who complain to the police of being blackmailed for participation in homosexual offences are sometimes, in consequence, charged with those offences. The following case is an example:—

Case I

A., aged 49, met B., aged 35, in a cinema. Afterwards they went to A's flat and committed buggery.

For a period of about seven years B. visited A's flat regularly, and the men committed buggery together on each occasion.

B. then commenced to demand money from A., from whom, in the course of about three months, he obtained some £40.

A. finally complained to the police. The facts were reported to the Director of Public Prosecutions, who advised that no action should be taken against B. for demanding money by menaces, but that both men should be charged with buggery.

Both men were thereupon charged with two offences of buggery committed with each other, and, after pleading guilty, were sentenced to nine months' imprisonment. Neither man had any previous convictions, nor were any other offences taken into consideration.

If the law were to be amended in the sense we propose, acts such as those which took place between A. and B. would no longer be criminal offences, and men in A's position could accordingly go to the police without fear of prosecution. It is, however, interesting to note that A. said in his statement to the police:—

"I sent the money because I thought from his letters that if I did not do so he would tell the people at the shop and where I live that I had had sexual intercourse with him."

In this case, therefore, the fear of social exposure was uppermost, though as we have suggested above, this is probably conditioned by the present law. Blackmail is a pernicious social evil, and we regret that any unnecessary obstacle should be put in the way of bringing it to light. We feel that, except for some grave reason, proceedings should not be instituted in respect of homosexual offences incidentally revealed in the course of investigating allegations of blackmail.

113. At present, extortion by a threat to accuse of buggery and certain other crimes carries a specially heavy penalty. From the point of view of blackmail, we see no reason why the law should differentiate between buggery and other homosexual acts, and we accordingly recommend that Section 29 (3) of the Larceny Act, 1916, be extended so as to apply to all homosexual offences.

Jurisdiction of the Courts

114. At present, in England and Wales, all cases of gross indecency must be tried on indictment (that is, before a jury) when the offence is committed by a person over seventeen. Many of these cases are, in our view, of a nature suitable for trial in a magistrates' court. Moreover, as will be apparent from Table IVA in Appendix I, by far the greater proportion of offenders convicted of gross indecency by the higher courts receive sentences which would be within the competence of a magistrates' court. In 1955, the 831 persons so convicted were dealt with as follows:—

Absolute discharge	28
Conditional discharge	114
Bound over	45
Fine	316
Probation	148
Imprisonment for not more than six months	71
Imprisonment for more than six months and up to one year	56
Imprisonment for over one year	40
Borstal	7
Otherwise dealt with	6
	831

It will be seen that no less than 722 (87 per cent.) of the offenders were dealt with in a way which would have been open to a magistrates' court. It is possible also that of the 56 offenders who received sentences of imprisonment of over six months but not over twelve months, some were convicted of more than one offence, so that a similar sentence could have been passed in these cases by a magistrates' court. Provided that the accused has the right to claim trial by jury if he so wishes, we feel that the offence of committing an act of gross indecency with another male person should be triable summarily. We accordingly recommend that the offence be added to the first schedule of the Magistrates' Courts Act, 1952.[1] Adoption of this recommendation would serve also to remedy an anomaly to which we call attention in paragraph 126 below.

---

[1] Our attention has been called to a decision of the English courts (*Fairclough* v. *Whipp*, 35 Cr. App. R., 138) that an invitation to another person to touch the invitor does not, even if accepted, amount to an assault on the invitee. If therefore, a man persuades a child to touch his person (and such cases are not uncommon), he is not guilty of an indecent assault. If the invitee is a boy, the man can clearly be charged with gross indecency. If our recommendation in paragraph 114 is adopted, such cases could be dealt with in magistrates' courts in the same way as indecent assaults, instead of having to go for trial as at present.

Procuring or Attempting to Procure Acts of Gross Indecency

115.([1]) If acts of gross indecency between consenting adults in private are no longer to be criminal offences, it follows that an adult ought not to be guilty of an offence merely by reason of procuring or attempting to procure the commission of such an act in private between another adult and himself. If the attempt takes the form of public solicitation the law already deals with it, as explained in the following paragraph, and should continue to do so. But we recommend that Section 13 of the Sexual Offences Act, 1956, be amended in such a way that a person is not guilty of an offence against that section merely because he procures or attempts to procure the commission with himself of an act which is no longer a criminal offence.

At the same time, we do not wish to encourage the activities of third parties who might interest themselves in making arrangements for the commission of homosexual acts, even if those acts are to be no longer illegal. Exploitation of the weaknesses of others is as objectionable in this field as in any other, and we should not wish to seem to be countenancing anything which approximated to living on immoral earnings. We do not think it would be appropriate to draw up a complex code corresponding to that which relates to the procuration of women (see Chapter XII below) and we accordingly simply recommend that it should continue to be an offence, punishable with a maximum of two years' imprisonment, for a third party to procure or attempt to procure an act of gross indecency between male persons, whether or not the act to be procured constitutes a criminal offence.

Persistent Soliciting or Importuning

116. It is an offence, punishable with six months' imprisonment on summary conviction or with two years' imprisonment on indictment, for a male person persistently to solicit or importune in a public place for immoral purposes. "Immoral purposes" is not defined, but where it is clear from the circumstances that the "immoral purposes" in contemplation involve homosexual behaviour the offence may be regarded as a "homosexual offence."

117. A curious difference between English and Scottish practice emerged from our enquiry. In England, the provisions in Section 1 of the Vagrancy Act, 1898, relating to importuning by male persons (now replaced by Section 32 of the Sexual Offences Act, 1956) have been used to deal almost exclusively with males importuning males for the purpose of homosexual relations, though occasionally they are used to deal with males soliciting males for the purposes of heterosexual relations—that is, touting for clients on behalf of prostitutes. In Scotland, however, the corresponding provision (Section 1 of the Immoral Traffic (Scotland) Act, 1902) seems never to have been used in connection with males importuning males for the purposes of homosexual relations, the authorities apparently taking the view (for which support may be found in the long title of the Act) that the provision was not intended to deal with this type of offence.

118. It is of interest to note that on being asked, on the first reading of the 1898 Bill, to explain its objects, the Home Secretary replied that it was intended—

> "for the purpose of bringing under the operation of the Vagrancy Act, 1824, as rogues and vagabonds, those men who lived by the disgraceful earnings of the women whom they consorted with and controlled. Against these enemies of society, commonly called 'bullies,' a Bill had already been introduced by an Hon. Member, but it was open to considerable objection, which this Bill avoided."([2])

([1]) See Reservation I (c), page 121.
([2]) Parliamentary Debates, 1898, Vol. 54, Col. 1538 (14th March, 1898).

Nothing was said about homosexual importuning, and there is some foundation for the suggestion that has been made([1]) that Parliament provided the police with the powers to deal with homosexual importuning entirely by inadvertence.

Nevertheless, there is no doubt that the section, as worded, includes homosexual importuning, and it seems clear from the parliamentary debates on the Criminal Law Amendment Bill, 1912,([2]) which sought among other things to increase the penalties laid down in the 1898 Act, that the section was then being used in England and Wales to deal with homosexual importuners, so that Parliament has, at least since 1912, recognised its application in this connection.

119. There are no reliable figures relating to males dealt with by the courts for importuning prior to 1954, since up to that year the offences of importuning and living on immoral earnings were aggregated in the criminal statistics. In 1954, however, 460 males were dealt with by magistrates' courts for this offence, and 21 were committed for trial at higher courts. In 1955, 498 were dealt with by magistrates' courts and 23 were committed for trial. These offenders were dealt with as shown in Table V in Appendix I.

120. Of 425 convictions at magistrates' courts in England and Wales during 1954, 323 related to offences committed in London. Outside London, the highest figures were 49 at Birmingham and 20 at Portsmouth. It seems, therefore, that the problem is almost confined to London and a few other large towns; and our evidence shows that it is largely concentrated on certain public conveniences. We have been surprised to find how widely known among homosexuals, even those who come from distant parts of the world, the location of these conveniences has proved to be. Occasionally, men are detected in the streets importuning male passers-by; the men so detected are usually male prostitutes. But for the most part, those convicted of importuning are in no sense male prostitutes; they are simply homosexuals seeking a partner for subsequent homosexual behaviour.

121. This particular offence necessarily calls for the employment of plain-clothes police if it is to be successfully detected and prevented from becoming a public nuisance; and it is evident that the figures of convictions, both for importuning and for indecencies committed in such places as public lavatories, must to some extent reflect police activity. It has been suggested by more than one of our witnesses that in carrying out their duty in connection with offences of this nature police officers act as *agents provocateurs*. We have paid special attention to this matter in our examination of the Commissioner of Police and other senior police officers, and we are satisfied that they do everything they can to ensure that their officers do not act in a deliberately provocative manner. We also made a special point of examining some of the constables engaged in this work. Those whom we saw were ordinary police constables, normally employed on uniformed duty but occasionally employed in pairs, for a four weeks' spell of duty on this work, between substantial periods on other duties. We feel bound to record that we were on the whole favourably impressed by the account they gave us of the way in which they carried out their unpleasant task. It must, in our view, be accepted that in the detection of some offences —and this is one of them—a police officer legitimately resorts to a degree of subterfuge in the course of his duty. But it would be open to the gravest

---

([1]) "The Practitioner," April 1954 (Article by Mr. John Maude, Q.C.).
([2]) Parliamentary Debates, 1912, Vol. 43, Col. 1858 (12th November, 1912).

objection if this were allowed to reach a point at which a police officer deliberately provoked an act; for it is essential that the police should be above suspicion, and we believe that if there is to be an error in the one direction or the other it would be better that a case of this comparatively trivial crime should occasionally escape the courts than that the police as a whole should come under suspicion.

122. Some of our witnesses have suggested that the offence with which a person is charged does not always correspond with the actual behaviour of the offender. We have seen one case, and have heard of others, in which the facts would seem to sustain a charge of gross indecency, or attempting to procure the commission of an act of gross indecency, rather than a charge of importuning, though the offender was charged with the latter offence. It has been suggested that the police sometimes advise persons found committing acts of gross indecency in public lavatories to plead guilty at the magistrates' court to importuning in order to avoid going for trial before a jury on a charge of gross indecency. How often this happens we cannot say; the statements of persons who plead guilty to offences which they subsequently deny must be treated with a certain amount of reserve. But if our recommendation[1] that gross indecency should be triable summarily is accepted, there would be no encouragement to the offender to enter a false plea of guilty to importuning in order to avoid going for trial in respect of an act of gross indecency which had been committed, and no temptation to the police to frame a charge with a view to enabling the magistrates' courts to dispose of a case they could not otherwise properly deal with.

123. As a general rule, a person charged in England and Wales with an offence for which he is liable to imprisonment for more than three months may claim to be tried by a jury. Male persons charged with importuning are, however, excluded from the benefit of this rule. We see no reason why a person charged with this offence should not enjoy the general right. On the contrary, we see every reason why he should. Frequently, conviction of this offence has serious consequences quite apart from any punishment which may be imposed. Moreover, behaviour which seems to establish a *prima facie* case of importuning and so leads up to an arrest may occasionally be attributable to innocent causes; and in cases such as this, where actions are susceptible of different interpretations, it is clearly right that the defendant should be entitled to have the issue put to a jury. We recommend accordingly.

124.[2] We call attention to the fact that the possible penalties for this offence are substantially greater than those which we have recommended in relation to solicitation by females for the purposes of prostitution (paragraph 275 below). The very fact that the law can impose severe penalties is, however, a considerable factor in producing the present situation that the amount of male importuning in the streets is negligible and that consequently male importuning is not nearly so offensive or such an affront to public decency as are the street activities of female prostitutes. Having regard to the modifications we have recommended in the law relating to homosexual offences, we do not think that it would be expedient at the present time to reduce in any way the penalties attaching to homosexual importuning. It is important that the limited modification of the law which we propose should not be interpreted as an indication that the law can be indifferent to other forms of homosexual behaviour, or as a general licence to adult homosexuals to behave as they please.

---

[1] See paragraph 114.
[2] See Reservation IV (*b*), page 127.

Bye-law Offences

125. Some local authorities have power to make bye-laws for the good rule and government of their areas and for the prevention and suppression of nuisances. Local authorities providing public lavatories and sanitary conveniences have power to make regulations or bye-laws as to the conduct of persons entering or using them. Bye-laws made under these powers frequently provide penalties for indecent behaviour, and these apply to homosexual behaviour as much as to other forms of indecency. The bye-laws are subject to Ministerial confirmation, and may not impose a penalty exceeding a fine of five pounds.

126. A curious situation arises at the present time in places in England and Wales where such bye-laws are in force. A man found to be persistently importuning may be dealt with summarily and becomes liable, if so dealt with, to imprisonment for not more than six months. If, however, he is detected in an act of indecency with another man, he may be charged either with gross indecency under Section 13 of the Sexual Offences Act, 1956, in which case he must, if he is over 17, be tried on indictment, thus becoming liable to imprisonment for up to two years; or with indecency under the bye-law, in which case he is dealt with summarily but the penalty cannot exceed a fine of five pounds. Where there are no aggravating circumstances and where the offender has no previous convictions for similar offences, the police are naturally and quite properly reluctant to proceed on indictment, which involves time and expense, if a summary remedy is available. Accordingly, in such cases they usually bring the offender before the magistrates' court on both charges, intimating to the court that they have no objection to the case being dealt with under the bye-law if the court sees fit to do so. In the majority of cases the suggestion is accepted by the court. The Cambridge survey shows that out of 448 men charged with gross indecency in 1947, no fewer than 386 (86·2 per cent.) were dealt with in this way. It seems to us anomalous that a man who actually commits an indecent act in a public place should be liable only to a fine of five pounds if dealt with summarily, while a man who searches unsuccessfully for a partner is liable on summary conviction to six months' imprisonment for importuning.

If our recommendation that offences against Section 13 of the Sexual Offences Act, 1956, should be triable summarily is accepted, we should expect that proceedings in respect of acts of indecency committed in lavatories and other public places would be taken under that section and not under a bye-law, on the principle, recognised in Section 249 (1) (4) of the Local Government Act, 1933, that bye-laws ought not to be used to deal with offences which can be dealt with summarily under statutory provisions. This would remedy the present anomalous situation.

General

127. Apart from such exceptions as are mentioned in this report, the general criminal law and procedure apply to homosexual offences as to other offences. Persons charged with homosexual offences are brought to trial and tried in the same way as other offenders; and the various methods by which the courts can deal with persons charged with criminal offences generally are equally available in respect of persons charged with homosexual offences. So, too, an attempt to commit a homosexual offence is itself a criminal offence, just as is an attempt to commit any other offence; and compounding or aiding or abetting a homosexual offence, or conspiring or inciting to commit a homosexual offence, is an offence in the same way as compounding or aiding or abetting, or conspiring or inciting to commit, any other offence.

Where we have considered it necessary to deal especially with some specific aspect of the general law or procedure in its particular application to homosexual offences we have done so in the appropriate parts of our report.

Police Procedures

128. The application and administration of the law are no less important than its precise formulation and its penalties. Discrepancies in the administration of any law are almost inevitable if that law does not commend itself as satisfactory to those who are charged with administering it. Such discrepancies not only bring the law into disrepute, and thus reduce its efficacy as a safeguard for society, but also inculcate a feeling of injustice and unfairness in the minds of those who are brought to trial. They may feel—and with some justification—that the incidence of punishment falls haphazardly, if what is done with seeming impunity in one part of the country is severely treated in another, both by the police and by the courts. And the very existence of this haphazard element in its administration is a strong argument against the present law, since it is evident that this law does not command the universal respect of those who are charged with enforcing it.

129. To some extent the laws relating to homosexual offences, and for that matter to other sexual offences, are bound to operate unevenly. Obviously many homosexual acts, especially those committed by consenting parties in private, never come to light, so that the number of those prosecuted in respect of homosexual acts constitutes but a fraction of those who from time to time commit such acts. But over and above this obvious fact, we have found that there are variations in the ways in which different police forces administer these laws. In some parts of the country they appear to be administered with " discretion "; that is to say, in some police districts no proceedings are initiated unless there has been a complaint or the offence has otherwise obtruded itself upon the notice of the police, for instance by a breach of public order and decency. In other parts of the country, on the other hand, it appears that a firm effort is made to apply the full rigour of the law as it stands. The following examples, extracted from police reports, will serve to illustrate this contrast:—

Case II

Two youths aged 17 and 15 years, were found in a field, their cycles having been seen at the roadside by patrolling police officers. The youths were interrogated by the officers and admitted mutual masturbation. Eventual enquiries and admission by these youths involved five other youths in offences of buggery, gross indecency and attempted buggery.

This led to what the police refer to as " intense police enquiry " in the district.

The following extracts from the police report illustrate the methods by which the police uncovered some of the offences:

" As a result " (*i.e.*, of the intense enquiry put in hand by the police) " it was learned that a man named A., aged 39 years, of (address), was being frequently mentioned as the type of person likely to be engaged in homosexual practices, although no such allegation or complaint was made regarding him to the police. Discreet enquiry regarding him, by police, disclosed that he was associating with a man named B., aged 24 years, of (address). B. was interviewed by police and it was put to him that unnatural practices were taking place between A. and himself. He 'broke down' and admitted that this was true. He then made a statement, after caution, admitting the extent of his malpractices with A.

A. was seen on the following day and a copy of B.'s statement handed to him. After reading it he alleged that it was not the truth and upon being cautioned made a statement."

Case III

(Extracted from the same police report)

"A man, C., aged 60 years, of (address) had, for many years, been considered by the police as likely to be engaged in homosexual practices. It was found that D., 27 years, of (address) had been lodging with C. (a single man) and had left abruptly for no apparent or known reason. It was suspected, however, that malpractices had taken place between them. D. was seen by the police and after the possibility had been put to him, he admitted acts of gross indecency had occurred between C. and himself. D. subsequently called at............Police Station and made a further statement regarding his association with C. As a result, copies of the statment made by D were served on C., who after being cautioned, made a statement giving his account of the events occurring between D. and himself."

Case IV

E., aged 53, was convicted of buggery with F., aged 31. To quote from the police report,

"The offence was discovered when it was observed by police that E., a man known to spend a great deal of his leisure time in company with men considerably younger than himself, was, during the evening, returning to the shop at...............where he was employed. He was joined by F., and the two men frequently did not leave the shop until after midnight. Observation could not satisfactorily be carried out on the premises and F. was interviewed by the police. He made a statement admitting that over a period of two years he had at regular intervals committed buggery with E. E. was interviewed and made a statement admitting buggery with F."

Case V

(Extract from police report)

"At the present time a number of complaints have been received from residents in a street in this City concerning the conduct of a house in the neighbourhood. Enquiries have been made and it has been ascertained that the house in question is occupied solely by four homosexuals and that naval personnel are taken there nightly, usually after the public houses have closed.

Although the residents freely complain, it has not been possible as yet to find two persons who are willing to swear their complaint before a Justice and thereby enable the Police to commence proceedings under the existing legislation."

It is interesting to contrast Case II with Case V. In Case II, though the police had received no complaint regarding the activities of the men concerned, they felt it was their duty to interrogate them. In Case V, although the police had received complaints from residents, they evidently felt that it would not be proper to question either the known homosexuals or the sailors resorting to their house merely on the basis of suspicion.

130. Wide currency has been given, not only in this country but abroad, to a suggestion that a prosecution which took place not long before we were appointed was part of a nation-wide " witch-hunt " against homosexuals. We have found no evidence of any " drive " on a national scale. The absence of uniformity in police practice which we have mentioned is enough to disprove this suggestion. For instance, in the whole of the Metropolitan Police District, in only 10 cases (each involving two men) were men over 21 convicted during the three years ended March 1956, of homosexual offences committed in private with consenting adults. In five of these cases, the offenders were caught *in flagrante delicto* by someone who reported the matter to the police. In the remaining five cases, the offences came to light in the course of enquiry into other matters, for example, larceny or blackmail. It seems to us that in some areas—it may be in most—the police deal only with such matters as obtrude themselves on their notice, not going out of their way to substantiate suspicions of covert irregular behaviour. What we have found is that there may from time to time arise particular local campaigns against this kind of offence, either as the result of a deliberate drive by the police or by reason of local public indignation.

131. We should not wish to imply that it would never be proper for police officers to follow up offences on mere suspicion. But where no clear public interest is involved, we would deprecate any out-of-the-way prying which could soon give rise to suspicions of " witch-hunting " and so bring, if not the law, at least the police into disrepute.

132. There are several ways in which homosexual offences committed in private between consenting parties may come to the notice of the police. We have obtained reports on this point from the police in relation to the 480 men who were convicted in England and Wales during the three years ended March 1956 of homosexual offences committed in private with consenting adult partners. These show that 19 of the men were prosecuted as the result of a report made to the police by one of the parties to the offence. 53 were caught *in flagrante delicto* by someone who intruded, accidentally or otherwise, on their privacy. Offences committed by the remaining 408 came to light in a variety of ways, of which Cases II, III and IV above provide some examples; but by far the greater number of the men (304) were convicted of offences revealed in the course of investigating another offence committed by one or other of the partners. Usually this other offence was also of a homosexual character, but in 34 instances it was of a different type, for example, larceny.

133. It appears from reports furnished to us by the police that police forces differ in their practices in relation to the interrogation of suspected offenders. In some, the interrogation and resulting statement seem to be confined to the particular offence under investigation. In others, they seem to range much more widely. The following is a pattern which we encountered frequently: A man is questioned by the police about an offence under enquiry, and in the course of the interrogation admits having indulged in homosexual behaviour with men whom he names. These men are then confronted with the statement made by the first man, and, in turn, make statements, inculpating further men. The process repeats itself until eventually a large number of men may be involved.

134. The police sometimes take considerable trouble in following up alleged offences revealed in this way, and their enquiries often bring to light offences committed some years earlier. The following are a few examples:

Case VI

A., aged 20, was being questioned by the police regarding other offences (not homosexual offences), and made a statement admitting acts of gross indecency with B., aged 38, some twelve or eighteen months earlier; in the course of his statement he also said that he had witnessed acts of mutual masturbation between B. and two youths of 17 some three years earlier. B. and the two youths were questioned by the police and made statements admitting the acts which A. had witnessed. Eventually B. and the two youths (by now young men of 20) were prosecuted in respect of these acts. The Chairman of Quarter Sessions, in discharging the younger men absolutely, expressed his disapproval of the proceedings against them.

Case VII

X., a nineteen-year-old serviceman stationed in Egypt, who was apparently being questioned by the service police in connection with homosexual offences which had occurred at the Station at which he was serving, made a statement which included references to an offence which had occurred five years earlier between Y., a man of 47, and himself, in a cinema in his home town. Y. was in due course questioned by the police in this country, to whom X.'s statement had evidently been passed by the service police, and made a statement admitting this offence and a number of other offences over a period of years, including some with Z., a man of his own age, which had taken place some six or seven years previously. There had, so far as is known, been no offences between Y. and Z. for over six years, but Z. was charged with, and convicted of, an offence which had taken place six years previously. Z. was not charged with any other offences.

Case VIII

C., aged 45, was observed by the police to be associating with men younger than himself and his movements were watched. As a result of this observation it came to the notice of the police that he had, on a particular night, shared a single room, at the hotel where he was employed, with D., aged 21 years. D. was accordingly questioned by the police and admitted offences with C. on the night in question and other similar offences which had occurred a few nights previously.

C. was then questioned by the police, and admitted not only the offences with D, but also a number of other offences going back for some twenty years. Among the offences so admitted were acts of gross indecency committed some twelve or thirteen years earlier with E., then a youth of 17. There was no suggestion that any offences had been committed with or by E. during a period of at least ten years prior to the date at which C. was being questioned.

The police nevertheless questioned E., by now a man of 30, occupying a responsible position and happily married with two children. E. admitted that acts of mutual masturbation had taken place with C. over a period of seven months some thirteen years earlier. On the advice of the Director of Public Prosecutions, no proceedings were taken in respect of the offences between C. and E. owing to the lapse of time.

135. If an offence comes to the notice of the police, it is their duty to investigate it and to prosecute it if their investigations produce the necessary evidence. As the law stands at present, they may lay themselves open to criticism by the courts if they fail to do so. But we do not think that any public interest is served by pursuing stale offences such as those we have mentioned above. We would not go so far as to say that proceedings should never be taken in respect of a stale offence. Cases may occur for example, in which a person who has committed a serious assault or a series of assaults successfully conceals his whereabouts and so evades proceedings for a substantial period. In such cases, it is right that proceedings should be taken despite the lapse of time. But we recommend that, except for cases of indecent assault (and offences committed with boys under 16 will, except for the special case mentioned in the footnote to paragraph 114 above, always come into this category), the prosecution of any homosexual offence more than twelve months after its commission should be barred by statute.

Differences between English and Scottish Criminal Procedure

136. It will have been observed from the figures in paragraph 51 above that the number of men prosecuted in Scotland for homosexual offences committed in private with consenting adult partners is infinitesimal in comparison with the number so prosecuted in England and Wales. From our examination of Scottish witnesses, including the police and legal and medical witnesses, we are led to believe that homosexuality and homosexual behaviour are about as prevalent in different parts of Scotland as in comparable districts in the rest of Great Britain, and it seems to us that the disparity in the number of prosecutions is due to some fundamental differences in criminal procedures.

137. In Scotland, the homosexual offences listed in paragraph 77, like most other criminal offences, are prosecuted by a public prosecutor " in the public interest." They are prosecuted, usually in the Sheriff Courts, by the Procurator-Fiscal, a legal officer appointed by the Lord Advocate. It is the duty of the Procurator-Fiscal to initiate and conduct proceedings in the Sheriff Court in any case in which he considers the circumstances warrant such action, but he is not bound to institute proceedings in every case brought to his notice, though he would of course be answerable to the Lord Advocate in the event of his failure to do so where the public interest so required. But the overriding consideration is the public interest, and since no obvious public interest is served in the prosecution of stale offences such as those exemplified in paragraph 134 above, it is most unlikely that proceedings in cases such as these would be instituted in Scotland; and if there is little likelihood of a prosecution going forward, the police are not likely to waste time in pursuing enquiries into old offences.

138. We have already explained([1]) that in Scotland the court in which an offence shall be tried, and hence the maximum sentence which may be imposed, is decided by the prosecution, who have regard, in making the decision, to the gravity of the offence. No proceedings may, however, be commenced in a court of summary jurisdiction, including the Sheriff Court, in respect of any statutory offence committed more than six months previously, unless the statute specially provides. While it would still be open to the Procurator-Fiscal to commence proceedings with a view to the accused being tried on indictment after that time had elapsed, it seems to us unlikely that he would so proceed in respect of an isolated or comparatively trivial act of indecency. All cases in which the offence is more than six months old

---

([1]) See Note (b) to the table relating to Scotland in paragraph 77.

must, in any event, be reported in detail by the Procurator-Fiscal to the Crown Office before proceedings are taken and these can then be taken only on instructions from that Office. These considerations, too, possibly have some effect on the extent to which the police pursue enquiries into stale offences.

139. Another factor influencing the intensity of police enquiry is the standard of proof required by the law, and this seems to us to be higher in Scotland than it is in England and Wales. By the law of Scotland, no person can be convicted of any of the homosexual offences listed in paragraph 77 unless there is evidence of at least two witnesses implicating the person with the commission of the offence with which he is charged, or corroboration of one witness from such proved facts and circumstances as lead clearly to a conclusion of guilt. A written statement by the offender admitting his offences would, as in England and Wales, afford the necessary corroboration, but it seems to us that the rules relating to the admissibility of statements made by an accused person are much more stringent, or at least are more stringently interpreted, than they are in England.

140. In Scotland, the position is as follows. Where an offence has been committed it is the duty of police, subject to what follows, to question any person from whom it is considered that useful information may be obtained. A police officer is not entitled to question a person with the object of causing him to incriminate himself; and if in the course of questioning the officer seriously comes to the view that the person may be the perpetrator of the crime he must cease putting any questions and, if the information in his possession justifies this course, caution and charge the person. The caution should be in the following terms: " You are not obliged to say anything in answer to the charge, but anything you do say will be taken down in writing and may be used in evidence." After the person has been cautioned and charged, no further questions may be put to him. If he makes any reply it must be noted. If he wishes to write a reply he must be permitted to do so. If a person in police custody, at some time after he has been cautioned and charged, states that he wishes to make a statement, he has the right to have a solicitor present and any such statement is, where at all possible, to be taken by a magistrate or, in any event, by an officer who has not been directly concerned with the investigation of the offence with which the accused is charged. No questions must be put to the accused except such as may be necessary to clear up any obscurity, and even these must not go beyond elucidation. In brief, therefore, a man who is in custody and charged with an offence must not be questioned at all, except perhaps to clear up some particular point (for example, of time or place) in a statement previously made by the accused, though even this is looked on very critically by the courts. And at an earlier stage, questions are permissible so long as the police are investigating an occurrence, but once they get to know or have reason to believe that the person being questioned is the individual who has committed the offence, then the questioning must cease.

141. In England and Wales the position is summarised in what are known as the " Judges' Rules;" these are not rules of law, but are a set of rules drawn up by Her Majesty's Judges for the guidance of the police. The court may rule out a statement if it thinks it unreliable even though full compliance has been made with the Rules. Conversely, the fact that the Rules have not been fully complied with does not of itself render a statement inadmissible.[1] The effect of the Rules is as follows. When a police officer is endeavouring to discover the author of a crime, there is no objection to his

---

[1] *R.* v. *Best* (1909) 1 K.B., 692.

putting questions in respect thereof to any person or persons, whether suspected or not, from whom he thinks that useful information can be obtained. When a police officer has made up his mind to charge a person with a crime, he must, before asking him any questions, or any further questions as the case may be, warn such person that he is not obliged to say anything, but that anything he says may be given in evidence. Persons actually in custody must not be questioned without first being cautioned. This rule is not intended to encourage or authorise the questioning of a person in custody, even after he has been cautioned, on the subject of the crime for which he is in custody; but in some cases it may be proper or necessary (for example, for the purpose of removing some ambiguity in what he has said in a voluntary statement) to put questions to such a person, and the rule is intended to apply to cases of this kind.

142. The fact that the police in England may, subject to caution, question a suspect right up to the time at which he is formally taken into custody seems to us to account in a large measure for the fact that in the great majority of the English cases we have seen the offender was prosecuted on the strength of a written admission of his offences. We understand that such admissions are made by the great majority of persons accused of criminal offences generally, but it is striking that of the 480 men convicted in England and Wales during the three years ended March 1956 of homosexual offences committed with consenting adults in private, no fewer than 449 (94 per cent.) made written statements to the police admitting their offences. Only one of the nine men so convicted in Scotland during the same period made a written admission. In some cases, one party to the offence made a written statement admitting it and the other party refused to make any statement, with the result that one offender was successfully prosecuted while no proceedings could be taken against the other owing to lack of the necessary corroborative evidence.

143. We express no opinion as to the respective merits or demerits of the English and Scottish rules on this point; they operate over the whole field of criminal law and are not peculiar to homosexual offences. We recognise, moreover, that the criminal law fails when a guilty man escapes judgment no less than when an innocent man is convicted, so that the police have a duty to take all proper steps to secure the necessary corroborative evidence when they have reason to suspect that a criminal offence has been committed. But whereas some offences can be corroborated by external evidence (for example, fingerprints, photographs or the presence of stolen goods), it frequently happens in the case of a homosexual offence that the only incontrovertible corroboration that can be obtained is a written statement by the offender admitting his guilt. Accordingly the police may feel that they are placed in a greater necessity of obtaining written statements in cases of this kind than they would be in relation to cases where satisfactory corroborative evidence could be obtained by other means. And on the part of the offender, there is a greater anxiety to avoid publicity than there would be in relation to an offence which did not come under the same degree of social condemnation; this leads to a greater readiness to co-operate in disposing of the proceedings expeditiously in the hope of thereby minimising any public scandal. These factors, in our view, place before the police a temptation which does not exist in the same degree in relation to criminal offences generally; and for this reason it is particularly important to ensure that the Judges' Rules are strictly applied in relation to homosexual offenders.

Offences in Disciplinary Services and Establishments

144.([1]) We recognise that within services and establishments whose members are subject to a disciplinary régime it may be necessary, for the sake of good management and the preservation of discipline and for the protection of those of subordinate rank or position, to regard homosexual behaviour, even by consenting adults in private, as an offence. For instance, if our recommendations are accepted, a serving soldier over twenty-one who commits a homosexual act with a consenting adult partner in private will cease to be guilty of a civil offence or of an offence against Section 70 (1) of the Army Act, 1955 (which provides that any person subject to military law who commits a civil offence shall be guilty of an offence under that section, and hence liable to be dealt with by court-martial). The service authorities may nevertheless consider it necessary to retain Section 66 of the Act (which provides for the punishment of, *inter alia*, disgraceful conduct of an indecent or unnatural kind) on the ground that it is essential, in the services, to treat as offences certain types of conduct which may not amount to offences under the civil code.([2]) Similar problems may arise in relation to other services and establishments.

Offences by Inmates of Approved Schools([3])

145. Our attention has been called to some of the difficulties experienced by headmasters and managers of approved schools in dealing with indecent acts among boys committed to their charge. Since boys in approved schools cannot, like boys in ordinary boarding schools, be expelled or removed by their parents, the sanctions available to those responsible for the management of these establishments are limited. Indecencies of a trivial character can quite properly be, and usually are, dealt with within the establishment as breaches of school discipline. But there arise occasionally more serious cases —for instance, where boys are being persistently bullied or victimised by another boy or boys—where some more severe action against the offender is called for.

146. This is another matter on which there is some divergence of practice as between England and Wales on the one hand and Scotland on the other. In Scotland, the managers of approved schools are given discretion to deal with all indecent or homosexual acts by pupils and are free to decide whether or not to report particular incidents to the police. The action taken in such cases must, however, be recorded in the punishment book or log book of the school, whichever is appropriate. But in England and Wales, the managers of approved schools, while they are given discretion to deal with indecencies of a minor character as breaches of school discipline, are required to report to the police and the Home Office not only cases of victimisation but also all cases in which buggery or attempted buggery is detected or alleged.

147. We see no reason why the physical nature of the act should be the criterion by which the question whether or not to report to the police should be decided. We are informed that the requirement to report such cases to the police is not intended to secure that approved school boys are necessarily prosecuted for indecency committed by them; its purpose is to ensure that boys are not shielded, by reason of their being in approved

---

[1] See Reservation I (*d*), page 122.

[2] *Cf.* Report of the Select Committee on the Army Act and the Air Force Act, 20th October, 1953 (H. of C. Paper 289), paragraph 43.

[3] See paragraph 161 below.

schools, from the legal consequences of their actions, and that managers do not usurp the functions of the police. But it seems to us that the police have no greater (and no less) duty to concern themselves with what goes on in an approved school than they have in relation to any other establishment, and we feel that subject to any special safeguards necessitated by the circumstances in which the inmates are there, the heads and managers of approved schools should enjoy the same measure of discretion as those responsible for the management of any other educational establishment. The fact that such cases must be reported to the Home Office seems to us to be sufficient to ensure that boys who are likely to be a menace, or who have been a menace, to others are properly dealt with, either by transfer to another approved school or by prosecution where necessary, and to safeguard the interests of boys whose parents or guardians cannot remove them and who are victims or potential victims of other boys.

CHAPTER VI

The Treatment of Offenders

148. From our terms of reference, it is clear that we are concerned with the various ways in which convicted offenders are dealt with by the courts, and that the word "treatment" is not intended to be confined in its meaning to any specific kind of medical attention.

149. The punishment prescribed by law for homosexual offences (other than bye-law offences) is imprisonment. This is in accordance with customary legislative practice; but the general criminal law provides other methods by which the courts can deal with persons brought before them on criminal charges. These methods apply to persons convicted of homosexual offences just as they apply to other offenders, and in practice only a minority of homosexual offenders are sent to prison. For instance, in 1955,[1] only 30 per cent. of the persons found guilty by the English courts of homosexual offences punishable with imprisonment were, in fact, sent to prison; and in Scotland, during the same year, only 37 per cent. of those convicted of recorded homosexual offences were so dealt with. We think, therefore, that it may be helpful, as a background to our consideration of this part of enquiry, to review briefly the more important alternatives to imprisonment available to the courts at the present time.

(a) England and Wales

150. In appropriate cases, the following alternative methods of treatment may be applied to persons found guilty of criminal offences, including homosexual offences:

(i) absolute discharge
(ii) conditional discharge
(iii) binding over
(iv) probation
(v) fine
and, in the case of younger offenders,

---

[1] No later statistics are available.

(vi) borstal training (for offenders aged 16 to 21)
(vii) detention in a detention centre (for offenders aged 14 to 21)
(viii) committal to an approved school ⎫ (for offenders
(ix) committal to the care of a fit person ⎭ under 17)
(x) attendance at an attendance centre (for offenders aged 12 to 17).

Absolute and Conditional Discharge
151. " Absolute discharge " is self-explanatory, and is appropriate where the court is of opinion, having regard to all the circumstances of the case, including the nature of the offence and the character of the offender, that it is inexpedient to inflict punishment and that a probation order is not appropriate. As an alternative to absolute discharge, the court may discharge the offender subject to the condition that he commits no further offence for a specified period not exceeding twelve months. This is known as " conditional discharge." An offender committing another offence during the period of conditional discharge is liable to be sentenced for the original offence.

12 per cent. of the persons convicted during 1955 of homosexual offences punishable with imprisonment were absolutely or conditionally discharged.

Binding Over
152. Where a court considers that the circumstances of a case make such a course expedient in the interests of justice it may, instead of imposing any punishment, require the convicted person to enter into recognisances, with or without sureties, to come up for judgment if called upon. The binding over is usually for a specified period, and it is usual to require the convicted person, during that period, to keep the peace and be of good behaviour. If he fails to do so, he may be brought up and sentenced for the offence in respect of which he was bound over. This method is not so frequently used as the more modern conditional discharge; but it is still used, and about 3 per cent. of the persons convicted during 1955 of homosexual offences punishable with imprisonment were bound over.

Probation
153. Probation is a development of the system of binding over. Where the court by which the person is convicted is of opinion that having regard to the circumstances, including the nature of the offence and the character of the offender, it is expedient to do so, it may, instead of sentencing him, make a probation order. This method is frequently used by the courts in dealing with homosexual offenders, and 24 per cent. of the persons convicted during 1955 of homosexual offences punishable with imprisonment were put on probation.

154. A probation order requires the offender to be under the supervision of a probation officer, whose duty is to " advise, assist and befriend " him for not less than one or more than three years. The order may require the offender to comply with such additional requirements (including requirements as to residence) as the court, having regard to his circumstances, considers necessary for securing his good conduct or for preventing repetition by him of the same offence or the commission of other offences. Unless the offender is under fourteen years of age, a probation order can be made only if he expresses his willingness to comply with its requirements.

155. Where a court is satisfied, on the evidence of a duly qualified medical practitioner appearing to be experienced in the diagnosis of mental disorders, that the mental condition of an offender, though not such as to justify certification under the Lunacy or Mental Deficiency Acts, is such as requires and may be susceptible to treatment, it has power to include in the probation order a requirement that the offender shall submit, for a specified period not exceeding twelve months, to suitable treatment. This treatment may be:

(a) treatment as a voluntary patient under Section 1 of the Mental Treatment Act, 1930;

(b) treatment as a resident patient in a place approved for the purpose by the Minister of Health;

(c) treatment as a non-resident patient at a place specified in the order; or

(d) treatment under the direction of a medical practitioner specified in the order.

The precise nature of the treatment is at the discretion of the doctor in charge of the case.

The court may not impose such a requirement unless it is satisfied that the necessary arrangements can be made.

156. A probationer who fails to comply with the terms of the probation order may be brought before the court and fined up to £10 or, if of appropriate age, ordered to attend at an attendance centre, the probation order remaining in force in either case. Alternatively, he may be dealt with for the offence in respect of which he was placed on probation. He can also be dealt with for the original offence if he commits a further offence during the period of the order.

157. Conviction of an offence in respect of which an order of absolute or conditional discharge or a probation order is made is not regarded as a conviction for the purpose of any future proceedings against the offender, except where an offender over seventeen is subsequently sentenced for the offence in respect of which he was conditionally discharged or placed on probation. In any event, the conviction of an offender who is placed on probation or discharged conditionally or absolutely must be disregarded for the purposes of any enactment imposing any disqualification or disability on convicted persons or authorising or requiring the imposition of any such disqualification or disability.

Fine

158. A court before which a person is convicted of any of the homosexual offences punishable with imprisonment may fine the offender instead of sending him to prison. The courts frequently avail themselves of this alternative, and 30 per cent. of the persons convicted in 1955 of homosexual offences punishable with imprisonment were fined instead.

Borstal Training

159. Where a person over sixteen but under twenty-one years of age is convicted on indictment of an offence punishable by imprisonment the court may, in lieu of any other sentence, pass a sentence of borstal training where it is satisfied, having regard to the character and previous conduct of the offender and to the circumstances of the offence, that such a course is expedient for the offender's reformation and the prevention of crime. And

where a person between the ages stated is convicted by a magistrates' court of an offence punishable on summary conviction with imprisonment, he may be committed to quarter sessions with a view to the passing of a sentence of borstal training, but in this case the court must, before committing the offender for sentence, consider any report or representations made by or on behalf of the Prison Commissioners on his physical and mental condition and his suitability for borstal training.

A person sentenced to borstal training is to be detained in a borstal institution for such period, not exceeding three years, as the Prison Commissioners may determine, but the Prison Commissioners may not release him in less than nine months unless required to do so by the Home Secretary.

The object of borstal training is to develop character and the moral, mental, physical and vocational capacities of the offender, with particular emphasis on the development of responsibility and self-control through giving trust which increases as the offender makes progress.

Borstal training is not frequently used by the courts in dealing with homosexual offenders. In 1955, only 19 youths were sentenced to borstal training for indictable homosexual offences; during that year 236 youths between seventeen and twenty-one were convicted of such offences.

Detention in a Detention Centre

160. Detention centres are available, on a limited scale, for the treatment of persons between fourteen and twenty-one years of age. Treatment at these centres is disciplinary, and is of the nature of a "short sharp shock" for those who are thought to need it. The sentence is normally one of three months. This method of treatment is to be used only where the court has considered every other method (except imprisonment) by which the offender might be dealt with and is of the opinion that none of those methods is appropriate. It is available only in those cases where the offence is one in respect of which a sentence of imprisonment could have been imposed if it had been committed by an adult, and may not be used where the offender has been previously sentenced to imprisonment or borstal training, nor may it be used in the case of an offender over seventeen who has previously been detained in a detention centre. In areas where detention centres are not available, the court may order an offender between fourteen and seventeen years of age to be detained for up to one month in a remand home.

Seven youths out of a total of 170 within the prescribed ages convicted during 1955 of indictable homosexual offences were ordered to be detained in one of these centres.

Committal to an Approved School

161. A court by which a person under seventeen years of age is found guilty of an offence punishable in the case of an adult by imprisonment may order him to be sent to an "approved school." Approved schools, which come under the general supervision of the Home Office, are run by boards of voluntary Managers or, in some cases, by local authorities. In them an attempt is made to provide such education and training, under residential conditions, as is most suitable for the needs of the individual concerned. Of the 225 boys under seventeen convicted during 1955 of indictable homosexual offences, 21 were committed to approved schools.

Committal to the Care of a Fit Person

162. As an alternative to committing the offender to an approved school, the court may commit him to the care of a "fit person," whether a relative or not, who is willing to undertake the care of him. Where an order is made

committing the offender to the care of a fit person, a probation order may also be made. A local authority may be a "fit person" for this purpose, and in practice most offenders committed to the care of a fit person are committed to the care of a local authority, which, through its Children's Committee, makes such arrangements as it considers best for the offender's welfare, either in one of its own homes or by boarding him out with foster parents. One boy convicted of a homosexual offence was committed to the care of a "fit person" in 1955.

Attendance at an Attendance Centre
163. Attendance centres are available, also on a limited scale, for the treatment of boys between twelve and seventeen years of age found guilty by a court of summary jurisdiction of an offence for which an adult could be imprisoned. The primary objects of this method of treatment are to indicate the authority of the law and to educate the boys in the proper use of leisure time. The court may order the boy to attend the centre for not more than twelve hours in the aggregate. Arrangements for his attendance must be such as to avoid interference, so far as practicable, with his school or working hours. The boy cannot be required to attend the centre on more than one occasion in any one day, or for more than three hours on any one occasion. This method of treatment cannot be used if the offender has been previously sentenced to imprisonment, borstal training or detention in a detention centre, or has been ordered to be sent to an approved school. Three boys found guilty during 1955 of indictable homosexual offences were ordered to attend one of these centres.

Persistent Offenders
164. The criminal law contains special provisions applicable to offenders whom normal methods of punishment have failed to deter, or normal methods of training to reform. These provisions divide persistent offenders into two categories. First, those who, while they are clearly committed to a criminal career if not stopped in time, are yet not so far beyond hope of correction that a period of intensive and constructive training may not succeed in diverting them. Secondly, those who by their age, criminal history and character seem to be beyond this type of correction and can be restrained only by prolonged detention. For the first category, the law provides a form of sentence known as "corrective training"; for the second, a form of sentence called "preventive detention."

165. A sentence of corrective training for a term of not less than two nor more than four years may be imposed on a person not less than twenty-one years of age who is convicted on indictment of an offence punishable with imprisonment for a term of two years or more, if he has two or more previous convictions of such an offence since attaining the age of seventeen. Like borstal training, the aim of corrective training is the reformation of the offender and the prevention of crime by trying to stop those who have already engaged in crime on a number of occasions from developing into habitual criminals. The system aims at providing opportunities for the prisoners to exercise self-determination and responsibility. Corrective training is carried out in special prisons where there is more free association among the prisoners than is possible at an ordinary prison with a heterogeneous population, and selected assistant governors are appointed to take special responsibility for the individual training of groups of men. A prisoner sentenced to corrective training becomes eligible for release on conditional licence when he has served two-thirds of his sentence. Only one man convicted of a homosexual offence in 1955 was sentenced to corrective training.

166. Where the court is satisfied that this is expedient "for the protection of the public," a sentence of preventive detention for a term of not less than five nor more than fourteen years may be passed on a person not under thirty years of age who is convicted on indictment of an offence punishable with imprisonment for a term of two years or more, if that person (*a*) has three or more previous convictions of such an offence since attaining the age of seventeen, and (*b*) has served two or more sentences of imprisonment, corrective training or borstal training. A sentence of preventive detention is in its nature aimed at the detention of confirmed criminals for a prolonged period in conditions of maximum security and strong disciplinary control, but effort is also made to do what is possible to send these hardened offenders out of prison both able and willing to avoid relapsing into crime. Five men convicted of homosexual offences in 1955 were sentenced to preventive detention.

(b) Scotland

167. The methods of treatment available in Scotland differ from those mentioned above in the following respects:—

(i) "Conditional discharge" does not exist, but courts may adopt the somewhat similar procedure of deferring sentence for a period, with or without conditions adjected.

(ii) The court may dismiss the offender with an admonition.

(iii) "Binding over" is a term unfamiliar to Scots law, but Scottish courts may use the similar method of requiring offenders to find caution for their good behaviour.

(iv) Probation may be used only if the offender, whatever his age, expresses willingness to comply with the order. Courts of summary jurisdiction do not proceed to conviction before making a probation order or granting an absolute discharge. Where an offender has been convicted on indictment and placed on probation or discharged absolutely, the conviction is regarded as a conviction only for the purposes of the proceedings in which the order is made and of any subsequent proceedings which may be taken against the offender for a similar offence; the usual consequences of conviction apply, however, where the offender is seventeen or over and is subsequently sentenced for the original offence.

(v) There are at present no detention centres in Scotland, and there is no statutory provision for attendance centres.

(vi) Sentences of borstal training may be passed by sheriffs and stipendiary magistrates as well as by the High Court. No minimum period of training is prescribed (although in recent years no trainee has been released until he has been detained for at least nine months).

(vii) Sentences of preventive detention may be passed only by the High Court of Justiciary.

168. The figures relating to such homosexual offences as are separately recorded show that out of eighty persons against whom the charges were proved during 1955 fifty were dealt with by one or other of the above methods. Of these, forty were fined, seven were absolutely discharged or put on probation without a conviction being recorded, one was put on probation following conviction, and two were dismissed with an admonition.

Selection of the Appropriate Method of Disposal

169. In general, to decide the most appropriate method of treatment of a particular offender is a much more difficult problem for the courts than the decision as to his guilt, and this is particularly true of the offences with which we are here concerned. It is, however, of the utmost importance, not only to the offender but to the whole community, that the sentence should be right and effective. Harsh treatment can undoubtedly create in the offender a sense of injustice and induce in him a frame of mind likely to make him more inclined to commit further offences. On the other hand, leniency may not only have the same effect, by encouraging the offender to believe that he has nothing to fear if he commits further offences, but may also encourage potential offenders to believe that they have nothing to fear if they commit similar offences.

170. It is, we understand, now generally accepted that apart altogether from any considerations of retribution the objectives of penal sanctions are deterrence, prevention and reformation. Thus the law provides for the punishment of certain acts in the hope that persons will be deterred from committing such acts. Where the law itself has not proved a sufficient deterrent, it may be necessary, for the protection of others, to prevent the offender from doing further wrong, even by putting him in prison. And for the common good it is desirable that an offender should be subjected to such form of treatment as is most likely to improve his character and make him a better citizen.

171. The courts are faced with the problem of reconciling, in an individual case, these three main objectives, which are not always compatible. It is not enough to look only to the details of the offence or the circumstances of the offender. In doing justice to the individual offender the courts cannot overlook their duty to protect other citizens and to ensure respect for the criminal law, and they must necessarily ask themselves in every case which of these three objectives should be paramount before considering the method most likely to be successful in a particular case. Thus, for example, when a particular offence is rife at a particular time or in a particular place, it may be right for the courts to attach more weight to the deterrent and preventive aspects than would otherwise be the case. At the same time, the ultimate purpose is more likely to be achieved if the treatment of the offender is constructive and not merely punitive, and it follows that the personality of the individual offender must be a decisive factor in determining the appropriate treatment.

172. It will be apparent from the figures we have quoted above, and from the more detailed figures set out in the Tables in Appendix I, that the courts, in dealing with persons charged with homosexual offences, frequently use the alternative methods of treatment available to them.

Disparity in Sentencing[1]

173. We have had brought to our notice an opinion widely held among, and causing concern to, those well qualified to know, that the sentences imposed by the courts for homosexual offences show an undue disparity between one case and another. We are bound to record that this opinion is widespread, and to the extent to which it is believed to be true it increases the feeling of arbitrariness and injustice to which we have already referred.

---

[1] In consequence of his appointment as one of Her Majesty's Judges, which took place during the course of our enquiry, Mr. Justice Diplock felt obliged to withdraw from our deliberations so far as they related to matters dealt with under this heading.

174. It is clear to us from our examination of police reports that the circumstances in which the offences are committed vary considerably. In some cases, the act takes place between fully and freely consenting parties; in others, it is clear that the consent of one of the parties amounts to no more than a grudging submission. In some cases the act takes place between partners of roughly comparable age and status; in others between partners of very disparate age or status. In some cases the offender is a man in a position of authority. In some cases the act takes place in private; in others public decency is offended. And when, as frequently happens, a person is convicted of a series of offences, several of these elements may be present in varying combinations.

175. Even where two persons are convicted of committing an offence together, the fact that the courts must have regard not only to the offence itself but also to the individual offender means that it may be right, and very often is right, to discriminate between the two. One of the offenders, for example, may be of tender years and not known to have been previously guilty of any offence against the law; or he may have reached an advanced age without having broken the law and may have yielded to circumstances of such a kind that they are not likely to recur and at the same time may fairly be regarded as extenuating his offence. The other partner, on the other hand, may be a hardened and persistent offender. Further, homosexual acts do not occur spontaneously; there must be some initiative from one or other of the partners, and the circumstances in which the offence was instigated no doubt weigh to some extent with the courts.

176. We recognise the difficulty experienced by the courts in fitting the sentence both to the offence and the offender in this type of case. Nevertheless, making every allowance for the factors we have mentioned, we cannot avoid the conclusion that there are disparities in sentences wide enough to justify the concern expressed in paragraph 173.

177. Having indicated this lack of uniformity in the treatment of offenders by the courts, which sometimes gives the appearance of arbitrariness, it is less easy to suggest a remedy. The present penal system applies to all criminal offences, and the consideration of any fundamental change in the whole penal system (for example, the introduction of indeterminate sentences or reviewing tribunals) would raise issues far beyond our terms of reference. Short of some such fundamental change it must remain for the individual court to decide, subject only to the maximum prescribed by Parliament, the penalty to be imposed in all the circumstances of a particular case. There are elements present, in the offences with which we are concerned, which arouse in many people feelings of disgust and indignation, and it would be surprising if varying human reactions found no expression in the sentences imposed. We have no ground for doubting that within the limits of these natural differences all those responsible for the administration of justice recognise their obligation to take a dispassionate view of the offences and offenders before them. For reasons which will be apparent from what is said in paragraphs 174 and 175 above, it would be quite impossible, and indeed contrary to the principles of modern penology, to devise any "tariff" of "standard" sentences to be imposed in given circumstances. While we are therefore not able to suggest any positive remedy, we call attention to the matter and to the desirability of the courts' dealing dispassionately with every homosexual offence, giving proper weight to the reformative as well as to the deterrent or preventive aspects.

178. We have been made aware that in sentencing to imprisonment men convicted of homosexual offences, the courts sometimes intimate to an offender

that he will receive medical treatment for his condition in prison. In some cases, the courts even suggest that the offender is being sent to prison for this purpose. We are strongly of the opinion that such statements ought not to be made. A great deal is done in the prisons in the way of psychiatric or other treatment of those offenders in whom such treatment offers some prospect of success, but as we explain later, the proportion of such cases is very small. To hold out to a convicted offender a hope of treatment which does not materialise is to inculcate in him a sense of grievance which is bound to render him less responsive to such elements in prison treatment in its broader aspects as might conduce to his reformation.

179. Even where the information before the court holds out a substantial hope of successful treatment, the duration of the sentence should not be fixed by reference to any estimate of the time which treatment is likely to take. If the primary consideration in the mind of the court is successful treatment, there are means by which convicted offenders can be required to submit to this without going to prison. If, on the other hand, the seriousness of the offence is such that a prison sentence is necessary, this should be awarded, as it were, on its own merits, in the knowledge that within the limits of the resources available anything possible will be done in prison for an offender in whose case there is a reasonable probability that psychiatric or other treatment will be successful.

180. In the latter connection, one important point has been brought to our notice. The prison medical service is understaffed and incompletely integrated with the national health service. Its members do much valuable and devoted work. But there are not enough full-time prison medical officers, not enough of them have had an adequate psychiatric training—out of the forty-six full-time doctors at the time of our enquiry, only six held the Diploma in Psychological Medicine, though another twenty-two had had experience in mental hospitals or other fields of psychiatric medicine before joining the prison service—and in many parts of the country it is not possible for them to call on enough help from the psychiatric consultants of the national health service. There is a national shortage of psychiatrists; and it is to be expected that a substantial proportion of those who elect to take public appointments will prefer the wider and more varied experience offered by the mental hospitals and other psychiatric services within the national health service. If the most effective use is to be made of the limited supply of qualified psychiatrists, it is essential that there should be a two-way flow between the prison medical service and the national health service through the Regional Hospital Boards. This would be for the mutual benefit of both. We accordingly recommend that the organisation, establishment and conditions of service of the prison medical service be urgently reviewed with these considerations in mind.

Medical Reports

181. It has been urged on us that in every case in which a person is found guilty of a homosexual offence, the court by which he is found guilty should be required to obtain a report on his mental condition before deciding how to deal with him. The ground for this suggestion is the alleged frequency of psychiatric abnormality in the homosexual offender. The suggestion is that this should be a report to the court, as distinct from any reports which had been offered as evidence while the case was being tried, and that it should be furnished by a member of a panel of consultant psychiatrists nominated by some appropriate authority. The purpose of such a report would be to indicate to the court (*a*) whether the offender was suffering from any condition which would result in diminished responsibility; (*b*) whether the

offender's condition could be modified by some form of treatment which the court had power to require him to undergo, and the prospects of success of such treatment; and (c) what part, if any, in that treatment, should be taken by medical men.

182. At the present time, it frequently happens that expert psychiatric advice is furnished to the court during the hearing of the case. In some cases, the offender will have been medically examined while on remand. In others, medical evidence is called by the defence. In some cases, both happen. Some courts attach considerable weight to such evidence; others, less. It is at present within the competence of the court, if it should so wish, to obtain a report between the finding of guilt and the passing of sentence. The proposal made to us is therefore, in effect, that what is now within the discretion of the courts should become a universal requirement in relation to all persons found guilty of homosexual offences, and that a body of independent consultants should be available for the purpose.

183. The proposal presents several difficulties. First, it is not clear to us that homosexual offenders should be singled out, from all offenders, for this special procedure. We have already given our reasons for thinking that the commission of a homosexual offence is not *prima facie* evidence of disease in the offender or of a condition to which can be attributed any relevant diminution of responsibility. We have, at the same time, indicated that homosexual offences may sometimes be due in whole or in part to a recognisable disease; but this possibility attaches to any other crime, and there is no obvious reason for distinguishing, on this ground, between homosexual offences and other offences. If a report of the kind proposed is to be compulsorily required in the case of homosexual offenders, there seems to be no reason why the requirement should not be extended at least to other sexual offenders; for it could well be argued that the conduct of many persons guilty of heterosexual offences was as likely to be attributable to some disease as that of the homosexual offender. Indeed, outside the range of sexual offences altogether, there are other crimes which seem to need medical investigation no less.

184. Secondly, it is not clear that much would be gained by making obligatory what is at present within the discretion of the court. It is important to remember that the court's responsibility for imposing sentence is, within the limits prescribed by law, absolute. This responsibility cannot properly be abdicated; and while it is desirable that the courts should be as fully informed as possible about the mental and physical state of offenders brought before them, it would be contrary to the principles of criminal jurisprudence in this country if the courts were to hand over to doctors the essentially judicial duty of passing sentence on a person convicted of a crime. Further, if a court is not disposed to use its present discretionary power to call for a report, it is doubtful whether it would be greatly influenced by a report which it was compulsorily required to obtain. Our evidence suggests that the courts are ready to call for medical reports where there are any grounds, either in the facts of the case or in the convicted person's previous history (which is always before the court) for supposing that a medical report would be helpful. A survey of homosexual offenders remanded to Brixton prison in 1946 showed that out of 66 prisoners, 34 had some recognisable abnormality. Of the 66, the magistrates had called for a report in 39 cases, and this number included 29 of the 34 mentally abnormal cases. The Cambridge survey indicates that in dealing with homosexual offenders other than those convicted of bye-law offences, the courts called for medical reports in approximately

20 per cent. of cases, and in the case of indecent assaults the proportion was as high as 31·7 per cent.

185. Finally, there are practical difficulties. If all men found guilty of homosexual offences are to be examined and reported on, a good deal of expert time will be taken up. There are some parts of the country in which it would be difficult to find the necessary experts at short notice, and even if this difficulty could be overcome there would in some cases be a serious delay. To arrange and conduct an examination and report of the kind we are considering would take time; the consultant might require more than one interview with the offender, and by the time he had made his report the court might have ended its sitting. This is particularly liable to happen if the trial takes place on the last day of an assizes or quarter sessions. It is obviously desirable that the offenders should be sentenced by those who originally tried them. If a man were found guilty on the last day of an assize, it would be necessary to take him to whatever town the particular judge happened to be sitting at when the report became available, and this might be many miles from the venue of the trial. In the case of quarter sessions, the delay might be considerable. There would be difficulties in fixing a date for the resumed hearing; recorders and chairmen of quarter sessions are usually busy barristers, and in the case of county sessions a date convenient for four other magistrates as well as the chairman has to be found. Again, a judge of assize or a recorder or chairman of quarter sessions has so many cases—often a dozen or more pleas a day—that it must be difficult for him to keep in mind the detailed facts of a particular case for any length of time. A just sentence is more likely to be given at the conclusion of all the evidence—or possibly after " a night to sleep on it "—than after a lapse of time, when the facts of the case and the impressions made by witnesses are no longer clear in the judge's mind. We appreciate that difficulties of this sort do not exist to the same extent when the case is one which can be dealt with by a magistrates' court; nor do they exist to the same extent in Scotland. If our recommendation that gross indecency should be triable summarily is accepted, the number of such cases going to assizes and quarter sessions would be substantially reduced; and if homosexual acts between consenting adults in private ceased to be criminal offences, there would be a further reduction in the number of cases at present dealt with by the higher courts. The overall number of offenders to be dealt with would not, however, be substantially affected, and the difficulty about the local shortages of experts would remain.

186. In the light of the foregoing objections, we do not recommend that the court should be required to obtain a report on the mental condition of every person found guilty of a homosexual offence before deciding how to deal with him. Short of this, it has been suggested to us (and one of our members favours this suggestion) that the court should be required to obtain such a report before sentencing to imprisonment for the first time a person found guilty of a homosexual offence. We share the desire of our witnesses that no homosexual offender should be sent to prison if a recurrence of his offences can, consistently with the interests of justice, be prevented by other means. We are anxious also that the courts should be aware of any factors which might diminish the offender's responsibility for his offences. But even this modified proposal is open to many, if not most, of the objections we have mentioned. In particular, we see no reason why this requirement should be limited to persons convicted of homosexual offences. Further, it seems to us that it would be inappropriate to require a court to obtain a medical report just because it had it in mind to impose a particular form of punishment, and that the decision whether or not a medical report should be called

for should rest on other grounds. It might, for example, be much more important that a report should be obtained in the case of a young first offender who offered some hope of successful treatment though his offence was not serious enough to justify a prison sentence, than it would be in the case of a persistent offender whom other methods of treatment had failed to deter and who must necessarily be detained for the protection of others.

187. There is a case for requiring the courts to obtain a medical report in respect of every young person convicted for the first time of a homosexual offence. So far as treatment is likely to be effective, the probability of success is greater among young persons; indeed, this is one of the considerations that have weighed with us in leaving as a criminal offence homosexual behaviour by young persons under twenty-one. As we have said earlier, we do not contemplate that all such cases should come before the courts. If our recommendations are accepted, persons under twenty-one will be charged with homosexual offences only where their homosexual behaviour has been accompanied by conduct of a patently criminal or vicious nature, or where it is apparent that the offender would benefit from being placed on probation with a view either to treatment or to supervision of a more general kind. In these cases, it is likely that the conduct or environment of the offender will have been such as to suggest some maladjustment which a course of treatment opportunely undertaken might remedy, and in any event a talk with an experienced doctor may well be salutary. We accordingly recommend that a court by which a person under twenty-one is found guilty of a homosexual offence should be required by law, before passing sentence on that person, to obtain and consider a psychiatric report.

188. Others who ought always to be referred for examination are those who appear obviously disturbed or dull, those with unsatisfactory home backgrounds, and those whose first offence occurs late in life; in such cases, the existence of some mental abnormality which might account for the offence is a distinct probability. Courts should always be ready, too, to refer for examination those who seem genuinely to want help with their problem; as we explain later, psychotherapy often depends for its success on the co-operation of the patient, and this co-operation is likely to be forthcoming if the offender has a genuine desire to be helped.

189. Whenever circumstances such as those we have mentioned in the preceding paragraphs suggest that a medical examination is called for in the case of an offender who is committed on bail for trial at assizes or quarter sessions, we consider it desirable that the committing magistrates should make use of their power[1] to require the offender to submit to medical examination while on bail. This examination should be carried out by a medical practitioner experienced in the diagnosis of mental disorders. No further examination would then be necessary if the superior court wished to consider the possibility of putting the offender on probation with a requirement that he submits to medical treatment with a view to the improvement of his mental condition.[2]

Therapeutic measures

190. We are aware that in this section of our report we are dealing with professional matters of a complex and technical kind. The following paragraphs set out the assessment which has been reached by the Committee

---

[1] Magistrates' Courts Act, 1952, Section 26 (4).
[2] See paragraph 155 above.

as a whole of the evidence submitted to us on these matters. The non-medical members of the Committee recognise that to some of their medical colleagues this assessment, expressed, as it must be, in non-technical language and from the layman's point of view, may well seem inadequate. We hope therefore that the Note([1]) appended to this Chapter by Dr. Curran and Dr. Whitby will be taken as supplying the necessary professional supplement to the eighteen paragraphs which follow.

191. We have earlier made it clear that although homosexual behaviour in some cases may result from disease, the evidence placed before us has not established to our satisfaction the proposition that homosexuality is a disease. This does not mean, however, that it is not susceptible to treatment. As we explain elsewhere, psychiatrists deal regularly with problems of personality which are not regarded as diseases. It seems to us that the academic question whether homosexuality is a disease is of much less importance than the practical question of the extent to which, and the ways in which, treatment can help those in whom the condition exists.

192. In this connection, it is important to consider what the objectives of this help should be. It seems to us that these may be one or more of the following. First, a change in the direction of the sexual preference; secondly, a better adaptation to life in general; and thirdly, greater continence or self-control. Success in achieving one of these objectives may help in achieving another.

193. The first implies such an alteration of a man's sexual propensity that instead of being directed towards his own sex it will be directed towards the other sex. The notion of a complete reorientation rests, however, on the conception of homosexuality and heterosexuality as absolute conditions, whereas the probability is, as we have explained earlier, that these conditions can co-exist in an individual, and the degree to which they co-exist in an individual can vary during different epochs in his or her life. We were struck by the fact that none of our medical witnesses were able, when we saw them, to provide any reference in medical literature to a complete change of this kind. Some of them have since sent us one or two examples in which such a change is claimed, but it is extremely difficult to assess the results in such cases. This difficulty is well illustrated by the case of an elderly married man who sought advice, at his wife's instigation, for impotence. It transpired that he had always been entirely homosexual by propensity. He had married in the hope of cure, but had achieved intercourse only with the aid of homosexual fantasies. To all outward appearances this would have seemed a striking example of change in sexual orientation, but it was clear that he had always been and remained a homosexual. Our evidence leads us to the conclusion that a total reorientation from complete homosexuality to complete heterosexuality is very unlikely indeed. At the same time, there is evidence that the homosexual who is of a Kinsey rating lower than 5 or 6 provides opportunity for treatment with a better prospect of success in this sense. It should be noted, however, that behaviour does not necessarily correspond with propensity, so that a shift along the homosexual-heterosexual continuum would not necessarily be accompanied by a change in the form or extent of sexual activity.

194. Short of any alteration in the direction of the sexual urge, however, treatment may successfully lead to a better adaptation to life in general. A homosexual, like any other person who suffers from maladjustment to society, may be regarded as successfully treated if he is brought to a more

---

([1]) See page 72.

nearly complete adjustment with the society in which he lives. This can happen without any radical change in his propensity itself. It can happen by his being made more fully aware of his condition, and by processes which are directed not to changing it, but towards his fuller understanding of it and of the problems which it raises for him in relation to society. The object of the treatment is to relieve mental stress by producing a better adjustment. It is perhaps worth adding that for this reason there may be good grounds, from the medical point of view, for not attempting any fundamental reorientation of the sexual propensity of a homosexual who is already well adjusted and is a useful member of society.

195. Treatment may have yet another purpose. It may be directed simply towards making the man more discreet or continent in his behaviour, without attempting any other change in his nature. This is not to be despised as an objective, for if it is successful such treatment will reduce the number of homosexual offences and offenders. It is here that the use of oestrogens, to which we refer later, has its place.

196. From whichever of the foregoing points of view it may be regarded, treatment itself will vary through a wide range, if only to match the diversity of individual personalities. It is important to remember that "treatment" need not necessarily, or even often, imply any active steps to be taken by a physician or by a psychiatrist. Often it will be desirable that various methods of treatment should be applied simultaneously, bringing into service a combination of many helpers. Treatment will not always be conducted under the direct supervision of a doctor, though the responsibility for the original advice will be his. Nor will it always involve psychotherapy. As often as not, it will be a matter of guiding the patient to help himself, not only by personal influence but also by helping to manipulate environmental factors. And in this work there is a place for the clergyman, the psychiatric social worker, the probation officer and, it may be added, the adjusted homosexual, as well as for the doctor. Indeed, the Oxford survey suggests that in those cases where probation with a requirement to submit to medical treatment had produced successful results, these were due as much to the work of the probation officer as to that of the doctor.

197. There are many obstacles to success in psychotherapeutic treatment. These include lack of co-operation from the patient and a low level of intelligence, and many homosexual offenders show one or both of these features. Some of them do not wish to be changed, either in propensity or behaviour, if only because they are afraid of losing, without any sure prospect of anything to take its place, the one form of sexual satisfaction which they know; others are more concerned with escaping further criminal charges than with anything else; others are of a general level of intelligence so low as to prevent the establishing of the proper relationship between patient and psychiatrist. Out of 1,065 men in prison in 1955 for homosexual offences, only 158 (15 per cent.) were regarded by the prison medical officers as possible subjects for treatment, and only 65 (6 per cent.) were ultimately accepted for treatment at the psychiatric units at Wakefield and Wormwood Scrubs. Of the 907 regarded as unsuitable for treatment, 245 (27 per cent.) evinced no anxiety or real wish for treatment, and no less than 385 (42 per cent.) were found to be unsuitable on account of their age, inadaptability or inadequate character or intelligence. On the basis of these figures, it is not possible to expect dramatic results from widespread treatment of homosexual offenders by way of psychotherapy. To say this is not to belittle the work which has been, and is being, done by individual or group therapy, and it is estimated that of those selected for such treatment at the prisons during 1954 nearly one-half benefited therefrom.

198. From the medical, as distinct from the penal, point of view, there is much to be said for a wider use of probation with a requirement that the offender submits to medical treatment with a view to the improvement of his mental condition.[1] The Oxford survey indicates that only 68 persons convicted of homosexual offences were put on probation with such a requirement in 1953. This is out of a total of approximately 2,200 convictions. It is true that this method of treatment is of limited application; it is appropriate only where a psychiatrist is satisfied that the offender's mental condition is such as requires and may be susceptible to treatment, and these desiderata are not met in the majority of cases. Moreover, this procedure can be used only where the court is satisfied that arrangements can be made for the necessary treatment. This may be either at outpatient clinics—and this may well be the appropriate place for most cases—or in mental hospitals. In any case, this method can be used only with the offender's consent. And there is the overriding consideration that it must be for the court to decide, in each case, whether or not such a procedure is compatible with the protection of other persons from a man who has been convicted of a homosexual offence.

199. In this connection, the power of the courts to include in the probation order a requirement that the offender should submit to treatment as a voluntary patient in a mental hospital does not always ensure that other persons are adequately protected. Any person received into a mental hospital as a voluntary patient is entitled to leave there on giving seventy-two hours' written notice of his intention to do so.[2] It is true that a probationer who voluntarily discharges himself from a mental hospital which he has entered as a voluntary patient in pursuance of a probation order breaches the conditions attached to the order, and becomes liable, as explained earlier, to be dealt with for the offence in respect of which he was placed on probation. In practice, however, the mental hospital authorities deprecate prosecutions for breaches of probation orders in cases such as this, since they tend to give rise to the impression that persons not certifiably of unsound mind can be detained in mental hospitals by the power of the law against their own will. Out of forty-two cases covered by the Oxford survey, no fewer than ten probationers in whose cases a requirement to submit to medical treatment was attached to the probation order, discharged themselves from treatment against medical advice, and none of these ten was brought before the court for breach of probation when this breach consisted only of non-attendance or self-discharge. Considerations such as this doubtless weigh with the courts, and a reluctance to use this procedure is understandable in cases where the conduct of the offender has been such as to suggest that the protection of the public must be a decisive factor in determining how to dispose of him.

200. Nevertheless, the figures we have quoted suggest that there is room for a more extensive resort to probation with a condition of medical treatment. In saying this, we are not moved only by consideration for the offender. A prison sentence can, in many cases, detrimentally affect any prospect of successful treatment, so that the offender remains in a state of mind predisposed to the repetition of his offence. If, by the use of other methods, the offender can be successfully brought to a state of better adjustment to society in which he is less disposed to repeat his offence, then clearly society gains. The Cambridge survey, however, shows that the proportion of homosexual offenders subsequently reconvicted was almost the

---

[1] See paragraph 155 above.
[2] Mental Treatment Act, 1930, Section 1 (5).

same in the case of offenders who had been placed on probation (29·8 per cent.) as it was in the case of offenders who had been sent to prison (30·1 per cent.).

Prison as a Form of Treatment

201. The problem of dealing with the homosexual offender cannot be solved merely by substituting psychiatric or other forms of treatment for punitive methods. There is the consideration that the deterrent and preventive aspects of punishment are important, whether the question is considered merely from the point of view of what is best for the offender or from the wider view of what is best for the protection of society. The problem must be looked upon as one in which neither the considerations of therapeutic treatment nor the considerations of punishment can be disregarded. There must be effective methods of punishment and custody for the protection of the public, but the application of these methods should permit and encourage the use of therapeutic treatment in all suitable cases. In any case, the objections to imprisonment as a form of treatment for homosexual offenders can be over-emphasised. There are some men for whom a prison sentence is in itself a salutary shock, as an expression of society's disapproval of their behaviour; and although there doubtless are some homosexual offenders—as there are some burglars or embezzlers—to whom prison does more harm than good, yet there undeniably are others to whom it teaches an important lesson.

202. The fact must be faced that there will always be some men whom it is necessary to submit to some form of compulsory detention for the protection of others. Of 1,022 men in prison for homosexual offences in 1954, no fewer than 590 (58 per cent.) were involved in offences against boys aged 15 or under. 236 of these had previous convictions for homosexual offences. Further, of the 1,022 prisoners, 211 (21·6 per cent.) had four or more previous convictions of one kind or another recorded against them, and of these 102 (10 per cent.) had seven or more. These previous convictions were not necessarily related to homosexual offences, but there is a strong probability that most of them were; the Cambridge survey indicates that two-thirds of the sexual recidivists under review had previous convictions for sexual offences only, and that generally there was a similarity between the repeated offences.

203. The Cambridge survey also indicates that the proportion of offenders who have been sent to institutions for mental defectives in recent years is much higher among sexual offenders than among offenders generally, and there are other indications that sexual offences, especially where they are repeated, are frequently committed either by men who are too dull to appreciate the real nature or seriousness of their conduct or by men who seem quite incapable of controlling their urges. In such cases it is futile to think of imprisonment in terms of deterrence and reform. At the same time such men must obviously be submitted to some form of compulsory detention for the protection of others.

204. Where they are certifiable as persons of unsound mind or as mental defectives, what to do with them presents no special problem since they can be detained in the appropriate institutions. Where, however, they fall into neither of these categories, the only way in which they can be compulsorily detained is through the normal process of the criminal law, and it is difficult to see how it could be otherwise. If the detention is not to be related to conviction of a criminal offence, it would be necessary to relate it in some way to the offender's mental state, and this would be tantamount to introducing a conception of mental disorder not recognised by the laws relating

to mental illness and mental defect. The question whether the definitions of mental illness and mental defect are satisfactory in the light of present knowledge has been under consideration by the Royal Commission on Mental Illness and Mental Deficiency. If the Royal Commission's findings are accepted, they will result in a new definition of mental illness or mental defect which would embrace a certain number of homosexual offenders and provide for their compulsory detention otherwise than in prison; but we do not think that it would be practicable to introduce, in order to deal with the homosexual offender, a conception of mental disorder not recognised by the laws relating to mental illness and mental defect in general, and it follows that offenders whose detention is imperative and who cannot be detained under those laws must continue for the time being to be detained under the provisions of the criminal law.

205. But if such persons are not to be detained in prison, where are they to be detained? Some of our witnesses have advocated the establishing of a special institution, part prison and part mental hospital, for this purpose.

206. We see serious objections to this proposal. It is open to many of the criticisms which are brought in this connection against prisons; indeed, to some of them it would be even more vulnerable than prisons are, since a community composed exclusively of men convicted of homosexual offences is likely to be an even more discouraging background for treatment and cure, in any sense of the word, than an ordinary prison. No doubt the presence of homosexuals in prison can be a nuisance, and is liable to have an unsettling effect on other prisoners, and from this point of view there might be some advantage in segregating them. But we are not convinced that homosexual offenders either deserve or need this segregation more than do offenders of other kinds. Moreover, it would not be appropriate to assign an offender to a special institution of the kind proposed merely on the basis that he had committed a homosexual offence. To do so would be to ignore two facts; first, that men who are not predominantly homosexual by propensity sometimes lend themselves to homosexual practices from a variety of motives, and secondly, that there are at any given time in prison a number of homosexuals who are there because they have committed offences other than homosexual offences.

207. Some of our witnesses hoped that the proposed East-Hubert Institute would be used for the treatment of homosexual offenders. This institute is, however, intended primarily for offenders who are likely to benefit from psychiatric treatment, and the number of homosexual offenders in this category would be small. To send them to this particular institute would presuppose that they were proper subjects both for the forms of treatment it would provide and for living together with its other members. For a few carefully selected persons this might well be the best solution; but it cannot be a general answer to the problem.

208. In brief, therefore, prison will always have its place as a method of dealing with the homosexual offender, whether as a salutary deterrent for some offenders, or as a place of detention for those who in the last resort must be put away for the protection of the community. Offenders in the latter category will occasionally qualify for preventive detention and be dealt with accordingly. But there are others who have committed many offences which have escaped detection, with the result that they do not qualify for preventive detention, though their conduct clearly indicates that they need to be put away for a considerable time for the protection of others. Many of these offenders are, as we have said earlier, of low mentality and unable to appreciate the seriousness of their conduct. Since, however, the primary

consideration in such cases is the protection of the public and not the punishment, deterrence or reform of the offender, it seems equitable that the offender should be subject to a régime less rigorous than that imposed on the general run of prisoners, and more akin to that which prevails in institutions for mental defectives. We have already said that a special institution for homosexual offenders would be undesirable; but it is not only among homosexual offenders that the dullard recidivist is found. A substantial proportion of the prison population consists of men with long criminal records, and we are told that about one-eighth of the prison population consists of non-certifiable dullards. It seems likely, therefore, that there are sufficient dullard recidivists among the prison population to justify their being treated separately and subjected to a régime which, while it would afford the necessary protection of the public, would not entail a code of discipline more rigorous than this and the requirements of orderly institutional government demand. If it were possible to set aside an establishment for use as a "maximum security, minimum discipline" establishment for the reception of mentally sub-normal recidivists who are not certifiable or treatable, this would take its quota of homosexual offenders, but we recognise that this is a question of general prison administration and not one peculiar to the treatment of homosexual offenders.

Oestrogens

209. While, as we have said earlier, we see little likelihood of any "cure" of homosexuality in the sense of changing the nature and object of a man's sexual desires, it is possible in some cases to diminish the strength of these desires by physical means. The strength of a man's desires may well be an important factor in his behaviour, and if the strength of the desire can be diminished it is not unreasonable to suppose that the disposition to commit offences will be correspondingly lessened. In this connection we have given some consideration to the possible use of hormones (oestrogens), which affect the strength, though not the direction, of the sexual desire or libido, in the treatment of convicted homosexual offenders. At present, the use of oestrogens is forbidden in prisons in England and Wales (though not, we understand, in Scotland) even where the prisoner himself expresses a desire for oestrogen treatment.

210. The reluctance of the authorities to permit the indiscriminate administration of oestrogens for this purpose is understandable. Certainly there can be no question of departing, in respect of this form of treatment, from the general law that the consent of a patient must be given before medical treatment is administered. Nevertheless, where a prisoner himself clearly wishes to undergo oestrogen treatment, which may indeed have a beneficial effect, we think it wrong that he should not be afforded the opportunity.

211. We have made careful enquiry about two particular points in connection with oestrogen treatment: (i) the possibility of ill-effects of the treatment, and (ii) the permanence or transience of its effect upon sexual desire. On the former point we have been reassured by the evidence of doctors who have used this treatment in practice outside prisons. They were able to tell us that they had encountered no definite case of lasting impairment of general health. On the second point, the answer was the one that might have been expected, that the permanence of the cure depends on the regularity, continuity and persistence of the patient's obedience to his doctor's instructions. If he abandons the treatment as soon as he finds it to be temporarily effective, or as soon as he is freed from the threat of a criminal charge, the results are, naturally, transitory. If he perseveres with it, the

relief from desire will persist. There are certainly cases in which this form of treatment is helpful to a patient who is undergoing psychiatric treatment. We have therefore come to the conclusion that the ban on oestrogen treatment which is at present in force in prisons in England and Wales should be removed. We accordingly recommend that where a prisoner desires to have oestrogen treatment, he should, if the prison medical officer considers that this would be beneficial either as treatment *per se* or as an element in other forms of treatment, be permitted to do so.

Castration
212. We are aware that in some countries castration is practised, with the consent of the offender. We understand, however, that there is no guarantee that this operation removes either the desires or the ability to fulfil them; it would clearly have no effect, in the latter respect, in the case of the man who is addicted to the passive role of acts of buggery, or to other forms of homosexual behaviour not involving the use of his own genitalia. For many reasons, we do not believe that this operation would commend itself in this country.

Note by Dr. Curran and Dr. Whitby[1]

1. We are of the opinion that the assessment reached by our non-medical colleagues in paragraphs 191 to 212 calls for expansion in certain respects.

2. Our reasons are that in our view—
   (i) These paragraphs have over-simplified the variety of problems and the number of factors to be taken into account in justly assessing an individual accused of a homosexual offence;
   (ii) There has been an over-simplification of the varieties of treatment that may be applicable;
   (iii) An appearance of unjustified pessimism has been shown in assessing the outlook for many homosexuals, with or without treatment;
   (iv) We consider that a section on treatment should not lay so much emphasis on the deterrent and preventive aspects. These have been amply dealt with elsewhere in the report;
   (v) The difficulties, rather than the constructive opportunities, have been unduly stressed.

3. *Clinical Varieties.*—In order to deal adequately with an individual convicted of a homosexual offence, the court must assess not only the social gravity of the crime, but its significance in the individual offender. The same act may have a totally different significance, both as regards prognosis and treatment, in different individuals. For example, the same criminal act may be committed as a piece of adolescent experimentation; or it may be the result of temporary or permanent mental or physical disorder or disease; or it may be part of the individual's life style. When deciding what is the best treatment of the individual—and this is part of the court's function,

---

[1] See paragraph 190 above.

although not the only one—account must be taken of the prognosis and of the nature of any specific treatment, if called for, that is advisable in the individual case concerned.

It is not enough to seek answers of a purely general kind, for these may not clarify individual problems. For example, whilst the assessment of an individual on the homosexual-heterosexual continuum (his " Kinsey rating ") may give a good *general* guide on the prognosis for sexual reorientation, a general classification of this type ignores the clinical criteria that are essential in attempting to assess the treatment and prognosis of the *individual*, not only from the point of view of sexual reorientation, but from other points of view as well.

A few illustrations of representative types met with in practice—the headings being drawn from a valuable, although as yet unpublished, memorandum presented to the Committee—are set out below. The brief amplifications under these headings are our own. It must be understood that what follows indicates only a few of many possible variations:—

(i) *The adolescent and mentally immature adult,* many of whom are still in the transitional stage of psycho-sexual development. Quite often they mistake the part for the whole and erroneously suppose that the recognition of a homosexual component indicates that they are irretrievably homosexual. " Latent " heterosexuality can exist just as much as can " latent " homosexuality. Such individuals can and do react with shame and misery, or over-compensate by bravado. And they can meet an attractive girl, fall in love and all's well.

(ii) *" Severely damaged personalities."* Examples are obviously effeminate and flauntingly exhibitionistic individuals (these, contrary to popular belief, are quite rare); grossly inadequate, passive, weak-willed persons; or deeply resentful anti-social types.

(iii) *Homosexuality in relatively intact personalities,* otherwise well socialised. Many of these are valuable and efficient members of the community, quite unlike the common conception of the homosexual as being necessarily, or probably, vicious, criminal, effete or depraved.

(iv) *Latent and relatively well-compensated homosexuals,* who are either not aware of their real difficulty, or else have struggled successfully against it for long periods.

(v) *A homosexual predisposition co-existing with serious mental disability or disease,* for example, intellectual defect, brain damage or decay, serious mental illness or gross personality disorder (" psychopathy ").

The theoretical acceptance of these general propositions, that there is a great variety of problems, that the significance of offences varies with the individual offender, and that individual cases may require individual treatment, does not always lead to their application in practice. There is no clear and simple rule for making discriminations that are inherently complex and difficult. But in view of the varied nature of the problems, it will be seen that an informed medical report would often be of help to the court, and in some cases will be essential.

4. *Aims of Treatment.*—As mentioned in paragraph 192, there are broadly three possible objectives: (i) a change in the direction of sexual preference; (ii) a better adaptation to the sexual problem and to life in general, and (iii) greater continence or self-control. Treatment is not generally specifically aimed at achieving only one of these objectives and, when successful, modifications often occur in more than one way.

(i) *Change in Preference.*—If the aim of treatment be restricted to the total reorientation of a well-established homosexual propensity of the "Kinsey 6" type, there is justifiable pessimism, as is fully emphasised in paragraph 193. In practice, such cases form a minority of those reaching the psychiatrist. For example, in one well-known clinic, "Kinsey 6" formed 14 per cent. and "Kinsey 5" 26 per cent. of the cases seen; so that 60 per cent. were of a lower Kinsey rating—or in other words bi-sexual. Other clinics give comparable figures, and the experience of prison medical officers is similar. As will be seen later, there are grounds for reasonable optimism for change in sexual orientation in this majority group. In this connection, the large group of youngsters and young men with what is often called "transitional" homosexuality is especially important.

Another way of looking at this problem has been raised by Dr. T. C. N. Gibbens, in a valuable paper entitled "The Sexual Behaviour of Young Criminals," based upon the study of two hundred borstal lads. (Reference: Journal of Mental Science, Vol. 103, p. 535—the July number for 1957.) He states: "Perhaps the most important point that has to be made about homosexuality is that it should not be considered in isolation from heterosexuality. The issues are those of sexuality, with homosexual and heterosexual components in each case."

The encouraging fact is that many pass through a homosexual phase satisfactorily and without medical help. It is noteworthy in this connection to observe that Kinsey found that 8 per cent. of "Kinsey 6" homosexual males past adolescence indulged exclusively in homosexual acts for over three years, but only 4 per cent. did so throughout their lives. The inference is that a shift occurred, certainly in performance and probably in preference as well. The same phenomenon is often found in ordinary psychiatric casetaking when going over a patient's past history. Many factors are at work in producing this result, including both maturation and the most variable and diverse environmental influences. For example, individuals may not be attracted to girls (*a*) because they are highly homosexual; or (*b*) because the girls they have met are very dull; or (*c*) because they are shy (and this may arise from a multitude of causes ranging from the quite simple to the extremely complex), and so on.

(ii) *Better Adaptation.*—The better adaptation to the homosexual problem and to life in general must take into account the high proportion of homosexual cases with associated psychiatric abnormality. Thus, in one clinic, this was estimated at 57 out of 113 cases, and somewhat similar figures have been obtained from prison medical officers. In one series from a remand prison, 3 per cent. were found to be insane and 9 per cent. certifiably defective. (Reference: Taylor, F. H. (1947), British Medical Journal, 2, 525.) Treatment therefore cannot be confined to the homosexual problem alone, although treatment of the psychiatric abnormality may have a beneficial effect in this field as well.

(iii) *Better Control.*—The same considerations apply. It is noteworthy that, although the homosexual impulses remained, an improvement in this respect was claimed in 21 out of 77 cases by one clinic.

5. *Varieties of Treatment.*—The conception of therapeutic measures is apt to be construed too narrowly as meaning individual psychotherapy

involving many interviews over a long time. In fact, however, psychiatric treatment consists of a mixture of physical, psychological, social and environmental measures, in varying proportions according to the case. This will be illustrated later.

Whilst it is true that only a minority of homosexuals, for the reasons given in paragraph 197, are suitable for prolonged individual psychotherapy, the same is true for all other psychiatric conditions. Therefore, to emphasise that very few homosexuals in prison are suitable for such psychotherapy gives a false impression as to what can be done and what part can be played by other forms of psychiatric treatment, both in prison and outside.

Psychiatric treatment is a *positive* attempt to bring to bear any influence that may be helpful. In certain cases, individual psychotherapy may be the weapon of choice, although treatment will rarely be confined to this. In other cases, as mentioned briefly in paragraph 196, " psychiatric team work " is employed. In this, the doctor not only endeavours to treat the patient directly, but with the help of information obtained from the psychologist and the psychiatric social worker, he advises on suitable employment and leisure activities, attempts to reconcile the patient to his problems in a variety of ways, has discussions with friends and relations, and gives guidance on sexual matters or marital difficulties. By advice and support he encourages the patient to maintain progress and may enable new crises to be avoided or overcome. Treatment of this kind may well in many cases be delegated, as mentioned in paragraph 196, to psychiatric social workers and others. In this connection, we believe a special tribute should be paid to the work of the probation officers.

6. *Oestrogen Treatment.*—We agree with the recommendation made in paragraph 211 that, with the patient's consent, oestrogen treatment should be permitted in suitable cases in prison.

7. *Treatment as Voluntary Patients in Mental Hospitals under Section 4 of the Criminal Justice Act, 1948.*—We regret the implications drawn by our non-medical colleagues in paragraph 199 concerning the possible danger to the public should these patients take their discharge. That some patients do take their discharge is clear; but enquiry shows that no evidence of this possible danger to the public actually resulting has been brought before the Committee. The use of this section should surely be encouraged rather than discouraged in suitable cases. These we believe would usually be those with definite evidence of associated psychiatric disorder of a serious type. That some cases are unsuitable for this form of treatment and yet have it prescribed for them by the courts is a separate issue.

8. *The Results of Treatment.*—It is very difficult, when many factors are at work, to assess the part played by any one of them. This applies to the claims that can be made both for penal as well as for medical measures. For example, the assessment of the specific value of psychotherapy presents obvious difficulties, although its major importance in certain cases can scarcely be doubted.

Judged by whatever criteria, whether it be the recidivism rate or claims made by doctors, cautious optimism is justified in many homosexuals.

Thus, we are informed that the recidivism rate for homosexual offenders compares very favourably with that for other categories of offenders, both for those who have received prison sentences and those who have not. Better results, by the criterion of recidivism, have been claimed by prison doctors for those treated by psychotherapy when in prison than for those who have not been so treated, although it must be borne in mind that only cases with a better outlook would be so treated.

As regards medical claims, as pointed out in paragraph 197, although only a small percentage were accepted for specialised treatment in prison, nearly one-half were considered "improved." At out-patient clinics, where cases were less rigorously selected, encouraging results have also been reported. For example, in one clinic the results were regarded as "good" in 31 per cent. and "fair" in 32 per cent. In another clinic, 30 per cent. were regarded as "improved." Although many of these cases were referred for treatment by the courts, they were on the whole more favourable cases for treatment than the prison population, which would include a higher proportion of more difficult therapeutic problems.

It should be added that at out-patient clinics a wider range of possibilities in treatment, including environmental manipulation, is available than in prison, and the progress of patients can be better assessed in ordinary life than in a protected and restricted environment. This is an argument, from the purely therapeutic point of view, for a more extensive resort to probation with a condition of medical treatment, as is recommended in paragraph 200.

9. *In Summary* :—
   (i) The majority of those who are caught in or who indulge in homosexual acts are bisexual;
   (ii) The same act may have a totally different significance and prognosis in different individuals;
   (iii) A high proportion of homosexual offenders show associated psychiatric disorders;
   (iv) A medical report is therefore desirable in many of these cases and essential in some;
   (v) The outlook for the adolescent and transitional homosexual is often very good;
   (vi) In the changes that occur many factors play their part. Amongst these, treatment may be one; but not all cases need elaborate treatment;
   (vii) Complete pessimism in all regards is only justified in some homosexuals;
   (viii) From the purely therapeutic point of view, the more cases that can be treated without resort to prison the better;
   (ix) As recommended in paragraph 179, the duration of a prison sentence should not be decided on therapeutic grounds. This is not to say that a prison sentence may not have therapeutic value. Indeed, with one exception, our medical witnesses were unanimous that cases did occur in which a prison sentence could have therapeutic value.

DESMOND CURRAN.
JOSEPH WHITBY.

CHAPTER VII

Preventive Measures and Research

213. Our terms of reference are confined, strictly speaking, to the criminal law and the treatment of persons convicted of offences against that law. The law is, however, concerned with the prevention of crime no less than with its detection and punishment, and we have felt that it would not be proper to conclude our enquiry without giving some consideration to possible preventive measures.

214. Clearly, one of the most effective ways of reducing crime would be to eliminate its causes, if these could be identified and dealt with. Most homosexual behaviour is no doubt due to the existence of the homosexual propensity, in a greater or less degree, in one or both of the participants. As we have said earlier, various hypotheses have been put before us about the nature and origins of this propensity. But there is still a great deal of work to be done before any of the proffered explanations can be regarded as established, or any inferences from them accepted as wholly reliable. We have no doubt that properly co-ordinated research into the aetiology of homosexuality would have profitable results.

215. Secondly, there is much to be learnt about the various methods of treatment, their suitability to various kinds of patients, their varying chances of success, and the criteria by which that success is to be judged. Whether or not it is possible to establish the nature or origins of homosexuality, it is evident that psychiatric treatment has beneficial results in some cases. As we have said elsewhere, this treatment does not always involve psychotherapy, neither does it necessarily lead to any discernible change in the direction of sexual preference. But reliable information showing what type of person was likely to benefit, and in what way, from a particular form of treatment, would clearly be of great value as a preventive measure.

216. We therefore recommend that the appropriate body or bodies be invited to propose a programme of research into the aetiology of homosexuality and the effects of various forms of treatment. The actual carrying out of such research would necessarily be in the hands of those directly concerned with the treatment of the homosexual, since it is only from observations carried out over long periods by doctors treating individual cases that results can be established. These should include both prison doctors and psychiatrists working outside the prisons. The organisation of the research suggests the establishment, on the pattern familiar to the Medical Research Council, of a research unit which would include, for example, psychiatrists, geneticists, endocrinologists, psychologists, criminologists and statisticians. This unit could well be based on some establishment (for example, a University Department) experienced in socio-medical research and having access to prisons, psychiatric clinics and other centres where homosexuals are undergoing treatment. We hope that such work will form part of a wider study of forensic psychiatry, not confined to homosexuality, for which this country has fewer facilities than some others. Research of this kind would also increase the two-way flow between the prison medical service and outside psychiatrists, which, as we have said earlier, we consider to be desirable.

217. Researches of the kind we have proposed will necessarily take a long time. We have, however, had suggested to us several other measures which might be taken to diminish the incidence of homosexual offences. Some of them are general and wide in their application, such as the desirability of a healthy home background; medical guidance of parents and

children; sensible education in matters of sex, not only for children but for teachers, youth leaders and those who advise students. Particularly, it is urged that medical students should be given more information about homosexuality in their courses, and that clergy and probation officers should be better equipped to deal with the problems about which they are often consulted.

218. The Press might do much towards the education of public opinion, by ensuring that reports of court cases concerning homosexual offences were treated in the same way as that in which matrimonial cases have been treated for some years past; for there is little doubt that the influence of detailed reports of such cases is considerable and almost wholly bad. We have, incidentally, encountered several cases in which men have got into touch with homosexual offenders whose convictions were reported in the Press, with the result that further homosexual offences were committed.

219. It has been suggested, especially, that more care should be taken by those responsible for the appointment of teachers, youth leaders and others in similar positions of trust, to ensure that men known to be, or suspected of being, of homosexual tendencies, should be debarred from such employment. In regard to teachers, we are aware, and approve, of the steps taken by the Ministry of Education and the Scottish Education Department to ensure that men guilty of homosexual offences are not allowed to continue in the teaching profession. But it appears that headmasters of private schools are sometimes lax in taking up references in respect of teachers whom they propose to employ, and it occasionally happens that a teacher who has been dismissed, or asked to resign, from one post because of misconduct with boys under his charge subsequently finds employment in another school, where his misconduct is repeated. As far as youth organisations are concerned, these vary so much in their nature and structure that it is not possible to devise watertight measures. But we hope that the Criminal Record Office would be ready to supply, to responsible officers of the Headquarters of recognised youth organisations, information about the convictions of persons who seek positions of trust in those organisations.

220. On a point of detail, it has been put to us that the number of lavatory offences would be substantially reduced if all public lavatories were well lighted; but the facts do not seem to support this suggestion, since some of the lavatories at which most of the offences take place are particularly well lit. Our own opinion is that if uniformed police officers in the course of their duties on the beat keep a vigilant eye on public lavatories, that is more likely to discourage potential offenders than anything else. We have been informed that in some places in Scotland there are in force bye-laws making it an offence to stay for more than a certain time in a public lavatory; and it is for consideration whether the wider adoption of some similar bye-law might further discourage the improper use of such places.

221. The preventive measures we have mentioned above are not, in our view, such as to call for legislation, but we put them forward for consideration by the appropriate bodies.

PART THREE.—PROSTITUTION

CHAPTER VIII

General Considerations

222. By our terms of reference we are required to consider—

"the law and practice relating to offences against the criminal law in connection with prostitution and solicitation for immoral purposes."

So far as our terms of reference relate to offences in streets and public places, the problems were examined by an earlier Committee (the Street Offences Committee) set up in 1927 under the chairmanship of the late Lord Macmillan (then Mr. Hugh Macmillan, K.C.); and we have studied the report of that Committee[1] in coming to our own conclusions.

223. It would have taken us beyond our terms of reference to investigate in detail the prevalence of prostitution or the reasons which lead women to adopt this manner of life. On the former point we have something to say below[2] in connection with street offences. On the latter point, we believe that whatever may have been the case in the past, in these days, in this country at any rate, economic factors cannot account for it to any large or decisive extent. Economic pressure is no doubt a factor in some individual cases. So, in others, is a bad upbringing, seduction at an early age, or a broken marriage. But many women surmount such disasters without turning to a life of prostitution. It seems to us more likely that these are precipitating factors rather than determining causes, and that there must be some additional psychological element in the personality of the individual woman who becomes a prostitute. Our impression is that the great majority of prostitutes are women whose psychological make-up is such that they choose this life because they find in it a style of living which is to them easier, freer and more profitable than would be provided by any other occupation. As one of our women witnesses put it—

"Prostitution is a way of life consciously chosen because it suits a woman's personality in particular circumstances."

224. Prostitution in itself is not, in this country, an offence against the criminal law. Some of the activities of prostitutes are, and so are the activities of some others who are concerned in the activities of prostitutes. But it is not illegal for a woman to "offer her body to indiscriminate lewdness for hire," provided that she does not, in the course of doing so, commit any one of the specific acts which would bring her within the ambit of the law. Nor, it seems to us, can any case be sustained for attempting to make prostitution in itself illegal. We recognise that we are here, again, on the difficult borderland between law and morals, and, that this is debatable ground. But, for the general reasons which we have outlined in Chapter II above, we are agreed that private immorality should not be the concern of the criminal law except in the special circumstances therein mentioned.

225. Prostitution is a social fact deplorable in the eyes of moralists, sociologists and, we believe, the great majority of ordinary people. But it has persisted in many civilisations throughout many centuries, and the failure of attempts to stamp it out by repressive legislation shows that it cannot be eradicated through the agency of the criminal law. It remains true that

---

[1] Cmd. 3231 (1928).
[2] See paragraph 230.

without a demand for her services the prostitute could not exist, and that there are enough men who avail themselves of prostitutes to keep the trade alive. It also remains true that there are women who, even when there is no economic need to do so, choose this form of livelihood. For so long as these propositions continue to be true there will be prostitution, and no amount of legislation directed towards its abolition will abolish it.

226. It follows that there are limits to the degree of discouragement which the criminal law can properly exercise towards a woman who has deliberately decided to live her life in this way, or a man who has deliberately chosen to use her services. The criminal law, as the Street Offences Committee plainly pointed out, " is not concerned with private morals or with ethical sanctions." This does not mean that society itself can be indifferent to these matters, for prostitution is an evil of which any society which claims to be civilised should seek to rid itself; but this end could be achieved only through measures directed to a better understanding of the nature and obligation of sexual relationships and to a raising of the social and moral outlook of society as a whole. In these matters, the work of the churches and of organisations concerned with mental health, moral welfare, family welfare, child and marriage guidance and similar matters should be given all possible encouragement. But until education and the moral sense of the community bring about a change of attitude towards the fact of prostitution, the law by itself cannot do so.

227. At the same time, the law has its place and function in this matter. We cannot do better than quote the words of the Street Offences Committee—

> " As a general proposition it will be universally accepted that the law is not concerned with private morals or with ethical sanctions. On the other hand, the law is plainly concerned with the outward conduct of citizens in so far as that conduct injuriously affects the rights of other citizens. Certain forms of conduct it has always been thought right to bring within the scope of the criminal law on account of the injury which they occasion to the public in general. It is within this category of offences, if anywhere, that public solicitation for immoral purposes finds an appropriate place."

The statement very clearly represents our own approach and attitude to this part of our enquiry. We are concerned not with prostitution itself but with the manner in which the activities of prostitutes and those associated with them offend against public order and decency, expose the ordinary citizen to what is offensive or injurious, or involve the exploitation of others.

228. We have found it convenient to deal with this part of our enquiry under five broad headings, namely—

(*a*) Street offences;

(*b*) Living on the earnings of prostitution;

(*c*) Premises used for the purposes of prostitution;

(*d*) Procuration;

(*e*) Miscellaneous.

CHAPTER IX

STREET OFFENCES

The Extent of the Problem

229. From the evidence we have received there is no doubt that the aspect of prostitution which causes the greatest public concern at the present time is the presence, and the visible and obvious presence, of prostitutes in considerable numbers in the public streets of some parts of London and of a few provincial towns. It has indeed been suggested to us that in this respect some of the streets of London are without parallel in the capital cities of other civilised countries.

230. Whether or not this particular problem is more serious at the present time than it has been in the past, and if so how much more serious it is, we have no exact means of knowing. The first and obvious place to look for evidence on this point is in the statistics of prosecutions of prostitutes for street offences; and Tables XII and XVI in Appendix II show the number of prosecutions over the past fifty years. But if the figures of prosecutions are read without regard to their background they may easily produce an erroneous impression. In the first place, the figures relate to the number of prosecutions, and not to the number of individual prostitutes dealt with during the course of a particular year. For instance, while the number of prosecutions in the West End Central Division of the Metropolitan Police District in 1953 was 6,829, the number of prostitutes involved was 808. Secondly, the number of prosecutions must depend to some degree on the number of police available for work of this kind and on the vigour of their activity; and this in turn may well depend on public opinion. At any given moment there may be a state of affairs in the streets which arouses public resentment; this may result in increased police activity and in an increased number of prosecutions. But this increased number of prosecutions does not necessarily represent an increase in the number of offences committed; it may be no more than an increase in the proportion brought to court of the existing number of offenders. Further it may then happen that, for one reason or another, police activity dies down, with the consequence that the number of prosecutions decreases without any decrease in the number of offences actually committed.

231. A striking example of this last possibility will be found in a comparison of the English figures for the years 1922 and 1923. In 1922, the number of prosecutions for street offences by prostitutes in the Metropolitan Police District was 2,231. In 1923, it fell to 595, the lowest figure ever recorded, and an equally significant drop was discernible in the figures for the rest of the country. The drop in the Metropolis was directly attributed by the then Commissioner of Police to the severe criticism passed on the police, in the Press and elsewhere, as the result of a case in which the London Quarter Sessions found, on appeal, insufficient evidence to show that a person alleged to have been accosted had been " annoyed." The effect of this criticism, according to the Commissioner, was to reduce police action to a minimum, and a year later he reported that the conditions existing in the parks and in some of the West End and other thoroughfares were much less satisfactory than they had been a year or two earlier. A similar drop for a similar reason took place in 1929. These examples show that it is dangerous to assume a direct correlation between the number of prosecutions and the number of offences actually being committed. Equally, it is possible that the substantial increase in the number of prosecutions in England and Wales over the past ten years reflects a conscientious attempt on the part of the police to answer the demand of public opinion that " the streets must be cleaned up."

232. However this may be, it is evident that the problem is no new one. A senior officer of the Metropolitan Police in his evidence to the Select Committee of the House of Lords on the law relating to the Protection of Young Girls said in 1881:—

" . . . the state of affairs which exists in this capital is such that from four o'clock, or one may say from three o'clock in the afternoon, it is impossible for any respectable woman to walk from the top of the Haymarket to Wellington Street, Strand. From three or four o'clock in the afternoon Villiers Street and Charing Cross Station and the Strand are crowded with prostitutes, who are there openly soliciting prostitution in broad daylight. At half-past twelve at night a calculation was made a short time ago that there were 500 prostitutes between Piccadilly Circus and the bottom of Waterloo Place . . ."

And from representations made to the Home Office by voluntary organisations concerned with public morality some forty years later it appeared that prostitutes then solicited in substantial numbers in the areas of Tottenham Court Road, King's Cross and Charing Cross.

We have, in short, no reliable evidence whether the number of prostitutes plying their trade in the streets of London has changed significantly in recent years. What has probably happened is that they have shifted the scene of their activities to other and more residential areas and thereby have given ground for complaints from those ordinary citizens who live in these areas and from those who cannot, in going about their daily business, avoid the sight of a state of affairs which seems to them to be an affront to public order and decency.

The Present Law

233. Since the report of the Street Offences Committee deals with the history of the present laws and of the attempts that have been made from time to time to amend them, we do not consider it necessary to go over this ground again ourselves. It will, however, be convenient that we should set out briefly the present law as we find it.

(a) England and Wales

234. In the Metropolitan Police District and the City of London, every common prostitute or night-walker loitering or being in any thoroughfare or public place for the purpose of prostitution or solicitation to the annoyance of the inhabitants or passengers is liable to a fine of forty shillings.[1]

There is no statutory definition of the term " common prostitute," but the courts have held that the term includes a woman who offers her body commonly for acts of lewdness for payment. (It is not necessary that there should be an act, or offer of an act, of ordinary sexual connection.)[2]

235. In urban areas outside the Metropolitan Police District, every common prostitute who in any street (which includes, for this purpose, any road, square, court, alley and thoroughfare or public passage) to the obstruction, annoyance or danger of the residents or passengers, loiters or importunes passengers for the purposes of prostitution, is liable to a fine of forty shillings or to imprisonment for not more than fourteen days.[3]

---

[1] Metropolitan Police Act, 1839, Section 54 (11); City of London Police Act, 1839, Section 35 (11).
[2] *R.* v. *de Munck* (1918) (1 K.B. 635).
[3] Town Police Clauses Act, 1847, Section 28.

236. A police constable may arrest, without warrant, any person committing within his view the offences mentioned in the two foregoing paragraphs.

237. A common prostitute wandering in the public streets or public highways or in any place of public resort in any part of England and Wales, and behaving in a riotous or indecent manner may be deemed an "idle and disorderly person," and as such becomes liable to a fine not exceeding five pounds or imprisonment for not more than one month.(¹)

A prostitute committing the offence after having been convicted as an "idle and disorderly person," whether in respect of a similar offence or of some other offence qualifying for this designation, may be deemed a "rogue and vagabond," and as such becomes liable to a fine not exceeding twenty-five pounds or to imprisonment for not more than three months.

A person convicted as a "rogue and vagabond" having previously been so convicted may be deemed to be an "incorrigible rogue" and as such may be committed to quarter sessions for sentence. Quarter sessions may impose imprisonment for a term not exceeding one year.

238. It is an offence for a male person persistently to solicit or importune in a public place for immoral purposes.(²) The maximum penalty is six months' imprisonment on conviction by a magistrates' court, and two years' imprisonment on conviction on indictment. The statute does not specify the sex of the persons solicited, and in addition to its application to the solicitation of males by males for the purposes of homosexual acts (as to which see paragraph 116 above) it would seem to apply also to (a) the solicitation of males by males for the purpose of immoral relations with females (for example " touting " on behalf of prostitutes) and (b) the solicitation of females by males for immoral purposes.

239. In some of the larger provincial cities there are in force local Acts containing provisions corresponding broadly with those of the Metropolitan Police Act, 1839. These acts operate concurrently with the Town Police Clauses Act or the Vagrancy Act.

240. There are other enactments which, while not specifically directed to offences by prostitutes, afford means by which prostitutes soliciting in such a manner as to cause a nuisance can be, and sometimes are, dealt with by the courts. The following are two examples:—

(a) Even when no offence has actually been committed, Justices of the Peace have power " to take of all them that be not of good fame, where they shall be found, sufficient surety and mainprise of their good behaviour towards the King and his People "—that is, to order a person to enter into recognisance and find sureties to keep the peace or to be of good behaviour, if there are reasonable grounds to fear that he may commit some offence.(³) Failure to comply with the order may be punished by imprisonment for not more than six months.

(b) Under Section 54 (13) of the Metropolitan Police Act, 1839 (and Section 35 (13) of the City of London Police Act, 1839), any person who, in any thoroughfare or public place, uses any threatening, abusive or insulting words or behaviour with intent to provoke a breach of the peace, or whereby a breach of the peace may be occasioned, is liable to a fine of forty shillings, and may be arrested without warrant by a police constable within whose view the offence is committed.

(¹) Vagrancy Act, 1834, Section 3.
(²) Sexual Offences Act, 1956, Section 32.
(³) Justices of the Peace Act, 1361.

241. There are also in force numerous bye-laws for the prevention and suppression of nuisances not otherwise punishable in a summary manner. These bye-laws frequently contain provisions directed against offensive behaviour in streets and other places of public resort and are occasionally used to deal with offensive behaviour by prostitutes. The maximum penalty for a bye-law offence is a fine of five pounds.

(b) Scotland

242. In all burghs other than Edinburgh and Aberdeen, every common prostitute or street-walker who in any street (which includes for this purpose any harbour, railway station, canal, depot, wharf, towing path, public park, links, common or open area of space, the strand or sea beach down to low water mark and all public places within the burgh) loiters about or importunes passengers for the purpose of prostitution commits an offence and is liable to a fine of forty shillings.([1])

243. In Edinburgh, every prostitute or street-walker who loiters about or importunes passengers for the purpose of prostitution is liable to a penalty of ten pounds or alternatively to imprisonment for sixty days; and Aberdeen has a similar provision.([2])

244. In all burghs other than Edinburgh, Aberdeen and Greenock, any person who in any street (defined as in paragraph 242 above) habitually or persistently importunes or solicits, or loiters about for the purpose of importuning or soliciting women or children for immoral purposes, commits an offence and is liable to a fine of forty shillings.([3]) There are no corresponding provisions in Edinburgh, Aberdeen or Greenock.

245. A person found committing any of the offences mentioned in paragraphs 242 to 244 may be arrested by a police constable without a warrant.

246. The prosecutor may include in the complaint charging either of the offences mentioned in paragraphs 242 and 244 a further charge that the contravention has been aggravated by a previous conviction within seven years of a like offence; and in the event of the charge and aggravation being proved a penalty not exceeding forty shillings, or thirty days' imprisonment without the option of a fine, may be imposed in respect of the aggravation in addition to the penalty imposed in respect of the offence itself.([4])

247. It is an offence for a male person persistently to solicit or importune in a public place for immoral purposes([5]) (see paragraphs 116 and 238 above). This provision is of general application throughout Scotland; as in England and Wales, the maximum punishment is six months' imprisonment on conviction by a court of summary jurisdiction, and two years' imprisonment on conviction on indictment.

248. As in England and Wales, there are in force in some areas bye-laws directed against offensive behaviour in places of public resort. While these

---

([1]) Burgh Police (Scotland) Act, 1892, Section 381 (22).
([2]) Edinburgh Corporation Order, 1933, Section 116 (A) (3); Aberdeen Corporation (General Powers) Order, 1938, Section 186 (*a*) (ii).
([3]) Burgh Police (Scotland) Act, 1892, Section 381 (23).
([4]) Burgh Police (Scotland) Act, 1892, Section 465.
([5]) Immoral Traffic (Scotland) Act, 1902.

are usually concerned with offensive behaviour in general, there are occasionally bye-laws related directly to solicitation, of which the following are examples:—

> "No person shall loiter for the purpose of prostitution, nor conduct himself or herself in an indecent manner therein (*i.e.*, in the park)."
>
> "No male person shall molest or importune any female, and no prostitute or street-walker shall loiter or importune any person in the park or islands."

The maximum penalty for a bye-law offence is a fine of five pounds.

Defects of the Existing Law

249. There was a wide measure of agreement among our witnesses that the present law is defective. But there was less agreement between their proposals for its amendment. Some thought that the requirement, in England and Wales, to prove "annoyance" should be dropped and the English law brought more into line with that which prevails in the Scottish towns; others felt that there should be no prosecution unless actual annoyance had been caused by words or behaviour offensive to public order and decency, and even then only on the evidence of the person alleged to have been annoyed. Some thought that the police should be given more adequate powers to keep the streets free from the more general annoyance caused by the mere visible and obvious presence of prostitutes; others that the mere presence of prostitutes carrying on their trade was no more, and no less, a matter for police intervention than the presence of street photographers or toy-sellers. Many thought that the present law applies unequally as between men and women (to the detriment of the latter), while others urged that the only way to clear the streets was a substantial increase in the present penalties for street offences. Particularly, it was widely felt that the present system whereby a prostitute is repeatedly brought before the courts and automatically disposed of on pleading guilty and paying a fine of forty shillings, which she regards as an indirect and not very onerous form of taxation or licence, is making a farce of the criminal law. It would obviously be impossible to devise any amendment of the law which would meet the several, and often conflicting, points of view which have been put to us. We have therefore asked ourselves two questions: first, whether the law should be amended at all; and secondly, if so, in which direction. So far as the first question is concerned, the general agreement that the law is unsatisfactory seems to us a clear indication that the law should be amended, if by amending the law a more satisfactory situation can be brought about. As to the second, we feel that the right of the normal, decent citizen to go about the streets without affront to his or her sense of decency should be the prime consideration and should take precedence over the interests of the prostitute and her customers.

250. The disagreement among our witnesses turns, in effect, on the two controversial questions which, as the Street Offences Committee found, have always arisen when any attempt is made to redefine the laws relating to street offences by prostitutes. The first of these is whether "annoyance" should (as in England and Wales) or should not (as in Scotland) be a specific ingredient of the offence. The second is whether the common prostitute should be the subject of express legislation, as at present she is.

The Requirement to Establish " Annoyance "

251. In England and Wales it is necessary, for the purposes of a conviction for loitering or soliciting for the purposes of prostitution, to establish that the conduct of the prostitute caused "annoyance" to the inhabitants (or residents) or passengers. The standard of proof of annoyance required by the courts seems to have varied from time to time and from place to place, but at the present time it would appear that the courts are, generally speaking, content to infer from the circumstances of the case that annoyance has been caused. Experience has shown that men solicited by prostitutes almost invariably decline to give evidence. Usually the prostitute pleads guilty, but if she does not the courts are usually prepared to accept the evidence of a police officer who witnessed the offence, to the effect that a person or persons accosted appeared to be annoyed.

252. Many of our witnesses considered it unsatisfactory that a police officer's attribution of a state of mind to a person accosted should decide the question whether an offence has been committed. We agree that it is unsatisfactory; so did the Street Offences Committee. At the same time, like the Street Offences Committee, we recognise it as an irrefutable fact that in general persons accosted will not attend the courts to give evidence. Consequently, to enact that there should be no conviction unless the person alleged to have been annoyed gave evidence and proved personal annoyance would be to enact a dead letter. If only for this reason, we feel unable to recommend legislation along the lines of the Public Places (Order) Bill put forward by some of our witnesses as a basis for legislation. This Bill is designed to repeal all provisions in the existing law referring to solicitation by common prostitutes, and also certain other provisions not explicitly referring to solicitation but sometimes used for dealing with cognate offences, and to replace them by a single enactment directed against any person wilfully causing annoyance to any person in any public place by words or behaviour offensive to public order or decency. There is a proviso that no person shall be convicted of such offence, except upon the evidence of the person aggrieved (which includes, for this purpose, as well as a person solicited or importuned by the accused, any resident or passenger other than a police officer on duty, or any person who carries on business in or near the place where the offence is alleged to have taken place). Our witnesses suggested to us that if the offence became one of simple annoyance or obstruction with no reference of any kind to " prostitute," " prostitution " or " immoral purposes " some, at least, of the present reluctance to appear as a witness in these cases would be overcome. We do not think this at all likely.

253. There is the further serious difficulty that in reality it is not so much the conduct of any particular prostitute that causes the annoyance as the presence of numbers of prostitutes in the same place; and this annoyance is to the inhabitants or passengers at large rather than to any individual. That this more general form of annoyance exists, and that it causes no less offence (and may well cause more offence) than individual acts of soliciting is very clear from the evidence we have received. Nevertheless the law must deal with the offenders individually, though the annoyance caused to the inhabitants or passengers in general might be unrelated to and, indeed, unrelatable to, any individual prostitute.

254. The Street Offences Committee distinguished between overt acts of importuning (by which they meant acts of molestation by offensive words or behaviour) and the frequenting of streets or public places for the purposes of

prostitution. In the case of the former, they recommended that the requirement of proving annoyance should be eliminated, largely on the ground mentioned above, namely, that to require the person alleged to have been annoyed to give evidence would be to enact a dead letter. But in recommending that it should be an offence for any person " to frequent any street or public place for the purpose of prostitution or solicitation so as to constitute a public nuisance " they recommended—somewhat inconsistently it seems to us—that the evidence of one or more of the persons aggrieved should be essential to a conviction.

255. The proposition that to require the person alleged to have been annoyed to give evidence would be to enact a dead letter applies to the person annoyed by the loitering of prostitutes no less than to the person annoyed by an act of importuning. It probably applies even more, since it is unlikely that a resident in a neighbourhood where annoyance is caused by the loitering of prostitutes would be prepared to go to the courts day after day to establish the fact that he was annoyed. Indeed it seems to us unreasonable that he should be required to do so. In our view both loitering and importuning for the purpose of prostitution are so self-evidently public nuisances that the law ought to deal with them, as it deals with other self-evident public nuisances, without calling on individual citizens to establish the fact that they were annoyed.

256. We accordingly recommend that the law at present in force in England and Wales be reformulated so as to eliminate the requirement to establish annoyance from the offences set out in paragraphs 234 and 235 above.

The Prostitute as the Subject of Express Legislation

257. The second of the two controversial topics which we mentioned above([1]) is the question whether the prostitute should be the subject of express legislation. It has been put to us with some force that the present law is unjust in that it selects a special class of women, designates them " common prostitutes " and provides penalties solely for them, leaving their customers unpunished. It is argued that if there were no customers there would be no prostitutes, and to seek to punish the prostitute while the man is uncondemned is the negation of justice. We should agree that from the moral point of view there may be little or nothing to choose between the prostitute and her customer. But, as we have explained above (and as most of our witnesses would agree), it is not the duty of the law to concern itself with immorality as such. If it were the law's intention to punish prostitution *per se*, on the ground that it is immoral conduct, then it would be right that it should provide for the punishment of the man as well as the woman. But that is not the function of the law. It should confine itself to those activities which offend against public order and decency or expose the ordinary citizen to what is offensive or injurious; and the simple fact is that prostitutes do parade themselves more habitually and openly than their prospective customers, and do by their continual presence affront the sense of decency of the ordinary citizen. In doing so they create a nuisance which, in our view, the law is entitled to recognise and deal with.

258. We encountered, however, other and more specific objections to the use, in the several statutes mentioned above, of the expression " prostitute " or " common prostitute " in defining a particular offence. Especially, it

---

([1]) See paragraph 250.

has been represented to us that this denies to these particular women the degree of justice accorded to offenders generally. It has been argued (i) that the words " common prostitute " are nowhere defined by statute; (ii) that to define an offence by reference to the category of persons who commit it, while the same act might be committed with impunity by others, is a legal impropriety; (iii) that the affixing of this designation to any person charged with an offence introduces her to the court from the start as a person of low moral character, with an antecedent presumption of guilt; and (iv) that the affixing of this designation tends to brand convicted women and to render their reformation more difficult.

259. On the first point, while it may be true that there is no statutory definition of the term " common prostitute," the courts have evolved a working formula.([1]) On the second point, we would merely observe that in this context the words " common prostitute " are a description of a trade or calling that is not of itself unlawful, and that there are parallels for prohibiting to members of one trade or calling actions which for other persons are not offences. As regards the third point, we feel, as did the Street Offences Committee, that this is something which has been suggested rather than proved. It seems to us that the courts are well accustomed to this formula of description and we have no evidence that any injustice results from its use. It is indeed the first fact that has to be established if a charge is to be proved. It is worth recording that no evidence has been submitted to us either by prostitutes or on their behalf which suggests that they themselves feel grievance or fear injustice on this particular point. On the fourth point we should naturally be anxious to recommend any amendment of the law which might tend to assist in the reformation of a prostitute, provided that this could be done without impairing the law's effectiveness: but we have no evidence that this designation has ever interfered with reformation and for reasons which we explain below we believe the retention of the words to be necessary for the effective operation of the law.

260. Conscious of the strength of the feelings which underlie the representations which have been made to us, and recognising the sincerity (if not always the validity) of the arguments against this formula, we have tried to find some way of meeting them without sacrificing the safeguard from wrongful arrest which the formula seems to us to afford to women who are not " common prostitutes." For reasons which we have already explained, we find ourselves unable to recommend the formula put forward in the Public Places (Order) Bill and summarised in paragraph 252 above. We therefore explored the possibility of defining the offence by reference to a degree of habitualness or persistence rather than to a category of persons. We gave consideration, for instance, to such wording as " Any person who in any public place habitually or persistently loiters or importunes passengers for the purposes of prostitution." Here, however, we found ourselves up against two difficulties.

261. The first is a practical one, and concerns the measures which would be necessary to establish that the loitering was habitual and persistent. Prolonged observation by a plain-clothes officer or officers would almost certainly be necessary to establish a degree of habitualness or persistence sufficient to justify an arrest and subsequent proceedings. In effect, the police would have to employ in relation to the prostitute measures similar to those now employed in relation to the male importuner. Even as the law stands at present, the detection and prosecution of offences by prostitutes imposes a strain on the resources of police manpower, and if anything is to be done

---

([1]) See paragraph 234 above.

to clean up the streets we do not think that a formula of this sort would be workable. The problem of the prostitute is, in terms of numbers, far greater than that of the male importuner and, for that matter, far more of a public nuisance. In any event, we think it would be too easy to evade the formula by a game of "general post" in which an individual prostitute would not loiter in a particular place though the number of prostitutes in that place at a given time might be constant.

262. Our second difficulty related to the criteria which would enable the police to infer that a person was loitering "for the purposes of prostitution." We have in mind the possibility that any woman might, from ignorance or indiscretion, put herself in a position in which she might be said to be loitering, and by conduct which was quite innocent give rise to a suspicion in the mind of an observant policeman that she was loitering for the purposes of prostitution. She might, for example, be waiting for a friend who had been unexpectedly delayed, and from anxiety over the growing delay enquire the time of a number of male passers-by. While it is most unlikely that a woman in such circumstances would ever find herself convicted of an offence, a policeman might quite legitimately reach the *prima facie* conclusion that she was loitering for the purposes of prostitution and arrest her accordingly. We cannot help feeling, therefore, that the alternative formula we have considered would give rise to the possibility of the arrest of innocent persons, and we think this is a risk that ought not to be taken. We have accordingly come to the conclusion, with regret, that no alternative formulation is preferable to that which is already familiar to those concerned, and that, on balance, it is better to retain the words "common prostitute" in the definition of the offence.

263. It has been represented to us, as we have noted in paragraph 258 above, that the fact that a woman is charged as a "common prostitute" means that she is thereafter permanently labelled as such, and that to the police and for all record purposes she will always be a "common prostitute" even though she may have abandoned prostitution and lived respectably for many years. Consequently, it is urged, the prostitute feels that as long as she remains so labelled efforts at reform and rehabilitation are not worth while. It has accordingly been suggested that records of convictions as a common prostitute should be expunged after the lapse of a certain time from the date of the conviction.

264. We have been given no convincing reasons for believing that if a woman abandons the life of prostitution she has anything to fear from the fact that her earlier convictions are recorded, any more than has a person convicted of any other offence. The information recorded by the police has relevance only in the event of her being charged with further offences at some future date. Unless she is charged again, it never again comes to light. If on the other hand, she resumes her activities, there is no obvious reason why it should not. If, as has been suggested, the label militates against reformation in some cases, its removal may, in others, encourage the prostitute to feel that she is free to recommence her activities with a clean sheet after the stipulated lapse of time. We accordingly recommend no change on this point, relying on the discretion and good sense of the courts in this as in other cases.

265. Some of our witnesses have objected to the inclusion in the present law of the words "for the purpose of prostitution" on the grounds (a) that it is contrary to the principles of British law to make the "purpose" of an act an offence when the "purpose," if achieved, is not an offence; and (b) that "purpose" is something which cannot be substantiated by admissible corroborative evidence. If, however, the law is to impose penalties in respect

of a particular offence, it is necessary that the offence should be clearly defined, and while we recognise some force in the objection we are unable to suggest for this purpose any alternative to the present formulation. Further, this is not the only instance of the inclusion of a " purpose " in the statement of the law. Betting is not illegal; but loitering in the street for the purpose of betting is.

Non-urban Areas

266. It will have been observed that the present laws relating to loitering for the purposes of prostitution apply only to urban areas. No doubt at the time these were formulated the problem was peculiar to towns, as, indeed, it largely is to-day. But we have evidence that public nuisance is caused by women who loiter in certain places situated outside urban areas—notably in some places where there are service camps. If the conduct of such women is such as would constitute an offence if committed in a town, it is clearly right that the law should deal with it. We accordingly recommend that the laws relating to the offences dealt with in this chapter be made of general application.

" Kerb Crawling "

267. Our attention has been drawn to what we are informed is an increasingly prevalent form of solicitation by men of women, commonly described as " kerb crawling." The form this takes is that a motorist, driving slowly, and overtaking women pedestrians, halts by them with the intention of inviting them into his car. This is undoubtedly a serious nuisance to many well-behaved women, and it does not appear that, from the point of view of prosecuting those who are responsible for it, it fits conveniently into any existing category of offence except at the point where a specific invitation is addressed to an individual. To meet the problem it would be necessary to frame an offence the essential ingredient of which would be driving a motor-car for the purposes of immoral solicitation. Whilst we appreciate the reality of the problem, and we consider that it should be kept under review, the difficulties of proof would be considerable, and the possibility of a very damaging charge being levelled at an innocent motorist must also be borne in mind. We do not feel able to make any positive recommendation.

Police Procedures

268. Apart altogether from the actual formulation of the law, there are matters of police practice which are relevant to our enquiry. For instance, the methods employed to establish that the woman charged is a common prostitute vary. In London, the instructions issued to police officers provide that the first time a woman is seen committing either of the offences mentioned in paragraphs 234 and 237 above, she should be cautioned, particulars being recorded in the official pocket book; and that if she repeats the offence she should be arrested and charged. The caution need not have been given on the date of the arrest or by the arresting officer. If it can be proved that the woman has been recently and justifiably cautioned, that is generally regarded as presumptive evidence that she is a common prostitute. Sometimes the provision mentioned in paragraph 240 (*b*) above is invoked where the police are not able to establish with certainty that the woman is a common prostitute, provided that the woman has, in fact, used " threatening, abusive or insulting behaviour . . . . whereby a breach of the peace may be occasioned "; but officers are instructed that whenever practicable a caution should be given for a first offence.

269. In Glasgow, if a woman suspected of being a prostitute is observed in any street, she is watched by the police and if she is is seen to importune or accost men the police officer warns her that if she persists in her conduct she may be apprehended. Particulars of this caution are recorded by the officer in his official note-book. These particulars are also reported to a moral welfare worker, who then endeavours to get into touch with the prostitute. If, after being cautioned, the woman repeats the offence she is apprehended and taken to the police station where she is formally cautioned, particulars of the caution being recorded at the station for future reference. If, after these cautions, she repeats the offence, she is brought before the court, where evidence as to the conduct which has led to the cautions serves as presumptive evidence that she is a common prostitute. A similar system operates in Edinburgh, but here the woman is given two cautions on the street before being taken to the police station for the formal caution.

270. Street offences by prostitutes do not present, in the Scottish towns, a problem of the same magnitude as in London, so that the more elaborate machinery which operates there is not necessarily appropriate to London or other towns where a greater problem exists. It seems to us, however, that the system of formal caution at the police station has much to commend it as also has the system of reference to a moral welfare worker. It is possible that if some girls just starting on a life of prostitution are brought up short at this stage they will think twice before taking the further step which brings them into conflict with the courts. Moreover, if the recommendations which we make later on as to increased penalties are adopted, there is the possibility that the London prostitutes will be less ready to plead guilty than they are at present and that more elaborate steps than those at present taken will be necessary if the courts are to be satisfied that the woman charged is a common prostitute. We accordingly commend for consideration the rather more formal system of caution which now operates in the Scottish towns. We also recommend that consideration be given to the practicability of extending the practice of referring to a moral welfare worker or to some other officer (for example, a probation officer or court missionary), particulars of a prostitute cautioned for the first time.

271. A second point connected with police practice is this. We have more than once encountered the suggestion that prostitutes in the West End of London are arrested in turn about once a fortnight on some sort of rota. Our evidence does not support this suggestion. We have examined a record of the arrests of prostitutes in the West End Central Division during the year 1953, when there were 6,829 arrests involving 808 prostitutes. Of these 808 prostitutes, 181 were arrested on one occasion only. At the other end of the scale, one was arrested twenty-seven times. Between these two extremes, no regular pattern emerged in relation either to individual prostitutes or individual police officers.

395 (nearly one-half) of the 808 prostitutes were arrested on five or fewer occasions in the course of the year, and only 88 (11 per cent.) were arrested twenty times or more. In some of the cases in the latter category there did appear to be some rough sort of pattern about the dates of the arrests, but not such as to suggest anything in the nature of a pre-determined order of arrest.

272. We were told that the courts occasionally show themselves reluctant to impose the full penalty on a prostitute brought before them for a second time in quick succession. We also have the impression that some police officers are reluctant to arrest the same prostitute twice within a short space of time; the number of prostitutes that can be dealt with by the police

available at any given time is limited, and it would be surprising if the police did not exercise a certain amount of discrimination of this kind in making their arrests. These factors, combined with an element of chance and, perhaps, some aggressiveness on the part of a particular prostitute, may account for the impression of a rota.

Women Police

273. We should like to take this opportunity of recording our appreciation of the work of the women police in this whole field. It seems clear to us, from evidence we have heard, that women police are more effective in keeping prostitutes "on the move" than are their male colleagues, if only because prostitutes appear to resent being arrested by women much more than being arrested by men. But more important is the genuine concern felt by many of the women police about the young prostitute. Our impression is that within the limits of their public duty they are anxious to take every opportunity of diverting the young prostitute from the manner of life which she is in danger of adopting. We should not want to see the women police used exclusively, or even mainly, as a *police des moeurs*; but we hope that every encouragement will continue to be given to them to take every legitimate chance of dissuading young girls from adopting a life of prostitution, by advice and help rather than by involving them in the machinery of the law.

Penalties

274. The main reason for our proposal that "annoyance" should be removed from the statement of the law is our belief that an amendment of the law in this sense would ensure that an offender was charged in terms more appropriate to the facts of the situation. We do not expect that the elimination of the requirement to prove annoyance would materially affect the number of prostitutes brought before the courts and convicted. For although this requirement may occasionally have caused difficulties, it has not, in London at any rate, proved a serious obstacle to the arrest and conviction of offenders. So its removal is unlikely to reduce the number of convictions. It seems to us that it is not any major defect in its present formulation which causes the law to be ineffective in dealing with this problem. We have accordingly been obliged to consider whether or not the penalties attached to breaches of it are adequate or inadequate to discourage repetition of the offence.

275. The present maximum fine is forty shillings, for the first or any subsequent offence. This penalty seems to us quite inadequate, in two ways. The amount of the fine was fixed over a hundred years ago, when forty shillings was a not inconsiderable sum. We think that this amount should be brought more into line with the considerable change in monetary values since it was first fixed. Further, it is apparent from the figures of convictions fifty years ago that repeated fines of the same amount, though then an appreciable one, proved futile as a deterrent. They would, in our view, prove equally futile to-day, even at a higher rate than forty shillings. We therefore believe that if the problem is to be effectively dealt with a system of progressively higher penalties, such as applies in the case of many other offences, must be introduced. We accordingly recommend that the maximum penalty for a first offence should be a fine of ten pounds; that the maximum penalty for a second offence should be a fine of twenty-five pounds; and that the maximum penalty for a third or subsequent offence should be three months' imprisonment. We would stress that these are maxima, and we recognise that here, as for all other offences, the courts would be at liberty to award some lesser penalty.

276. Our decision to make this recommendation has not been lightly reached. We are well aware that in the vast majority of cases the prostitute must pay the fines from the proceeds of her prostitution, and that if the fines are increased she will attempt to recoup herself either by passing on the cost to her clients or by seeking more customers. If it could be assumed that the prostitute would resort to the first of these alternatives alone, then increased fines would at least have something to commend them in that they would tend to curb demand as well as supply. But the second possibility cannot be overlooked; and that would cause the prostitute to be more active on the streets, with the result that increasing the fine would defeat its own object.

277. For this reason, therefore, that increased and even graduated fines might in themselves prove inadequate, the sanction of imprisonment must in our opinion be available, in the last resort, for repeated offences. In making this recommendation we have two purposes in mind. The first is straightforward deterrence. We believe that most of the prostitutes loitering in the streets are those who are well established in their habits, whom repeated fines have failed to deter. We therefore feel justified in recommending that deprivation of liberty, which would be particularly unwelcome to these offenders, should be available as a sanction when, in an individual case, monetary fines have failed. But equally important is the other strand in our thinking, which may be called the reformative element in punishment. We do not deceive ourselves into thinking that a short term of imprisonment is likely to effect reform where repeated fines have failed. But we believe that the presence of imprisonment as a possible punishment may make the courts anxious to try, and the individual prostitutes more willing to accept, the use of probation in suitable cases. As the law at present stands, a probation order can be made in the case of an offender over fourteen years of age only if the offender expresses willingness to comply with its imposition and conditions. Since, as is at present the case, the alternative to probation is a fine of forty shillings, the prostitute frequently declines even to see the probation officer. This is regrettable, for we feel that many women who have adopted a life of prostitution could be led to renounce it by enquiry into their personal problems and by advice and treatment which the probation service is well equipped to give them. If the alternative to a probation order were not an insignificant fine but the possibility of ultimate imprisonment, it is probable that some of those who now refuse the help of the probation officer would be more ready to respond to the opportunity of probation if it were offered. The possibility that help of this kind might be accepted by some even of the most persistent offenders seems to us to be a strong argument for including imprisonment as an ultimate penalty.

278. We attach special importance to the use of probation in the case of the young prostitute. We believe that many of the hardened prostitutes on the streets to-day could have been deflected from the life if they could have been compelled to undergo some form of supervision when they first appeared before the courts. We recognise, however, that the willing participation of the probationer is essential to the success of probation as a method of treatment, and accordingly we feel that it would not be appropriate to recommend compulsory probation.

279. At the same time, we are anxious to ensure that the young prostitute should benefit fully from the kind of help with personal problems which the probation service and the other social services available to the courts are particularly fitted to provide, so that she may have every encouragement to abandon the life before she becomes hardened to it. We think that much useful work could be done if every young prostitute brought before the courts

at an early stage in her career were remanded for a few weeks, in custody if necessary, in order to enable a full social report to be furnished. This remand would provide an opportunity for probation officers and other social workers to get into touch where possible with the parents or guardians of the girl, to explore the possibilities of placing her in employment, to arrange for a medical or psychiatric examination if this were thought advisable, and so on. It has been found not infrequently that short remands such as we have in mind have enabled probation officers and other social workers to smooth out difficulties which have prevented young offenders from obtaining employment and so compelled or encouraged their continuance in crime.

280. We are aware that the courts have power to remand a convicted offender, in custody if necessary, up to three weeks, for the purpose of enabling enquiries to be made or of determining the most suitable method of dealing with the case.(¹) We understand, however, that some courts are reluctant to use this power of remand in relation to an offence for which they can ultimately only impose a fine. We accordingly recommend that courts should be given explicit power to remand, in custody if need be, for not more than three weeks, any prostitute convicted for the first or second time of a street offence, in order to enable a social or medical report to be furnished. In the meantime, we commend the practice of many courts in putting young offenders into touch with the probation officer and with voluntary organisations which exist to help girls in difficulty or trouble.

281. An alternative method by which young offenders could be brought under compulsory supervision has been suggested to us by some of our witnesses. This is that the age up to which young persons may be dealt with under the Children and Young Persons Acts as being in need of " care or protection " should be raised to twenty-one. We should ourselves like to see the age for " care or protection " raised at least to eighteen, and if it were practicable to raise it even higher this would be advantageous from the point of view of dealing with the young prostitute. We recognise, however, that this raises wider issues (involving, among other things, the liberty of the subject) not peculiar to the prostitute, and that a Committee (the Children and Young Persons Committee) is at present considering, *inter alia*, the working of the law relating to proceedings and the powers of the courts, in respect of juveniles brought before the courts as delinquent or as being in need of care or protection or beyond control. We have communicated to this Committee our concern about that part of its general field which falls within our own terms of reference and our hope that the Committee will, in reaching its conclusions, have due regard to the young prostitute.

282. It has been suggested to us that there might, with advantage, be a special system of punishment to include a period of detention in a special residential establishment with a view to rehabilitation. We do not think that this would be desirable, practicable or equitable. In particular, we think that it would be undesirable to segregate prostitutes in a residential establishment. It is clear from the evidence we have received from witnesses experienced in dealing with prostitutes detained in establishments of various kinds that it would be very difficult, in an establishment with this particular population, to provide any programme of rehabilitation which would be at all likely to succeed; nor do we believe that a community composed entirely of prostitutes is at all an encouraging background for the restoration of any one of them to a more normal form of living. It is in any event doubtful

---

(¹) England and Wales: Magistrates' Courts Act, 1952, Sections 14 (3) and 105; *R.* v. *Boaks* (1956). Scotland: Criminal Justice (Scotland) Act, 1949, Section 26.

whether a programme of rehabilitation would succeed against a background of compulsory detention; rehabilitation measures, in this as in other fields, depend to a large extent for their success on the willing co-operation of the person concerned.

283. Further, the punishment must bear some relation to the gravity of the offence. Prostitution is not an offence, and the prostitute does not come before the court because she is a prostitute but because, being a prostitute, she has committed some offence. If our recommendations are accepted, she would not be liable to imprisonment for that offence except on a third or subsequent conviction. To submit her to a prolonged period of compulsory detention (and rehabilitation may be a lengthy process) merely because she has committed such an offence would be inequitable. If our recommendations result in more prostitutes finding their way to prisons, borstals or approved schools, their segregation from other offenders in these establishments might have advantages for the other offenders, but this possibility does not justify a special system of punishment for prostitutes as such.

284. Some of our witnesses have suggested that the courts in dealing with prostitutes brought before them for street offences should make more use of the power, mentioned in paragraph 240 (a) above, to require the offender to enter into a recognisance or find sureties for good behaviour. We are aware that some courts use this power in these cases, and the effect is to render the prostitute liable to the payment of substantial sums of money, or imprisonment in default of payment, in the event of her repeating her offence. The power is traced to the Justices of the Peace Act, 1361, and the Commission of the Peace granted under the authority of that Act. Legal authorities are not agreed as to all the offences for which surety for good behaviour may be required; the procedure is normally used to prevent the commission or repetition of a serious offence, or conduct likely to lead to a breach of the peace. Our own view is that since Parliament has prescribed a specific and comparatively trivial penalty for this specific offence, it is not desirable that general powers of this kind should be used to attach, in effect, an inflated penalty to this offence. If, as we think, the present statutory penalties are inadequate, it is by Parliament that they should be increased.

Possible Consequences of Amending the Law

285. It will be apparent, from the recommendations we have made, that we are not attempting to abolish prostitution or to make prostitution in itself illegal. We do not think that the law ought to try to do so; nor do we think that if it tried it could by itself succeed. What the law can and should do is to ensure that the streets of London and our big provincial cities should be freed from what is offensive or injurious and made tolerable for the ordinary citizen who lives in them or passes through them.

286.([1]) If this is done, there will doubtless be consequences; and it is our business to try to assess them, at least in outline, lest curing one evil should result in greater evil of a different kind. It must be accepted that for so long as prostitution exists the prostitute will seek customers and the potential customer will seek prostitutes. If the prostitute is not allowed to find her customers in the streets, then presumably she and her customers will find other means of meeting each other. It has been suggested to us that to " drive

---

([1]) See Reservations I (e) and I (f), page 122.

the prostitutes from the streets" is to encourage the closer organisation of the trade, with greater opportunities for exploiting prostitutes and greater dangers that new classes of "middlemen" (*e.g.*, taxi-drivers and hotel porters) will arise. We think it possible, indeed probable, that there will be an extension of the "call-girl" system[1] and, perhaps, a growth in the activities of touts. These are dangers; but where they involve exploitation of the prostitute, we should expect the laws which already cover this kind of exploitation to be rigorously enforced and even, as we suggest in paragraph 331 below, extended in their range. Another possible consequence is an increase in small advertisements in shops or local newspapers, offering the services of "masseuses," "models" or "companions"; but we think that this would be less injurious than the presence of prostitutes in the streets.

287. It has also been suggested to us that if the prostitutes disappeared from the streets the police would be deprived of a useful source of information about crime in general. We have had no evidence that more than a small proportion of prostitutes are connected with serious crime or that any considerable amount of information leading to convictions is obtained from them. Nor could we accept the proposition, if it were put forward, that legislation relating to one field of crime ought to be determined by its consequences in making the work of the police easier or more difficult in another.

288. Suggestions have been made that the police are occasionally bribed by prostitutes with money or other favours; and we recognise that the increased penalties we have proposed may increase, both for the prostitute and for the police officer, the temptation to resort to bribery. We do not, however, consider that this risk is sufficiently serious to outweigh the advantages of the amendments we have proposed. Our opinion is that the general standard of the police in this respect is high; and although no process of recruitment, however stringent, will ensure that every man who joins a large force can be guaranteed to be blameless, we do not believe that the changes we have proposed are likely to result in markedly increased corruption. There are other fields of crime where the temptation to the police to succumb to bribery is, and will continue to be, much stronger than it is here.

289. In any event, there must be set against these disadvantages, which are to a large extent hypothetical, the clear advantage that the ordinary citizen would be able to go about his business without the constant affront to his sense of decency which the presence of these women affords. So even if this can be achieved only by risking the dangers we have outlined, we still feel that the time has come to rid the streets of this nuisance and that the risk must therefore be taken. Moreover, we think that the measures we have proposed, even if they can be made effective only at the risk of other evils, might serve, perhaps to a large extent, to discourage newcomers to the ranks of the prostitute. We attach great importance to this. Not only does the present law fail to discourage; its inadequacies afford an encouragement in that the very presence of the prostitutes on the streets provides an example which some young women, to whom a life of prostitution had not yet become a fully formed intention, might be tempted to follow. Again, while we fully recognise, as we have said earlier, that the prostitute could not exist in the absence of a demand for her services, demand and supply are not entirely unrelated, and the mere presence of the prostitutes on the streets stimulates a demand for their services. Many men, especially younger ones, who now avail themselves of the services of prostitutes would be less inclined to do so if these services were less readily and obviously available.

290. In short, therefore, we feel that the possible consequences of clearing the streets are less harmful than the constant public parading of the

---

[1] See paragraph 315 (*d*) below.

prostitute's wares. We do not feel that it is "mere hypocrisy" to say this. It would be if we were avowedly trying to extinguish prostitution, for in that case the less open carrying on of the trade would be as objectionable as the more overt. But having taken into account the dangers which might follow from the changes in the law which we have proposed, we think that they would be less injurious to the community in general than the present state of affairs.

Licensed Brothels

291. One or two of our witnesses have suggested to us that the obvious and most satisfactory method of clearing the streets is to institute licensed brothels. This course, it is claimed, would ensure that the streets were kept clear, would guarantee some control of the prostitutes in the brothels and would preserve public decency without giving the impression of interference by the criminal law in affairs of private morals.

292. We do not advocate this solution. We have already expressed our view that prostitution can be eradicated only through measures directed to a better understanding of the nature and obligations of sex relationships and to a raising of the social and moral outlook of society as a whole. The licensing and toleration of brothels by the State would make nonsense of such measures, for it would imply that the State recognised prostitution as a social necessity.

293. If, as we have already suggested, the presence of prostitutes on the streets encourages indulgence in promiscuous intercourse by men who might be less inclined to avail themselves of the services of prostitutes if these services were less readily and obviously available, the existence of tolerated or licensed brothels would provide an even greater encouragement. And if the presence of prostitutes on the streets encourages some women who might not otherwise have done so to enter their ranks, the existence of tolerated or licensed brothels would provide an even greater encouragement to their recruitment.

294. But an even more fundamental objection to the tolerated brothel is its close connection with the traffic in women and children. The continued existence of brothels must obviously depend on a steady supply of new women, and a special body of experts appointed by the League of Nations in 1927 to consider some of the problems connected with this traffic found definite evidence that the demand thus created was met by traffickers and was the cause of both national and international traffic. "It is the existence of licensed houses which supplies the traffickers and their accomplices with a sure and permanent market for their services."[1]

295. We are not impressed by the argument about "control" of prostitutes in so far as this implies some medical safeguard, for it is obvious that this is more apparent than real; a woman who is absolutely healthy at the time of examination may be infected shortly afterwards and infect others before her own infection is detected.

296. We think it significant that other countries which have given a trial to this alleged solution of the problem have recently closed their *maisons tolerées*. All but two European countries have now abolished them, and there are at the present time only 19 countries with tolerated brothels as against 119 "abolitionist" countries. In our view, the toleration of brothels by the State would be a retrograde step.

---

[1] Report of the Special Body of Experts on Traffic in Women and Children. League of Nations Document C. 52 M.52, 1927, IV, Part I, page 14.

Research

297. Such research work as has already been done in connection with female prostitution has been more often from the point of view of sociology and reform than from the point of view of deliberate scientific investigation. We still do not know at all precisely what element it is in the total personality of a woman which results in her adopting a life of prostitution, and this, too, would seem to offer a fruitful field for research. At the present time, it is unlikely that sufficient case-material would be available for clinical research; but if our recommendations, and more particularly those in paragraphs 278 to 280 which relate to young and first offenders, result in more case-material becoming available, we recommend that research into the aetiology of prostitution should be undertaken. As in the case of research into homosexuality, there would be need of team-work, in which psychiatric social workers would play an important part.

CHAPTER X

LIVING ON THE EARNINGS OF PROSTITUTION

298. It is an offence for a male person knowingly to live wholly or in part on the earnings of prostitution. For this purpose, a man who lives with or is habitually in the company of a prostitute, or who exercises control, direction or influence over a prostitute's movements in a way which shows he is aiding, abetting or compelling her prostitution with others, is presumed to be knowingly living on the earnings of prostitution unless he proves the contrary.[1] And it is an offence for a female for purposes of gain to exercise control, direction or influence over a prostitute's movements in a way which shows she is aiding, abetting or compelling her prostitution.[2] The maximum penalty in either case is six months' imprisonment on conviction before a court of summary jurisdiction and two years' imprisonment on conviction on indictment.

299. Where it appears to a justice of the peace (in Scotland, a court of summary jurisdiction) from information on oath that there is reasonable cause to suspect that any house or part of a house is used by a woman for purposes of prostitution, and that a male person residing in or frequenting the house is living wholly or in part on her earnings, the justice (in Scotland, the court) may issue a warrant authorising a constable to enter and search the house and to arrest the man.[3]

300. There are no reliable figures relating to males dealt with by the courts prior to 1954 for living on the earnings of prostitution. As explained in paragraph 119 above, up to that year the offence was combined in the English criminal statistics with the offence of importuning by male persons. In 1954, in England and Wales, 114 men were found guilty of the offence at magistrates' courts and 11 at the higher courts. In 1955, the figures were

---

[1] England and Wales: Sexual Offences Act, 1956, Section 30. Scotland: Immoral Traffic (Scotland) Act, 1902, Section 1 (1) and (3).

[2] England and Wales: Sexual Offences Act, 1956, Section 31. Scotland: Criminal Law Amendment Act, 1912, Section 7 (4).

[3] England and Wales: Sexual Offences Act, 1956, Section 42. Scotland: Immoral Traffic (Scotland) Act, 1902, Section 1 (2).

113 and 14 respectively. These offenders were disposed of as indicated in Table XIII in Appendix II. The number of women convicted of exercising control, direction, or influence over a prostitute's movements is negligible, and has not exceeded five in any recent year. No figures relating to either offence are available in respect of Scotland, since the figures for these offences cannot be identified separately from the list of crimes and offences used for statistical purposes.

301. In its simplest and most usual form, " living on the earnings of prostitution " consists of an arrangement by which a man lives with a prostitute and is wholly or mainly kept by her. Such a man is commonly known as a " ponce " or *souteneur*. Detection of this offence is not without its difficulties, and calls for prolonged observation, usually covering several days and nights, in which the attention of the police is directed to such questions as the following:—

(i) whether the man and woman are living together: this is difficult to establish when the couple live in flats or parts of houses;
(ii) whether the woman is, in fact, carrying on prostitution;
(iii) whether the man is doing any work;
(iv) whether the man watches the woman soliciting;
(v) whether the woman is seen to hand the man any money;
(vi) whether they go home together after the woman has finished accommodating her customers.

The difficulties are increased by the fact that many prostitutes—particularly those operating in the West End of London—live with their ponces at some distance from the area in which they carry on their trade.

There is little doubt that the number of prosecutions could be appreciably increased if sufficient manpower were available to undertake the prolonged observation necessary to obtain satisfactory evidence, but we are satisfied that within the resources available to them the police do all they can to deal with this particular offence.

302. Such evidence as we have been able to obtain on this matter suggests that the arrangement between the prostitute and the man she lives with is usually brought about at the instance of the woman, and it seems to stem from a need on the part of the prostitute for some element of stability in the background of her life. As one writer has put it:—

> " This man may be literally the ' bully,' which is another of his titles; he may have forced her into the mode of life and be compelling her continuance in it. But he may also be, whether her legal husband or not, the equivalent of a husband to the promiscuous woman; he is frequently the only person in the world towards whom she feels affection and sense of possession; he is usually her champion in disputes and her protector in a skirmish. He is deeply despised by the police and by the public outside his trade; but he may be nevertheless the one humanising element in the life of the woman on whom he lives."[1]

It may be the case that once the arrangement is established the " ponce " makes more and more financial demands on the prostitute. It may also be the case that he sometimes is " literally ' the bully.' " But in the main the association between prostitute and " ponce " is voluntary and operates to

---

[1] Hall. " Prostitution: A Survey and a Challenge." Williams and Norgate, 1933, page 40.

mutual advantage. To say this is not to condone exploitation; the "ponce" or "bully" has rightly been the subject of universal and unreserved reprobation, and we have already expressed the view that the law should deal with the exploitation of others.

303. We have no doubt that behind the trade of prostitution there lies a variety of commercial interests, to some of which we refer below. The evidence submitted to us, however, has disclosed nothing in the nature of "organised vice" in which the prostitute is an unwilling victim, coerced by a vile exploiter. This does not mean that there is not "organisation," in the sense of encouragement to willing girls and women to enter or continue upon a life of prostitution.

304. The present law seems to be based on the desire to protect the prostitute from coercion and exploitation. When it was framed, the prostitute may have been in some danger of coercion; but today, either through the effectiveness of the law or through changes which have removed some of the economic and social factors likely to result in a life of prostitution, she is in less danger of coercion or exploitation against her will.

305. The popular impression of vast organisations in which women are virtually enslaved is perhaps in part due to the indiscriminate use of words which suggest an entirely passive role for the women concerned. We have, for example, learned of an arrangement between several prostitutes and a car-hire firm whereby the firm made large sums of money out of the use of their cars by the prostitutes. The firm was said to "run" a group of prostitutes, with the implication that they organised the women's activities. Another group of prostitutes lived in rooms, at various addresses, of which one particular man was landlord. This man, who had several convictions for brothel keeping and living on the earnings of prostitution, was said to be "running several girls." In both cases, however much unpleasant exploitation there might appear to the outsider to be, and might indeed actually be, the association between the prostitute and the "exploiter" was entirely voluntary and operated to mutual advantage.

306. It is in our view an over-simplification to think that those who live on the earnings of prostitution are exploiting the prostitute as such. What they are really exploiting is the whole complex of the relationship between prostitute and customer; they are, in effect, exploiting the human weaknesses which cause the customer to seek the prostitute and the prostitute to meet the demand. The more direct methods with which we have dealt above are not the only means by which the trade is exploited; that it continues to thrive is due in no small measure to efforts deliberately made to excite the demand on which its prosperity depends. Abraham Flexner, in his work on "Prostitution in Europe," to which the Street Offences Committee made reference, says (page 41) " A very large constituent in what has been called the irresistible demand of natural instinct is nothing but suggestion and stimulation associated with alcohol, late hours and sensuous amusements." At the present time, entertainments of a suggestive character, dubious advertisements, the sale of pornographic literature, contraceptives and "aphrodisiac" drugs (sometimes all in one shop), and the sale of alcoholic liquor in premises frequented by prostitutes, all sustain the trade, and in turn themselves profit from it. With most of these evils the law attempts to deal so far as it can without unduly trespassing on the liberty of the individual; and, as in the case of prostitution itself, it is to educative measures rather than to amendment of the law that society must look for a remedy.

307.(¹) It has been suggested to us that the present penalties provided by the law for living on the earnings of prostitution are inadequate and should be increased. We feel that the maximum of two years' imprisonment for which the law provides is adequate for this offence.

CHAPTER XI

PREMISES USED FOR THE PURPOSES OF PROSTITUTION

The Present Law

308. It is an offence:—

(*a*) for any person to keep a brothel, or to manage, or act or assist in the management of, a brothel;(²)

(*b*) for the lessor or landlord of any premises or his agent to let the whole or part of the premises with the knowledge that they are to be used, in whole or in part, as a brothel, or, where the whole or part of the premises is used as a brothel, to be wilfully a party to that use continuing;(³)

(*c*) for the tenant or occupier, or person in charge, of any premises knowingly to permit the whole or part of the premises to be used as a brothel;(⁴)

(*d*) for the tenant or occupier of any premises knowingly to permit the whole or part of the premises to be used for the purposes of habitual prostitution.(⁵)

The maximum penalty in each case is a fine of £100 or imprisonment for three months or both. On a second or subsequent conviction it is a fine of £250 or imprisonment for six months or both. For the purposes of the higher penalties, a conviction of any of these offences counts as a previous conviction in the same way as a conviction of the offence charged. In Scotland, the higher penalties may be imposed only in the Sheriff Courts, and not in other courts of summary jurisdiction.

309. In England and Wales, a person who keeps a brothel also commits an offence at common law for which he is punishable with a fine or imprisonment at the discretion of the court. In practice, proceedings are usually taken under the statutory provisions outlined above.

310. In certain burghs in Scotland. there is in operation concurrently with the provisions outlined in paragraph 308, a further statutory provision under which it is an offence, punishable with a fine of £20 or imprisonment, without the option of a fine, for sixty days, to be the occupier of, or to

---

[1] See Reservation V, page 128.

[2] England and Wales: Sexual Offences Act, 1956, Section 33. Scotland: Criminal Law Amendment Act, 1885, Section 13 (1).

[3] England and Wales: Sexual Offences Act, 1956, Section 34. Scotland: Criminal Law Amendment Act, 1885, Section 13 (3).

[4] England and Wales: Sexual Offences Act, 1956, Section 35 (1). Scotland: Criminal Law Amendment Act, 1885, Section 13 (2), as amended by the Criminal Law Amendment Act, 1912, Section 4 (1).

[5] England and Wales: Sexual Offences Act, 1956, Section 36. Scotland: Criminal Law Amendment Act, 1885, Section 13 (2).

manage or assist in the management of, a brothel.([1]) Under this provision, a magistrate may, on a complaint by the burgh prosecutor, grant a search warrant in respect of any premises or place if he is satisfied, on the evidence of a senior police officer and at least one other person not holding any office under the Burgh Police (Scotland) Act, 1892, that there is reasonable ground for believing that the premises are being used as a brothel, and the warrant empowers any constable to arrest the occupier of the premises or any person found therein who manages or assists in managing the brothel.

311. In England and Wales it is an offence for the holder of a justices' licence to permit the licensed premises to be a brothel. The maximum penalty is a fine of twenty pounds, but a licensee convicted (whether under this provision or under the provisions outlined in paragraph 308) of permitting his premises to be a brothel automatically forfeits his licence.([2])

312. In England and Wales, where the tenant or occupier of any premises is convicted, under the provisions outlined in paragraph 308, of knowingly permitting the whole or part of the premises to be used as a brothel, the lessor or landlord may require him to assign the lease or other contract under which the premises are held by him to some person approved by the lessor or landlord. Approval for this purpose must not be unreasonably withheld. If he fails to do so within three months, the lessor may (without prejudice to the rights or remedies of any party thereto accrued before the date of the determination) determine the lease or contract, and the court by which the tenant or occupier was convicted may make a summary order for the delivery of possession of premises to the lessor or landlord. If the lessor or landlord, after having the conviction brought to his notice, fails to exercise these rights or, having exercised them by determining the lease or contract, subsequently grants a new lease or contract to the same person without having all reasonable provisions to prevent the recurrence of the offence inserted in the new lease or contract, he is deemed to be a party to any subsequent offence committed in respect of the premises while his landlord-tenant relationship with the convicted person subsists, unless he can show that he took all reasonable steps to prevent the recurrence of the offence.([3])

313. In Scotland, the conviction of any person under the provisions outlined in paragraphs 308 and 310 automatically voids and terminates any lease or arrangement to let relating to the premises concerned as from the date of the conviction; but the rights of the owner, for rent or otherwise, for the year current at the date of the voidance remain unaffected.([4])

314. It will have been observed from paragraph 308 that the law distinguishes between use of the premises "as a brothel" and use "for the purposes of habitual prostitution." The law may be summarised briefly and in non-technical language as follows:—

It is an offence—

(1) (a) for any person to keep or assist in keeping a brothel;
    (b) for a landlord (or his agent) knowingly to let premises for use as a brothel;

([1]) Burgh Police (Scotland) Act, 1892, Section 403. This Act extends to all burghs other than Edinburgh, Glasgow, Dundee, Aberdeen and Greenock which have, however, power to adopt the provisions of the Act or to have enacted local Act provisions of their own. Of the five excepted burghs, only Glasgow has adopted Section 403.

([2]) Licensing Act, 1953, Section 140.

([3]) Sexual Offences Act, 1956, Section 35.

([4]) Burgh Police (Scotland) Act, 1892, Section 403, as extended by Criminal Law Amendment Act, 1912, Section 6.

(c) for a tenant, occupier or person in charge to permit premises to be used as a brothel;

(2) for a tenant or occupier to permit premises to be used for the purposes of habitual prostitution.

Whatever the popular conception may be, in its present legal acceptance in this country a " brothel " means any place resorted to by persons of both sexes and habitually used for the purposes of illicit sexual intercourse. Such a place is a brothel within the meaning of the law whether or not those who resort to it or those engaged in the management thereof receive payment for their services.[1] Premises cannot, however, in law be a brothel unless there are at least two women using them for the purposes of illicit sexual intercourse or acts of lewdness.[2] Rooms or flats let separately to individual women, though they may be in the same building, constitute separate " premises " for this purpose.[3]

315. In practice, premises in respect of which prosecutions are instituted under the law relating to brothels at the present time consist mainly of—

(a) houses or flats the tenants of which allow two or more prostitutes to bring men there for the purposes of prostitution. The tenant may be a prostitute who also uses the premises for her own prostitution; cases of this sort frequently arise when the prostitute is in financial difficulty (perhaps as a result of having undertaken to pay key money and an exorbitant rent), and consequently allows one or more other prostitutes to bring men to the premises in return for a payment made on each occasion when they use the premises;

(b) hotels or boarding houses to which several prostitutes take different men; such premises are frequently used by prostitutes—particularly " part-timers "—who have no premises of their own available for the purpose;

(c) houses in which a number of rooms are let off to prostitutes who use them indiscriminately—*i.e.*, where it is apparent that there is no separate letting to individual prostitutes;

(d) " call-girl " establishments—*i.e.*, houses or flats to which men go and to which prostitutes are summoned by telephone message or some other arrangement.

316. As we have explained above, premises in the sole occupation of a woman who uses them for her own prostitution do not, in law, constitute a " brothel," even though they may be in the same building as other premises similarly used. They are, however, clearly " used for the purposes of habitual prostitution " within the meaning of the law; but in the latter context the law provides only for the punishment of the " tenant or occupier " who " permits " such user, and the courts have held (a) that a woman who is the sole occupier of premises which she uses for the purposes of her own habitual prostitution cannot be convicted of " permitting " the premises to be so used;[4] (b) that a lessee of premises of which he occupies part himself and lets another part to a woman who uses that part for the purposes of habitual prostitution commits no offence since he is, in effect, the landlord of the part sublet and the " tenant or occupier " only of what remains; [5] and (c) that

---

[1] *Winter* v. *Wolfe* (1931), 1 K.B.549. *Girgawy* v. *Strathern* (1925), J.C.31.
[2] *Caldwell* v. *Leach* (1913), 77 J.P.254.
[3] *Strath* v. *Foxon* (1955), 3 All E.R. 398.
[4] *Mattison* v. *Johnson* (1916), 85 L.J.K.B.741.
[5] *Siviour* v. *Napolitano* (1931), 1 K.B.636.

"tenant or occupier" means a tenant in occupation, so that a tenant who has parted with effective control by granting a subtenancy to a prostitute commits no offence.

317. It will be seen, therefore, that under the law as it stands at present several rooms in one building may be let to individual prostitutes with impunity so long as each prostitute reserves her room to her exclusive use. To all outward appearance, a building used in this way is in no way distinguishable from a similar building used by an equivalent number of prostitutes who use the rooms indiscriminately and thus turn the premises, in the eyes of the law, into a "brothel." It must be difficult for the ordinary citizen to understand why the appropriate authorities should be able to take action in respect of some premises while they can take none in respect of others which are, to all outward appearance, being used in exactly the same way. This, we think, accounts for complaints that have been made from time to time to the effect that the police are not sufficiently active as regards premises used for the purposes of prostitution.

Proposals for Amendment

318. It is evident that the prostitutes and their landlords are aware of the loopholes in the law and are quick to take advantage of them. Various suggestions for amending the law relating to these matters have been put to us by our witnesses. Some witnesses have gone so far as to suggest that the use by a convicted prostitute for her own habitual prostitution of premises of which she is the tenant or occupier should be an offence. By "convicted prostitute" our witnesses presumably meant prostitutes convicted of some offence ancillary to their profession—for example, soliciting—since prostitution is, of itself, no offence. To make it an offence for a prostitute to use for the purposes of her own prostitution premises of which she is the occupier would be tantamount to making prostitution itself an offence; and, as we have said earlier, no case for this can, in our view, be sustained. Moreover, the course suggested would be arbitrary in that it would discriminate between prostitution by a woman who has been convicted of soliciting and prostitution by a woman who has not, although the latter may have been conducting herself as a prostitute over a much longer period.

319. Another suggestion, which found more general favour among our witnesses, was that the legal distinction between premises used "as a brothel" and premises used "for the purposes of habitual prostitution" should be eliminated. It is at least arguable that the conduct of the landlord who knowingly lets individual flats or rooms to individual prostitutes differs in degree only, and not in kind, from that of the landlord who lets premises for use as a brothel; and the proposal is, at first sight, attractive. But it seems to us that it would be going too far to apply in its entirety to premises used for habitual prostitution the law relating to premises used as brothels. It would at once mean that it would be an offence knowingly to let premises to a prostitute for the purposes of her own prostitution or knowingly to be a party to the use of premises for this purpose.

320. As long as society tolerates the prostitute, it must permit her to carry on her business somewhere. That she ought not to be allowed to carry it on in public will be apparent from what we have said in an earlier chapter; and the law, for a variety of reasons, rightly frowns on the brothel. The only remaining possibility is individual premises. We have therefore reached the conclusion that it would not be right to amend the law in such a way as to make guilty of a criminal offence a person who lets premises to a prostitute who uses them, even with his knowledge, for the purposes of

her own habitual prostitution. It is perhaps not out of place to mention here that if premises are let with the intention of their being used for the purposes of prostitution, the lease is wholly unenforceable and the landlord cannot recover the rent or sue upon the lessee's covenants.(¹)

321. This does not, however, mean that a landlord should not have the right to recover possession of premises which are being put to unauthorised use, or that a landlord should be obliged to tolerate the use for the purposes of prostitution of premises of which he is the lessor. We are very conscious of the difficulties experienced by reputable landlords who are anxious to eradicate prostitution from their properties. The tenancy of premises occupied by a prostitute frequently constitutes the last link in a chain of leases and sub-leases, and in many such cases the superior landlords have let the premises *bona fide* and at normal rents. In some cases a superior landlord cannot refuse consent to the assignment of a lease or the granting of a sub-lease, and in others he can only refuse consent for some good reason. Usually, applications to assign or sub-let are supported by references so outwardly unimpeachable that no valid objection to the assignment or sub-letting can be made; yet a few months later the premises assigned or sub-let are found to be in use by a prostitute. In some cases, the fact that the premises are so occupied is observed by the landlord or his agent; in some, the first the landlord hears of the matter is that the tenant has been convicted of permitting the premises to be used as a brothel or for the purpose of habitual prostitution; and in some, the matter is brought to his notice in a cautionary letter from the police or local authority to the effect that the premises are being used as a brothel.

322. As we have explained above, in Scotland, the conviction of a tenant of permitting the premises to be used as a brothel automatically terminates the contract of tenancy. In England and Wales, there is no such automatic termination, but the landlord has the right to require the tenant to assign the lease to some suitable person within three months, and if the tenant fails to do this the landlord may then terminate the tenancy.

323. We do not think that a provision on the lines of the law in force in Scotland would work equitably in England and Wales, where leases providing for payment of a substantial premium and thereafter of a nominal rent are much more common. Automatic termination of the lease might, where it is of this nature, result in some cases in a penalty disproportionate to the circumstances of the offence. For the same reason, we do not consider it desirable that the landlord should have the right himself to determine the lease on the conviction of the tenant. We do consider, however, that the landlord should have the right, where the tenant has been convicted of a criminal offence in connection with the user of the premises, to apply to the courts for an order determining the lease. Further, we feel that this application could most appropriately be dealt with by the court by which the tenant was convicted. This court has before it, and fresh in its mind, the details of the particular case, and could appropriately draw up a single order embodying all the legal consequences of the conviction.

324. At present, the law gives the landlord the right to require the tenant to assign the lease if he is convicted of " permitting " the premises to be used as a brothel, but not if he is convicted of keeping, or managing, or acting or assisting in the management of, a brothel on the premises. This seems to us to be anomalous, and we consider that the rights and duties of the landlord should be the same in each case.

(¹) Halsbury's Laws of England. 2nd edn. Vol. 20, page 224.

325. We have already suggested that it would be going too far to apply in its entirety to premises used for the purposes of habitual prostitution the law relating to premises used as brothels. The present law distinguishes, however, as regards premises used for the purposes of habitual prostitution, between those of which the prostitute is herself the tenant and those of which she is not. As we have explained earlier, a prostitute commits no offence if she uses for the purposes of her own prostitution premises of which she is herself the owner or tenant; but a tenant who permits the premises to be used for the purposes of habitual prostitution commits an offence. We think it appropriate that the law should carry this distinction a stage further, and that where a tenant is convicted of permitting premises to be used for the purposes of habitual prostitution, the landlord should have the same rights, in regard to the determination of the tenancy, as he would have if the tenant had been convicted of permitting the premises to be used as a brothel.

326. We accordingly recommend that magistrates' courts in England and Wales, should be empowered, on convicting a tenant or occupier of—

(i) keeping or managing, or acting or assisting in the management of, a brothel; or
(ii) knowingly permitting premises to be used as a brothel; or
(iii) knowingly permitting premises to be used for the purposes of habitual prostitution,

to make an order

either

(i) determining the lease or contract of tenancy or licence to occupy (without prejudice to the rights or remedies of any party thereto accrued before the date of the determination);

or

(ii) requiring the tenant to assign the lease or contract of tenancy within a period of three months to some person approved by the landlord, whose approval for this purpose must not be unreasonably withheld.

327. We consider that the landlord should have the right to be heard, if he so desires, in regard to the making of such an order, and we accordingly further recommend that the police or other authority by whom the proceedings are instituted should be required to notify the landlord of the proceedings and to inform him of his right to apply for such an order in the event of conviction. We envisage that the landlord's application would be made in writing before the proceedings and dealt with by the court at the time when the tenant is sentenced. If he does not take advantage of this right to apply for an order, or if, in a case where an order is made, he subsequently grants a new lease or contract to the same person without having all reasonable provisions to prevent the recurrence of the offence inserted in the new lease or contract, he should be deemed to be a party to any subsequent similar offence committed by the tenant on the premises unless he can show that he took all reasonable steps to prevent the recurrence of the offence.

328. We are aware that difficulties are sometimes encountered in establishing the identity of the landlord in cases of this sort. To overcome these, we recommend that a magistrates' court should have power to require a tenant charged with any of the offences mentioned above, under pain of penalty, to disclose the name and address of the person to whom he pays his rent. Moreover, since as we have explained earlier, the tenancy in cases of

this sort frequently constitutes the last link in a chain of leases, we recommend that there should be similar power to require each immediate lessor in turn to disclose the name and address of his superior lessor. This is of special importance in cases where the premises are being used as a brothel, since in that case each of the superior lessors is in peril of the law as long as the user continues.

329. While the proposals we have put forward would, we think, be of considerable assistance to the landlord in cases where the tenant is convicted of an offence, we recognise that there are many cases where there is no conviction of a tenant but where a landlord experiences difficulty in ridding his premises of prostitution. Although, as we have said earlier, it ought not to be made an offence to let premises for use by a prostitute, we are certain that most reputable landlords would be anxious to free their properties from an encumbrance of this sort, and we have been made aware of some of the difficulties which the legal processes to this end entail. But if the letting of premises for use by a prostitute is not to be a criminal offence (and we have given reasons why in our opinion it ought not to be), it follows that any measures which may be necessary to evict her must be outside the field of the criminal law and hence outside our terms of reference.

330. Although, for reasons which will be apparent from what we have said earlier, we think that it would be neither desirable nor practicable to extend to premises used for the purposes of habitual prostitution all the provisions of the law relating to brothels, we have reason to believe that certain " flat farmers " derive considerable profits from high rents and key-moneys charged to prostitutes. Key-money is said to be in the neighbourhood of £100, and may even be as high as £200 in some areas, and the rental charged from £20 to £25 a week. Some flats that are let out on these terms are premises where the rent is controlled by law at 30s. a week, and this is the sum that is ostensibly charged by the lessor to the prostitute. False rent books are kept showing the maximum permitted charge, and the additional profits are often shared between the lessor and the agent who lets the premises.

331.([1]) It is clearly wrong that unscrupulous landlords and estate agents should profit from the opportunities which the present law affords for the letting of premises to prostitutes at exorbitant rents. We accordingly recommend that a landlord who can be shown to be letting premises at an exorbitant rent or demanding exorbitant key-money in the knowledge that they are to be used for the purposes of prostitution should be deemed, for the purposes of the law outlined in the preceding chapter of this report, to be " living on the earnings of prostitution," and that the same should apply to any agent who can be shown to have knowingly taken part in the transaction. We recognise that the receipt of exorbitant rents will not always be easy to prove; the prostitute is usually reluctant to take any action which might result in her losing her business premises. At the present time, however, even when police have been able to establish the receipt of exorbitant rents, it has not always been possible to secure convictions of the landlords, since some courts have held that the receipt of exorbitant rents does not amount to " living on the earnings of prostitution " within the meaning of the law.([2]) Adoption of our recommendation would serve at least to remedy this situation. We recognise, too, the difficulties attendant on the proof of guilty knowledge on the part of the lessor; but these difficulties arise at present in respect of

---

[1] See Reservation I (g), page 123.
[2] *R.* v. *Silver* and others. Central Criminal Court, 9th February, 1956.

premises used as brothels, and the procedure at present employed in respect of brothels can no doubt be adapted to premises used for the purposes of habitual prostitution.

332. We think the recommendations we have made go as far as the criminal law can be expected to go so long as prostitution in itself is not to be a crime. We have no doubt that in carrying out her trade the prostitute will continue to give offence to some people; and in this connection we have much sympathy with the respectable tenant who finds a neighbouring flat or house occupied by a prostitute who accommodates her customers there. The activities of prostitutes in these circumstances are the subject of many complaints from neighbouring residents who cannot understand why the police " do nothing about it." If, however, the prostitute exercises her trade in such a way as to cause a nuisance, there is a remedy available in the civil courts.([1])

Prosecution by Local Authorities

333. In London, the prosecution of offences relating to the use of premises for immoral purposes is usually undertaken by the metropolitan borough councils. This arrangement seems to stem from the historical developments of the laws relating to disorderly houses, and in particular from the absorption by the borough councils of the functions formerly vested in the overseers of the poor, upon whom the old enactments placed certain duties in this respect.

334. While the borough councils undertake the actual prosecution, the necessary observation now devolves on the police. If a complaint that premises are being used for immoral purposes is received by the borough council, it is referred to the police for enquiry and report. If the complaint is made to the police, the police make the necessary enquiries and report to the borough council. If the borough council considers that the report discloses evidence sufficient to justify proceedings, these are then instituted by the council. In practice, this arrangement has worked well, but cases have occasionally arisen in which the borough council concerned has been reluctant to institute proceedings though the police reports disclosed evidence sufficient to justify them; in such cases, the police have themselves sometimes prosecuted the offenders.

335. It has been represented to us by several of the metropolitan borough councils that the present arrangements are anachronistic, and that the police should carry out the prosecution, as well as the observation, of these offences, just as they do in the case of other criminal offences. Other councils would prefer to retain the function of prosecuting in these cases, on the ground that local authorities have a general duty to supervise the good governance of their areas, and that this problem does affect peaceful and orderly governance. It was also suggested that complainants in matters of this sort sometimes prefer to go to the local authority rather than to the police. It seems to us that these considerations, so far as they are valid at all, are equally applicable to numerous other offences, and that it would be difficult to justify the present arrangement on these grounds. While we see no serious objection to the retention of this initiative by any particular council which may wish to retain it, we consider it more satisfactory that there should be uniformity of practice and that such prosecutions should be undertaken by the police.

([1]) Cf. *Thompson-Schwab* v. *Costaki* (1956), 1 W.L.R.335.

Statistics

336. Tables XIV and XVII in Appendix II show the numbers of persons convicted during the five years ended 31st December, 1955, of the offences dealt with in this chapter. The tables also show how the offenders were dealt with by the courts.

CHAPTER XII

PROCURATION

337. It is an offence:—

*† (i) to procure a woman or girl to become, in any part of the world, a common prostitute;(¹)

*† (ii) to procure a woman or girl to leave the United Kingdom intending her to become an inmate of or frequent a brothel elsewhere;(¹)

*†(iii) to procure a woman or girl to leave her usual place of abode in the United Kingdom, intending her to become an inmate of or frequent a brothel in any part of the world for the purposes of prostitution;(¹)

*†(iv) to procure a girl under twenty-one to have unlawful sexual intercourse in any part of the world with a third person;(²)

† (v) to procure a woman or girl, by threats or intimidation, or by false pretences or false representations, to have unlawful sexual intercourse in any part of the world;(³)

†(vi) to apply or administer to, or cause to be taken by, a woman or girl any substance with intent to stupefy or overpower her so as to enable any man to have unlawful sexual intercourse with her;(⁴)

(vii) for a person who is the owner or occupier of any premises, or who has, or acts or assists in, the management or control of any premises, to induce or knowingly suffer a girl under the age of sixteen to resort to or be on the premises for the purpose of having unlawful sexual intercourse with men or with a particular man;(⁵) (A person charged with this offence may be found guilty of the offence described in paragraph 340 below, if the jury are not satisfied that he is guilty of the offence charged or of an attempt to commit it, but are satisfied that he is guilty of the other offence.)

---

* In England and Wales, a constable may arrest without warrant any person whom he has cause to suspect of having committed, or of attempting to commit, these offences.

† No person may be convicted of any of these offences on the evidence of one witness, unless the witness is corroborated in some material particular by evidence implicating the accused.

(¹) England and Wales: Sexual Offences Act, 1956, Section 22. Scotland: Criminal Law Amendment Act, 1885, Section 2.

(²) England and Wales: Sexual Offences Act, 1956, Section 23. Scotland: Criminal Law Amendment Act, 1885, Section 2.

(³) England and Wales: Sexual Offences Act, 1956, Sections 2 and 3. Scotland: Criminal Law Amendment Act, 1885, Section 3 (1) and 3 (2).

(⁴) England and Wales: Sexual Offences Act, 1956, Section 4. Scotland: Criminal Law Amendment Act, 1885, Section 3 (3).

(⁵) England and Wales: Sexual Offences Act, 1956, Sections 25 and 26. Scotland: Criminal Law Amendment Act, 1885, Section 6 (1) and (2).

(viii) to take an unmarried girl under the age of eighteen out of the possession of her parent or guardian against his will, if she is so taken that she shall have unlawful sexual intercourse with men or with a particular man (but a person is not guilty of this offence is he believes, and has reasonable cause to believe, that the girl is eighteen or over);([1])

(ix) to detain a woman or girl against her will on any premises with the intention that she shall have unlawful sexual intercourse with men or a particular man, or to detain her against her will in a brothel. (Where a woman or girl is on any premises for the purpose of having unlawful sexual intercourse, or is in a brothel, a person who, with the intention of compelling or inducing her to remain on the premises, withholds from her her clothes or any other property, or threatens her with legal proceedings in the event of her taking away clothes provided by him or on his direction, is deemed to be " detaining " her there; and a woman or girl is not liable to any proceedings, civil or criminal, for taking away or being found in possesion of any clothes she needed to enable her to leave the premises);([2])

(x) to procure a woman or girl who is a mental defective to have unlawful sexual intercourse in any part of the world;([3])

(xi) to take a woman or girl who is a mental defective out of the possession of her parent or guardian against his will, with the intention that she shall have unlawful sexual intercourse with men or with a particular man;([4])

(xii) for a person who is the owner or occupier of any premises, or who has, or acts or assists in, the management or control of any premises, to induce or knowingly suffer a woman or girl who is a mental defective to resort to or be on the premises for the purposes of having unlawful sexual intercourse with men or with a particular man;([5])

(xiii) to cause or encourage the prostitution in any part of the world of a woman or girl who is a mental defective. (In Scotland, this applies only to a person having the custody, charge or care of the woman or girl.)([6])

In England and Wales, a person is not guilty of the offences numbered (x) to (xiii) above if he does not know and has no reason to suspect the woman or girl to be a mental defective.

338. The maximum penalty for each of the offences mentioned in the preceding paragraph is two years' imprisonment, except as regards (vii), in which case, if the girl is under the age of thirteen, the maximum penalty is life imprisonment. In England and Wales these offences may be tried only at assizes. In Scotland they may be tried summarily in a Sheriff court if the prosecuting authorities so decide, and in that event the maximum penalty is three months' imprisonment.

([1]) England and Wales: Sexual Offences Act, 1956, Section 19. Scotland: Criminal Law Amendment Act, 1885, Section 7.

([2]) England and Wales: Sexual Offences Act, 1956, Section 24. Scotland: Criminal Law Amendment Act, 1885, Section 8.

([3]) England and Wales: Sexual Offences Act, 1956, Section 9. Scotland: Mental Deficiency and Lunacy (Scotland) Act, 1913, Section 46 (1) (*b*).

([4]) England and Wales: Sexual Offences Act, 1956, Section 21. Scotland: Mental Deficiency and Lunacy (Scotland) Act, 1913, Section 46 (1) (*e*).

([5]) England and Wales: Sexual Offences Act, 1956, Section 27. Scotland: Mental Deficiency and Lunacy (Scotland) Act, 1913, Section 46 (1) (*d*).

([6]) England and Wales: Sexual Offences Act, 1956, Section 29. Scotland: Mental Deficiency and Lunacy (Scotland) Act, 1913, Section 46 (1) (*c*).

339. It is an offence for the parent, guardian or any other person having the custody, charge or care of a girl under the age of sixteen years, to cause or encourage the prostitution of, or the commission of unlawful sexual intercourse with, or indecent assault on, the girl. In Scotland, the offence is extended to include causing or encouraging lewd, indecent and libidinous behaviour towards a girl between twelve and sixteen years of age. Where a girl has become a prostitute, or has had unlawful sexual intercourse or has been indecently assaulted (or, in Scotland, has been the victim of lewd, indecent and libidinous behaviour) a person is deemed for this purpose to have encouraged it if he knowingly allows her to consort with, or to enter or continue in the employment of, any prostitute or person of known immoral character.([1]) The maximum penalty is two years' imprisonment. In England and Wales, the offence may be tried either at assizes or quarter sessions; in Scotland, it may be tried summarily in a Sheriff court if the prosecuting authorities so decide, when the maximum penalty is again three months' imprisonment.

340. It is an offence for any person having the custody, charge or care of a child between the ages of four and sixteen years to allow that child to reside in or frequent a brothel.([2]) The offence is triable on indictment or summarily, and the maximum penalty is imprisonment for six months and a fine of £25.

341. Where it appears to a justice of the peace from information on oath laid by the parent, relative or guardian of a woman or girl, or by any other person who in the opinion of the justice is acting in her interests, that there is reasonable cause to suspect—

(a) that the woman or girl is detained in any place within his jurisdiction in order that she may have sexual intercourse with men or with a particular man; and

(b) that either she is so detained against her will, or she is under the age of sixteen or is a mental defective, or she is under the age of eighteen and is so detained against the will of her parent or other person having the lawful care or charge of her,

the justice may issue a warrant authorising a constable to search for her and to take her to and detain her in a place of safety until she can be brought before a justice of the peace. The justice before whom she is subsequently brought may cause her to be delivered up to her parent or guardian, or otherwise dealt with as circumstances may permit and require.([3]) In its application to Scotland, references in this paragraph to a justice of the peace include reference to a sheriff or sheriff-substitute.

342. The present laws against procuration, like those relating to brothels, owe their existence largely to the efforts in the nineteenth century of various societies formed in connection with one or other aspects of prostitution or regulation of vice. These efforts led eventually to the setting up, in 1881, of a Select Committee of the House of Lords to enquire into the law relating to the protection of young girls. This Committee, to whose report we have referred earlier, found that a certain number of girls had been induced by

---

([1]) England and Wales: Sexual Offences Act, 1956, Section 28. Scotland: Children and Young Persons (Scotland) Act, 1937, Section 13.
([2]) England and Wales: Children and Young Persons Act, 1933, Section 3. Scotland: Children and Young Persons (Scotland) Act, 1937, Section 14.
([3]) England and Wales: Sexual Offences Act, 1956, Section 43. Scotland: Criminal Law Amendment Act, 1885, Section 10. Mental Deficiency and Lunacy (Scotland) Act, 913, Section 46 (2).

agents in London to go over to the continent and placed in brothels there. The Criminal Law Amendment Act, 1885 (now replaced, in England and Wales, by the Sexual Offences Act, 1956), was the result.

343. Since that time, the international activities of the traffickers in women and girls have been considerably curbed by international action, first through voluntary societies and later through inter-governmental channels. Of recent years, these measures have been carried out through the machinery of the League of Nations and the United Nations with the co-operation of the voluntary bodies.

344. Very few cases of procuration come to the notice of the police in this country at the present time. It has been suggested that this is because the women or girls who become prostitutes do so because they want to and do not need to be " procured." In order to sustain a charge of procuring it is necessary to establish that some persuasion or influence has been brought to bear on the woman or girl, and this may be negatived by evidence which shows that she was not really " procured " because she needed no procuring at all and acted of her own free will.[1]

345. As regards England and Wales, no precise figures are available to show the number of procuration offences known to the police or dealt with by the courts prior to 1954, since the heading " procuration " in the criminal statistics includes the offence of living on the earnings of prostitution where this is dealt with on indictment. The average total of all offences recorded under this heading as known to the police over the past twenty-five years is, however, only 27 per annum so that the number of actual procuration offences is negligible. It is known that 6 men and 5 women were convicted of such offences during each of the years 1954 and 1955. In Scotland, figures are available from 1951 onwards. These show that no persons were proceeded against in 1951, 1952 or 1954. Two were proceeded against in 1953, one of whom was discharged without trial, the other being convicted and fined. One was convicted in 1955 and sentenced to imprisonment.

346. No evidence has been placed before us to suggest that the procuration laws are not working satisfactorily, and we make no recommendations concerning them.

CHAPTER XIII

MISCELLANEOUS PROVISIONS

Refreshment Houses, &c.

347. There are in force various statutory provisions for the punishment of keepers of licensed premises and refreshment houses who permit prostitutes to congregate on their premises.

348. In England and Wales, any holder of a justices' licence to sell intoxicating liquor who allows the licensed premises to be the habitual resort or meeting place of reputed prostitutes, whether or not the object of their resorting to or meeting at the premises is prostitution, is liable to a fine of £10 for a first offence and a fine of £20 for any subsequent offence. The licensee is not, however, prohibited from allowing such persons to remain

---

[1] *R. v. Christian* (1913) (78 J.P.112).

on the premises for the purpose of obtaining reasonable refreshment for such time as is necessary for that purpose.[1] In Scotland, it is a condition of a certificate granted for the sale by retail of excisable liquor that the certificate-holder shall not "knowingly permit or suffer men or women of notoriously bad fame ... to assemble" in the licensed premises.[2]

349. In England and Wales, any person licensed to keep a refreshment house (not being a place licensed by the justices for the sale of intoxicating liquor) who knowingly suffers prostitutes to assemble at, or continue on, his premises, is liable to a fine of £5 for a first offence. For a subsequent offence a fine of £20 may be imposed and the licence forfeited; the licensee may also be disqualified from holding a licence.[3] In burghs in Scotland, the occupier of any premises or place of public resort used for the sale or consumption of provisions or refreshments of any kind who knowingly harbours prostitutes or allows "persons of notoriously bad fame, or dissolute boys and girls" to assemble therein is liable to a fine of £10 or sixty days' imprisonment.[4]

350. In the Metropolitan Police District and the City of London, the keeper of any premises or place of public resort at which provisions, liquors or refreshments of any kind are sold or consumed who knowingly suffers prostitutes to meet together and remain there is liable to a fine of £5. If he holds a liquor licence, he is also subject to any penalties or penal consequences to which he may be liable for committing an offence against the tenor of his licence.[5]

351. It has been suggested to us that the street problem in London today might have been less acute if certain licensed premises known in former days as the rendezvous of prostitutes had continued in existence. It is right that the law should guard against the congregation in any one place of undesirables of any type, if only as a precaution against breaches of the peace, and we recommend no change in the law so far as it relates to the congregation of prostitutes in places of refreshment. At the same time, too rigorous an enforcement of the law in this respect might well have the effect, in some places, of driving prostitutes whose conduct at the present time is inoffensive, on to the streets, where their very presence would offend. In two large cities whose chief constables gave evidence to us, certain public houses, cafés and coffee stalls are known to be frequented by prostitutes who find their customers there, but in neither of these cities is there any significant street problem. We feel that the use of the statutory provisions we have mentioned might with advantage be confined to instances where the conduct of the prostitutes is such as to give offence to other users of the premises or to neighbouring residents.

Aliens

352. Where an alien is convicted of any offence for which a sentence of imprisonment may be awarded in the case of an offender of full age, or of any of the street offences mentioned in Chapter IX above, the court by which he or she is convicted may recommend that a deportation order (that is,

---

[1] Licensing Act, 1953, Section 139.
[2] Licensing (Scotland) Act, 1903, Sixth Schedule.
[3] Refreshment Houses Act, 1860, Section 32.
[4] Burgh Police (Scotland) Act, 1892, Section 380 (2) and similar local Acts.
[5] Metropolitan Police Act, 1839, Section 44. City of London Police Act, 1839, Section 28.

an order requiring the alien to leave and to remain thereafter out of the United Kingdom) be made. Such orders are made by the Secretary of State, who also has power to make a deportation order in any case in which he deems this course conducive to the public good.

353. An alien woman who marries a citizen of the United Kingdom and Colonies is entitled, on making application therefor to the Secretary of State and taking the oath of allegiance, to be registered as a citizen. The Secretary of State has no power to refuse such an application. It has been alleged that large numbers of foreign prostitutes contract abroad marriages of convenience with United Kingdom citizens in order to enable them to enter this country and operate here without being liable to registration as aliens and consequent supervision, and to deportation. While such cases have arisen, our information suggests that this problem has been much exaggerated. Of 372 prostitutes arrested for the first time by officers attached to the West End Central police station during the years 1953 and 1954, only 17 were of foreign birth. Of these, 8 had married British subjects under normal conditions before taking to prostitution, 3 remained single at the time of the enquiry, and 1 was an alien by marriage. Only 5 of the 17 women had contracted what seemed to be marriages of convenience, and we have no evidence to show that marriages with British subjects are being contracted on an organised basis in the furtherance of prostitution. It would be outside our terms of reference to propose any change in the law relating to the acquisition of citizenship of the United Kingdom. In any event, we doubt whether it would be practicable to give effect to legislation that distinguished between genuineness and otherwise of intention of the parties at the time of marriage without devising an elaborate procedure which this question does not seem important enough to justify. We are content therefore to call attention to the situation as we find it.

Punishment of Offences

354. In accordance with customary legislative practice, the statutes and bye-laws creating the " offences against the criminal law in connection with prostitution and solicitation for immoral purposes " provide for punishment of the offenders by way of fine or imprisonment. There are, however, in force a number of statutes of general application which provide alternative methods by which the courts can deal with persons brought before them charged with criminal offences. These alternative methods are outlined in Chapter VI of our report. In practice, they have only a limited application in relation to prostitution offences, but where appropriate they are used in dealing with these offences just as they would be in connection with other offences.

PART FOUR—SUMMARY OF RECOMMENDATIONS

355. The following is a summary of our Recommendations:—

(a) Homosexual Offences

We recommend :—

(i) That homosexual behaviour between consenting adults in private be no longer a criminal offence (paragraph 62).

(ii) That questions relating to "consent" and "in private" be decided by the same criteria as apply in the case of heterosexual acts between adults (paragraphs 63, 64).

(iii) That the age of "adulthood" for the purposes of the proposed change in the law be fixed at twenty-one (paragraph 71).

*(iv) That no proceedings be taken in respect of any homosexual act (other than an indecent assault) committed in private by a person under twenty-one, except by the Director of Public Prosecutions or with the sanction of the Attorney-General (paragraph 72).

(v) That the law relating to living on the earnings of prostitution be applied to the earnings of male, as well as female, prostitution (paragraph 76).

(vi) That the law be amended, if necessary, so as to make it explicit that the term "brothel" includes premises used for homosexual practices (paragraph 76).

(vii) That there be introduced revised maximum penalties in respect of buggery, gross indecency and indecent assaults (paragraphs 90, 91).

*(viii) That buggery be re-classified as a misdemeanour (paragraph 94).

(ix) That except for some grave reason, proceedings be not instituted in respect of homosexual offences incidentally revealed in the course of investigating allegations of blackmail (paragraph 112).

*(x) That Section 29 (3) of the Larceny Act, 1916, be extended so as to apply to all homosexual offences (paragraph 113).

*(xi) That the offence of gross indecency between male persons be made triable summarily with the consent of the accused (paragraph 114).

*(xii) That male persons charged with importuning for immoral purposes be entitled to claim trial by jury (paragraph 123).

(xiii) That except for indecent assaults, the prosecution of any homosexual offence more than twelve months old be barred by statute (paragraph 135).

(xiv) That subject to any necessary special safeguards, managers and headmasters of approved schools be allowed the same measure of discretion in dealing with homosexual behaviour between inmates as that enjoyed by those responsible for the management of any other educational establishment (paragraph 147).

(xv) That the organisation, establishment and conditions of service of the prison medical service be reviewed (paragraph 180).

---

* These Recommendations have application only in relation to England and Wales.

(xvi) That a court by which a person under twenty-one is found guilty of a homosexual offence be required to obtain and consider a psychiatric report before passing sentence (paragraph 187).

(xvii) That prisoners desirous of having oestrogen treatment be permitted to do so if the prison medical officer considers that this would be beneficial (paragraph 211).

(xviii) That research be instituted into the aetiology of homosexuality and the effects of various forms of treatment (paragraph 216).

(b) Prostitution

We recommend :—

*(xix) That the law relating to street offences be reformulated so as to eliminate the requirement to establish annoyance (paragraph 256).

(xx) That the law be made of general application (paragraph 266).

(xxi) That consideration be given to the possibility of introducing more widely the more formal system of cautioning prostitutes which is in force in Edinburgh and Glasgow (paragraph 270).

(xxii) That consideration be given to the practicability of extending the practice of referring to a moral welfare worker particulars of a prostitute cautioned for the first time (paragraph 270).

(xxiii) That the maximum penalties for street offences be increased, and that a system of progressively higher penalties for repeated offences be introduced (paragraph 275).

(xxiv) That courts be given explicit power to remand, in custody if need be, for not more than three weeks, a prostitute convicted for the first or second time of a street offence, in order that a social or medical report may be obtained (paragraph 280).

(xxv) That researches be instituted into the aetiology of prostitution (paragraph 297).

*(xxvi) That magistrates' courts be empowered, on convicting a tenant or occupier of

    (i) keeping or managing, or acting or assisting in the management of, a brothel; or

    (ii) knowingly permitting the premises to be used as a brothel; or

    (iii) knowingly permitting premises to be used for the purposes of habitual prostitution,

to make an order determining the tenancy or requiring the tenant to assign the tenancy to a person approved by the landlord (paragraph 326).

*(xxvii) That the landlord have the right to be heard in regard to the making of such an order (paragraph 327).

*(xxviii) That the courts be empowered to require a tenant or occupier charged with any of the offences mentioned in Recommendation (xxvi) to disclose the name and address of the person to whom he pays his rent; and that there be similar power to require each lessor of the premises, in turn, to disclose the name and address of his superior lessor (paragraph 328).

---

* These Recommendations have application only in relation to England and Wales.

(xxix) That a landlord letting premises at an exorbitant rent in the knowledge that they are to be used for the purposes of prostitution be deemed, in law, to be " living on the earnings of prostitution "; and that the same apply to any agent knowingly taking part in the transaction (paragraph 331).

*(xxx) That prosecutions in respect of premises used for immoral purposes be undertaken, as a general rule, by the police (paragraph 335).

J. F. WOLFENDEN.
JAMES ADAIR.([1])
MARY G. COHEN.([2])
DESMOND CURRAN.([3])
V. AUGUSTE DEMANT.
KENNETH DIPLOCK.
HUGH LINSTEAD
LOTHIAN.
KATHLEEN LOVIBOND.([4])
VICTOR MISHCON.
LILY STOPFORD.([5])
WILLIAM WELLS.
JOSEPH WHITBY.([6])

([1]) Subject to Reservation I below.
([2]) Subject to Reservations II and V below.
([3]) Subject to Reservations II and IV below.
([4]) Subject to Reservation V below.
([5]) Subject to Reservations II and V below.
([6]) Subject to Reservations II and III below.

W. C. ROBERTS,
Secretary.

E. J. FREEMAN,
Assistant Secretary.

12th August, 1957.

RESERVATIONS

I.—RESERVATION BY Mr. ADAIR

(a) Homosexual acts between consenting adults in private

1. It is with regret that I find it necessary to dissociate myself from the other members of the Committee on what is undoubtedly the most important recommendation in Part Two of the report—to take homosexual acts committed in private by consenting male adults out of the realm of the criminal law. I feel this regret the more deeply because of my recognition of the vast amount of care and thought bestowed by them on the question.

2. As I look at the matter, we are investigating in this part of our inquiry a course of conduct which is contrary to the best interests of the community, and one which can have very serious effects on the whole moral fabric of social life. It is one of those forms of conduct falling within the group to

---

* This Recommendation has application only in relation to England and Wales.

which the words of the Street Offences Committee, quoted in paragraph 227 of our report, apply as being " conduct it has always been thought right to bring within the scope of the criminal law on account of the injury which they occasion to the public in general." The influence of example in forming the views and developing the characters of young people can scarcely be overestimated. The presence in a district of, for example, adult male lovers living openly and notoriously under the approval of the law is bound to have a regrettable and pernicious effect on the young people of the community. No one interested in the moral, physical or spiritual welfare of public life wishes to see homosexuality extending in its scope, but rather reduced in extent, or at least kept effectively in check.

3. Existing homosexual trends and tendencies are currently the cause of much public concern and disgust, and the case for relaxing legal restrictions does not appear to me to be a compelling one. The more serious phases of such conduct have been recognised by our law as criminal for a continuous period of not less than 400 years, and a very heavy onus therefore rests on the advocates of the change now proposed to demonstrate by cogent evidence that the withdrawal of hitherto criminous conduct from the realm of criminal law is clearly justified.

4. I have studied carefully the evidence led before us, and find that it came in the main from four sources—official, medical, legal and sociological; and on the threshold I feel compelled to say that in each group there is in varying degrees a diversity of opinion on the proposal. Nor is it without significance that in those instances where it might be said that the majority of the group favoured the change now proposed, that majority was proportionately markedly smaller than that in the Committee now making this recommendation.

5. In much of the evidence we heard, particularly in the fourth group, I detect a marked degree of sentimentalism—a deep-rooted sympathy with and for the individual who is by nature homosexual and, therefore, considered of necessity a subject for medical and not legal attention. These considerations have been allowed to obscure the other type who, in the absence of any innate tendency, whether from monetary or other reasons, takes up this type of behaviour, and have tended, too, to obscure also the interests of the public in general and the decent self-disciplined citizen in particular. It seems to me significant that in the deliberations of a large proportion of organisations which made representations—including the two Churches—psychiatrist members or advisers played a prominent part.

6. While I have acquired over a long period of years the utmost confidence in the ability and opinions of many mental specialists, I have frequently found the views of others, as expressed on occasions, quite inexplicable and in not a few cases manifestly indefensible. When it is clear from evidence given before the Committee that many psychiatrists hold the view that the vast majority of criminal offenders, whatever the nature of their criminal acts, should be medically treated rather than be dealt with by the law, I may be excused if I look critically at such evidence and require corroboration from convincing sources before accepting a view which, though not without idealistic content, is scarcely compatible with the realities of communal life as now constituted.

7. Furthermore, it appears clear to me that many of those who considered the matter and were parties to the representations made to us were under the belief that if the individuals involved in homosexual practices were handed

over to the medical profession this would be an adequate answer to the problem. They were apparently unacquainted with the very limited powers of the medical profession in the bringing about of a change in either outlook or behaviour.

8. I feel obliged to make the following observations on some aspects of the course proposed by my colleagues:

(i) If the sanctions of the criminal law are removed, there is also removed one, if not the main, motive which at the present time influences homosexuals to consult medical advisers. The proportion of homosexuals who today consult medical advisers with regard to either their state or their behaviour is admittedly small. Of those who do, there is a considerable proportion who do so either because they have already found themselves in the hands of the police and have been sent for examination by the court, or because they desire expert evidence that may influence the court's outlook, or because circumstances have arisen that cause them to anticipate police attention. It appears, therefore, that even the small number who attend for medical examination will be reduced considerably if the proposed change be carried out.

(ii) If the sanctions of the criminal law are removed, there are also removed from the police opportunities to carry out important preventive work of social benefit to the community. It may be that my training and experience as a Procurator-Fiscal in Scotland, acting in close association with the police in the detection and investigation of crimes of all kinds, has coloured my view on the importance of such sanctions. It has certainly led me to take a different view from that of my colleagues as expressed in paragraph 58 of the report, and this view has not been modified by what has been a conscientious effort on my part to weigh impartially and without bias the relevant evidence submitted to the Committee. I have found on many occasions that in the knowledge that unlawful conduct was in contemplation a police officer could prevent it by a word in season or by making his presence known; this has been particularly so in the case of sexual offenders. To accept the recommendation here made is to take away from the police the only justification they have for operating in this practical and preventive fashion.

(iii) If the recommendation be adopted, the moral force of the law will be weakened. I am convinced that the main body of the community recognises clearly the moral force of the criminal law of the land. Many citizens, it must be admitted, regard the prohibitions expressly imposed by law as the utmost limits set to their activities and are prepared to take full advantage of any omission or relaxation. It would be surprising if there are not considerable numbers with this philosophy among those with whom we are concerned in this inquiry, and the removal of the present prohibition from the criminal code will be regarded as condoning or licensing licentiousness, and will open up for such people a new field of permitted conduct with unwholesome and distasteful implications.

What this may mean by way of increase in the behaviour can only be matter for speculation, but one thing seems to stand out—homosexual, like most practices, propagate themselves. To my mind enquiries as to what has occurred following a similar or other change in other countries gives but very slender ground for comparison and deduction. Not only have we differences of background, social philosophy, tradition, etc., but if the behaviour is made lawful the police authorities are freed from responsibility for investigating and assessing the volume of the conduct and, indeed, as has been pointed out, have largely lost their rights to enquire. In the result, the very nature of such conduct would tend to conceal itself from police notice, and might readily occur to an increasing extent without official recognition.

I think these comments are applicable to the reply given by the Swedish authorities, to which reference is made in paragraph 59 of the report. To my mind, the significant fact in relation to what has occurred in Sweden is that within such a short time there is already a move to raise the age for the consenting adult from eighteen to twenty-one—a move towards more, and not less, legal control.

Neither do I attempt to draw any deduction from the position in Scotland before and after adultery ceased to be a criminal offence, or to compare it with today's position.

(iv) If the recommendation be adopted, it will deprive young adult employees in those professions and occupations where the practices are particularly rife from a strong defence against corrupt approach by superiors and elders. Although it was not possible to assess from the evidence available the extent of homosexual practices in the theatrical profession and in some other occupations, it was clearly established that in certain of these quarters there were decided dangers of advances and influences having to be met and overcome. So long as the individual so approached knows that any compliance is a criminal offence, there are those who on this account will not only decline but who will feel in a stronger defensive position by having this answer.

(v) The present state of medical and mental science, and the limited knowledge and powers of the medical profession under existing circumstances to deal with homosexual patients, make the change recommended by the Committee premature and inopportune. I respectfully refer to the observations in the report on the limitations of present-day treatment and the need for enlightened research as adopted by medical and other members. I only add in this connection:

(*a*) Unless future research can evolve some course of treatment that will hold out much more hope to the individual there is little likelihood of patients seeking medical advice in such numbers as to lead one to expect any marked decrease in homosexual practices;

(*b*) Those who are not medically recognisable as homosexuals but who, for one reason or another, behave as such, are unlikely to attend for treatment; and

(*c*) Dealing as we are in this recommendation with persons over the age of twenty-one (or if the earlier age favoured by some members be accepted, eighteen), the pattern of each individual has become for all practical purposes immutable, and most are unlikely to be responsive to ready alteration. Many will, in fact, come within the category when little beyond advice as to conduct can be tendered.

(vi) The current relaxed attitude toward moral conduct and relationships, so prevalent everywhere, makes the present an inopportune time for loosening bonds and removing restrictions. A period so soon after two world wars, with the varied and abnormal conditions that are generally agreed as having contributed to the present state of affairs, not only in this but in other moral standards, is not a time when any suggestion which in the eyes of many signifies an approval of homosexual conduct should be introduced. So, too, when we see a definite and general increase in the number of offences being prosecuted and there is a general acceptance of the fact that this is but one of various evidences of a marked growth of homosexual practices, the time cannot be regarded as opportune for removing restrictions as recommended.

(vii) The fact that activities inherently hurtful to community life are carried out clandestinely and in privacy does not adequately justify the removal of such conduct from the criminal code. It is indisputable that many acts committed in private may be contrary to the public good and as such fall under the criminal law. In my view, homosexual acts are of this class, and the mere fact that the discrimination made by the majority of the Committee by which freedom from control is not recommended for persons between eighteen and twenty-one years of age is a definite recognition of this principle.

It is of the essence of most crimes that they are committed in privacy and secrecy, if for no other purpose than to avoid detection. In this connection, it is difficult to think of an act committed with more regard for privacy than the crime of incest, about which Blackstone, in a generic statement, quoted with approval by Hume, a distinguished Institutional writer on Scottish criminal law, said that it conflicted with "the due regulation and domestic order of the Kingdom, whereby the individuals of the State, like members of a well-governed family, are bound to conform their general behaviour to the rules of propriety, good neighbourhood and good manners, and to be decent, industrious and inoffensive in their respective situations."

The fact that the proportionate number of homosexual acts committed brought to the knowledge of the courts or the police is small is not an adequate reason for making the acts lawful. I would again quote Blackstone and Hume: "What though the forfeit of the law is not exacted in every instance? It no wise follows that it is, therefore, a useless law or without salutary influence on the masses of the people."

(b) The Definition of "in Private"

9. I find it necessary to supplement my dissent from the recommendation in paragraph 62 by commenting that if the recommendation is to permit acts in all places and circumstances in which heterosexual acts are outwith the provisions of the criminal law, it will make legal acts which have in the past been the subject of some notorious and highly objectionable cases. I refer to acts in rooms and cubicles of hotels, lodging houses and hostels where even the owner, occupier or manager may be a principal participant.

(c) Attempts to Procure the Commission of Acts of Gross Indecency

10. Apart from my general dissent from the proposal that homosexual behaviour between consenting males in private should no longer be a

criminal offence, I desire to record my dissent from the recommendation in the first portion of paragraph 115 of the report. The present law of public solicitation is restricted in its extent to instances of persistent importuning. This persistence may be directed either toward a number of other males or a series of insistent approaches toward one man. To give statutory authority to all adults to approach other adults and attempt by invitation or otherwise to get them to go to a private place for homosexual behavour is in my view a retrograde step and may readily lead to many undesirable scenes and to an increase in the amount of the behaviour itself.

(d) Offences in Disciplined Services

11. I appreciate that it is at all times possible for Parliament to include in the statutes relating to Her Majesty's Services provisions for treating as criminal offences acts committed by those in the Services which, if committed by civilians, would not be criminal. There seem to me to be very clear objections to increasing the number of such differentiating offences unless it be something peculiarly applicable to the Services and not likely to be met with in civilian life.

Such differentiations are always bound to provoke in Service members a feeling of injustice. It would probably mean that if the acts were between a serviceman and an adult consenting civilian, the former would be guilty of an offence and the latter not—even although, as past experience has demonstrated, the original suggestion, and even the payment of money as an inducement, was by the civilian. Even as between members of the Services, it is difficult to see legislation that would not result in differentiations that would give rise to feelings of injustice.

On the other hand, if military law is to follow the course of the civil law amended as proposed, I cannot but express a fear shared by officers of all Services, and by all who gave evidence on behalf of the Services, that as between those under and over the prescribed age there would be feelings of grave injustice and, as I assess the consequences, increase in the trend toward homosexual practices would be marked and intense, while the effect on the morale of members of the Services would be adverse and corrupting.

(e) Advertisements

12. While accepting paragraph 286 of the report as it stands, I foresee that the possibilities envisaged in the last sentence of that paragraph may lead to (a) the lucrative exploitation of prostitutes in certain cases; (b) notoriety of certain shops displaying such advertisements with consequent abnormal congregations of persons on foot pavements; and (c) advertisements referring to addresses in terms causing annoyance and inconvenience to respectable occupiers of premises there.

It is in my view desirable to prevent these consequences from the outset if possible, and I therefore recommend that provision should be made to control the nature and extent of any such advertising. This could be done by giving powers to local authorities to make bye-laws for regulating the terms and extent of all advertisements and announcements of the kind referred to in paragraph 286.

(f) "Middlemen"

13. Whatever we may think was the reason for importing into our legal code a charge of living on immoral earnings, it is clear that the general body of public opinion regards it as among the most shameful and reprehensible of offences. I therefore recommend that the terms of the two Acts dealing

with the subject be carefully revised with a view to including among the punishable third parties those who act as introducers to, or otherwise as agents for, prostitutes—referred to in paragraph 286 as " middlemen "—on the basis that they are living or partly living on immoral earnings and that their guilt will be presumed unless they disprove this.

(g) Letting of Premises for the Purpose of Prostitution

14. In my view, it is not only the landlord demanding exorbitant payments from known prostitutes who ought to be included in the proposed fresh legislation recommended in paragraph 331 of the report. While this recommendation will strike at a landlord against whom a single prostitute may complain that he has charged her an exorbitant rent, the landlord or factor who makes a business of letting rooms or other accommodation to prostitutes on a wholesale scale at rents which although high cannot be said to be exorbitant, is not struck at. Having in view the great difficulties there are in proving payments of exorbitant rents in this class of case, I recommend that where the circumstances show that the landlord or factor is making a business of letting houses, flats or rooms for the purpose of their being used for habitual prostitution, he should be presumed to be living on the earnings of prostitution unless he proves to the contrary.

JAMES ADAIR.

II.—RESERVATION BY Mrs. COHEN, Dr. CURRAN, Lady STOPFORD AND Dr. WHITBY

The Distinction Between Buggery and other Homosexual Offences

1. We agree, in the main, with the conclusions and recommendations of our colleagues. We do not, however, agree that there is any justification for the legal distinction between buggery and other forms of homosexual behaviour. As will be seen from Appendix III, such a distinction is not generally recognised in the laws of those European countries which make homosexual acts as such punishable.

2. We are of the opinion that the arguments set out in paragraph 79 of the report are sufficiently answered in paragraphs 80 to 83, and we agree with the conclusion as stated in paragraph 84, namely, that if the object of the higher sentence be based solely upon the treatment and deterrence (in the sense of the chances of recidivism) of the individual offender, there would appear to be no justification for a different sentence for buggery *per se*.

3. We feel that paragraphs 85 and 86 sufficiently dispose of the suggestion that heavier penalties should be attached to buggery because of the possibility of physical or psychological damage, and we agree with the conclusion set out in paragraph 87.

4. We do not consider that the more general arguments put forward in paragraph 88 of the report afford sufficient grounds for the distinction. Taking these arguments separately:

(*a*) That a long-standing tradition should not be held to debar the making of what we consider to be a just and equitable law has already been stated by the Committee in paragraph 60 in another connection, and we hold that this applies equally in this matter;

(b) That there is in the minds of many people a stronger instinctive revulsion from this particular form of behaviour than from any other homosexual act may be true of some, but it is not true of many others who would be more repelled by, say, the act of orogenital intercourse. In any case, we do not hold that such revulsion should be the grounds for a heavier punishment;

(c) That this act simulates the normal act of heterosexual intercourse would not, in our view, justify singling it out for heavier punishment unless it could be shown that it resembled heterosexual intercourse so closely that some persons, not predominantly homosexual, would come to prefer it to normal intercourse. Such a view is, in our opinion, untenable, and is contrary to medical experience and opinion;

(d) That it may sometimes approximate in the homosexual field to rape in the heterosexual and should therefore carry a similar maximum penalty ignores, in our view, the following considerations:

  (i) Rape can have serious consequences quite apart from the question whether physical or psychological damage is caused to the victim;

  (ii) Although the act of buggery is capable of causing physical injury, this is equally true of some other forms of homosexual behaviour, as explained in paragraph 85. Moreover, the general criminal law provides for punishment with imprisonment up to five years for acts causing bodily harm, and up to life imprisonment for acts causing grievous bodily harm. Alternatively, in a prosecution for indecent assault, the question of injury would be taken into account by the court as a relevant circumstance;

  (iii) The only other grounds for making a comparison between buggery and rape would appear to us to be based on the " instinctive revulsion " dealt with at (b) above, or the " simulation of normal intercourse " dealt with at (c).

5. Apart from the question of justice, there is another reason for abolishing this distinction. It is probable that the parents of a young victim of buggery would regard the offence with greater seriousness than some other homosexual offence. From the medical point of view, there is no reason to think that the one act does any more lasting harm than the other. What frequently causes more harm than either to the victim is the quite disproportionate amount of concern displayed by the parents, and the penalty of life imprisonment attaching to buggery serves to invest it with a special seriousness in their minds and thus to heighten this concern. We feel that if the law were changed so that buggery were no longer a special offence, this would help in producing a more rational public opinion, and would help to allay some of the unnecessary anxiety at present felt by parents and relatives, and this in turn would be of benefit to the victim.

6. We would therefore recommend that there should be no legal distinction between buggery and other homosexual offences, and would disagree with making a separate offence of category (a) in paragraph 91 (that is, buggery with a boy under sixteen, punishable with a maximum sentence of life imprisonment). We would include all such cases in the category of indecent assaults.

MARY G. COHEN.
DESMOND CURRAN.
LILY STOPFORD.
JOSEPH WHITBY.

III.—FURTHER RESERVATION BY Dr. WHITBY

Maximum Penalties for Homosexual Offences

1. I find myself unable to subscribe to the table of penalties suggested in paragraph 91 of the report. In my view, there should be only two categories of offence under these headings, namely:

   (a) Indecent assault; to include the offences described in (a) and (b) of paragraph 91, with a maximum penalty of ten years' imprisonment; and

   (b) Gross indecency; to include the offences described in (c) and (d) of paragraph 91, with a maximum penalty of two years' imprisonment.

2. The reasons for not making a special offence of buggery with a boy under sixteen, as proposed in paragraph 91(a), have already been given in the reservation also subscribed to by Mrs. Cohen, Lady Stopford and Dr. Curran.

3. Whilst I share the desire of the Committee as a whole to protect the young man between sixteen and twenty-one from the undesirable attentions of older men, I do not feel it to be just to separate acts of gross indecency with this age group from acts of gross indecency with older men, as suggested in paragraph 91(c). My reasons are as follows:

   (a) As pointed out in paragraph 67 of the report, it is hard to believe that a young man needs to be protected from would-be seducers more carefully than a girl. Seduction *per se* of a girl over sixteen is not a criminal offence at all;

   (b) Our medical witnesses were unanimous in stating that the effects of homosexual seduction in youth have been greatly exaggerated. As pointed out in paragraph 68 of the report, the main sexual pattern is generally fixed by the age of sixteen, and whatever moral damage may be done, the effect of seduction over this age is unlikely to be that of producing a homosexual deviation in one who is predominantly heterosexual;

   (c) The possibility of psychological damage or moral corruption must clearly be taken into account, but this is equally possible in the case of females, where the maximum penalty, even in cases of indecent assault—a graver offence—is only two years' imprisonment.

   (d) With no penalty for homosexual behaviour between consenting adults in private, two years' imprisonment should be a sufficient deterrent to the older man contemplating a more youthful partner, especially as the offence of gross indecency would still remain a crime if committed with a young man between sixteen and twenty-one even in private;

   (e) Where offences with several partners or victims are involved, the courts have power to award consecutive sentences. Where the penalty proposed fails to act as a sufficient deterrent and the offender persistently repeats his offences, the provisions of the criminal law relating to persistent offenders should apply to him as they apply to other offenders;

   (f) Whatever views may be held as to whether the adult homosexual who prefers a younger partner is more or less treatable than one who prefers another adult as partner, it has been pointed out in paragraph 179 of the report that the duration of sentence should not be fixed by reference to any estimate of the time which the treatment is likely to take.

4. The very fact that an offence with a young man may attract a heavier sentence would serve to invest it with a disproportionate seriousness in the minds of parents and relatives, and so lead to unnecessary fuss and concern over something which, from the point of view of the victim, is best forgotten as quickly as possible.

JOSEPH WHITBY.

IV.—FURTHER RESERVATION BY Dr. CURRAN

(a) Maximum Penalties for Homosexual Offences

1. I agree with Dr. Whitby in his reservation, and with his reasons, except on one point. I should like to go further and make the maximum sentence for indecent assault two years instead of ten years.

2. I agree with the opinion expressed by the Committee in paragraph 100 of the report concerning the lack of justification for the disparity in the maximum sentence for indecent assault on males (ten years) and females (two years). But to "assimilate" the maximum sentences by increasing the maximum sentence for indecent assault on females would seem to me to be a retrograde step.

3. The justification for heavy sentences rests doubtless upon a variable mixture of considerations and objectives, often summarised under the headings of retribution, deterrence and reformation.

4. Views on the justification of the retributive theory of punishment vary. Like many others, I do not regard retribution as a principle that is justified in itself or one that should properly guide decisions, whilst not doubting the importance of retribution as a motive. As Professor Weihofen put it in his recently published Isaac Ray Lectures, "The human thirst for vengeance, the human instincts of hate and fear, need no encouragement from the law. So long as they exist, we must of course take them into account, but we need not reinforce them and give them dignity by legal endorsement." ("The Urge to Punish" by Henry Weihofen—Victor Gollancz Ltd., London, 1957, p. 143.)

5. I agree with the important opinion expressed in paragraph 58 of the report: "It seems to us that the law itself probably makes little difference to the amount of homosexual behaviour which actually occurs; whatever the law may be, there will always be strong social forces opposed to homosexual behaviour." These strong social forces are, I believe, specially operative in the case of paedophiliacs, whose conduct is universally reprobated, not least by other homosexuals. Paedophiliacs act in isolation from the homosexuals, and are not accepted in homosexual coteries or groups.

6. I understand it has long been common ground in the opinion of those best qualified to judge that it is not the severity of the punishment that is most important for deterrence; it is the certainty—or high degree of probability—that punishment will actually result. If correct, this principle has special application to all homosexual crimes owing to the vast discrepancy between the number of criminal acts and the conviction rate. To say this is not to doubt that the possibility of imprisonment can have deterrent value. But I see little reason to suppose that the possibility of the maximum punishment of ten years as opposed to two years would have much, if indeed any, appreciable effect on deterrence. Only a small minority of the population know what is the maximum punishment for indecent assault. Only a minute fraction of the population know their criminal statistics and what punishments are awarded; and if

more did, they would know that the chances of getting sentences of more than two years for indecent assault would be small (about 1 in 18). Can it seriously be supposed that those who are guilty of indecent assault work out " betting odds " of this kind before they indulge in their acts? And if they did, what deterrent effect would it be likely to have?

7. As regards treatment as a ground for the length of sentence, I have nothing to add to paragraph 179 of the report.

8. It seems to me that the sole, and very proper, justification for long sentences is to keep out of harm's way those who have repeatedly shown themselves to be public menaces and concerning whom nothing else, in the present state of knowledge, can be done. This could, when necessary, be achieved (as Dr. Whitby suggests) by making sentences for multiple offences run consecutively; or, when applicable, by the imposition of preventive detention. The number of homosexual offenders so dealt with in 1955 was five (*cf.* paragraph 166), of whom two were convicted of buggery and three of indecent assault or attempted buggery.

9. An analysis of the 54 men who, in 1955 (Appendix I, Table IVA) received prison sentences for indecent assault, &c., in excess of two years, reveals the interesting point that 29 of them had no previous convictions for similar offences, and 21 of them no previous conviction for any indictable offence. Further, 32 of these 54 men had no similar offences taken into consideration, and 30 of them had no other offences of any kind taken into consideration. This suggests that in awarding these sentences, other considerations were involved than the protection of the public from sexual or other recidivists; and, of course, if, for example, the retributive view of punishment is justified, why not?

(b) Importuning

10. If the recommendation made in paragraph 62 of the report is accepted, so that homosexual behaviour between consenting adults in private should no longer be a criminal offence, I can see no logical reason why male importuning should be treated differently from female solicitation. The male importuner would be seeking a partner for an act that would no longer be illegal. I do not see why a heavier scale of penalty should be imposed for doing this unless male importuning is, or might become, more of a public nuisance than female solicitation.

11. The idea of male importuning is unquestionably more repellent to the general public than is the idea of female solicitation. But in fact male importuning is far less of a public nuisance than female solicitation. This is not, I think, only due to the much smaller numbers involved. Males seldom importune other males who do not give them encouragement. Their activities are less obvious, and more subtle and discreet, than is the case with female solicitation. Consequently, as I believe, the general public greatly underestimate (as do the criminal statistics) the amount of male importuning that goes on. Further, the number of male importuners who are prostitutes is admittedly extremely small; very few male importuners are out for financial gain.

12. The statement is made (paragraph 124): " The very fact that the law can impose severe penalties is, however, a considerable factor in producing the present situation that the amount of male importuning in the streets is negligible and that consequently male importuning is not nearly so offensive

or such an affront to public decency as are the street activities of female prostitutes." The inference is that a relaxation of the penalties would result in an increase in male importuning that would constitute a public nuisance of a particularly offensive kind. For a variety of reasons, I would regard the statement just quoted from paragraph 124 as a speculation with no sound foundation. But even if correct, I would suggest that the creation of a class of what would in effect be " common male importuners " on the same lines and with the same safeguards, and with the same penalties, as are proposed for " common prostitutes " would provide an adequate safeguard against the development of brazen activities on the part of male importuners that might be publicly offensive.

DESMOND CURRAN.

V.—RESERVATION BY Mrs. COHEN, Mrs. LOVIBOND AND Lady STOPFORD

Maximum Penalty for Living on the Earnings of Prostitution

1. We do not agree with the majority of our colleagues[1] that the maximum penalty of two years' imprisonment for the offence of living on the earnings of prostitution is adequate.

2. As explained in paragraph 92 of the report, the law must, in prescribing maximum penalties, have regard to the worst case that could arise, and we feel that the present maximum of two years' imprisonment is quite inadequate to deal with a person who makes a business of exploiting prostitution on a large scale.

3. The possibility that the increased penalties for street offences might encourage closer organisation of the trade and result in new classes of " middlemen " also seems to us to call for increased penalties for living on the earnings of prostitution; we think that increased penalties would counteract to some extent the dangers envisaged in paragraph 286 of the report.

4. We accordingly recommend that the maximum penalty for the offence of living on the earnings of prostitution be increased to five years' imprisonment.

MARY G. COHEN.
KATHLEEN LOVIBOND.
LILY STOPFORD.

---

[1] See paragraph 307 of the report.

APPENDICES

APPENDIX I
STATISTICS RELATING TO HOMOSEXUAL OFFENCES

(a) England and Wales

TABLE I

HOMOSEXUAL OFFENCES KNOWN TO THE POLICE

Table showing the number of indictable homosexual offences known to the police during the twenty-five years ended 31st December, 1955

Year	Buggery	Indecent assault, &c.	Gross indecency	Total
1931	73	371	178	622
1932	46	487	258	791
1933	82	554	210	846
1934	64	581	192	837
1935	78	535	227	840
1936	125	690	352	1,167
1937	102	703	316	1,121
1938	134	822	320	1,276
1939	146	766	280	1,192
1940	97	808	251	1,156
1941	177	757	390	1,324
1942	208	998	582	1,788
1943	245	1,208	623	2,076
1944	277	1,186	449	1,912
1945	223	1,318	459	2,000
1946	247	1,523	561	2,331
1947	255	1,839	690	2,784
1948	258	2,216	660	3,134
1949	562	2,409	852	3,823
1950	534	2,893	989	4,416
1951	452	3,272	1,152	4,876
1952	670	3,087	1,686	5,443
1953	700	3,305	1,675	5,680
1954	1,043	3,280	2,034	6,357
1955	766	3,556	2,322	6,644

TABLE II

PERSONS AGAINST WHOM PROCEEDINGS WERE TAKEN IN RESPECT OF HOMOSEXUAL OFFENCES

Table showing the number of persons against whom proceedings were taken in respect of indictable homosexual offences during the twenty-five years ended 31st December, 1955

Year	Number of persons proceeded against			
	Buggery	Indecent assault, &c.	Gross indecency	Total
1931	57	212	121	390
1932	32	242	170	444
1933	72	257	127	456
1934	57	305	153	515
1935	49	255	149	453
1936	82	308	164	554
1937	77	292	221	590
1938	71	428	220	719
1939	63	361	171	595
1940	53	361	131	545
1941	67	361	188	616
1942	113	397	211	721
1943	106	509	271	886
1944	121	441	244	806
1945	112	469	201	782
1946	120	470	281	871
1947	130	585	302	1,017
1948	149	714	395	1,258
1949	239	754	499	1,492
1950	271	881	514	1,666
1951	242	990	746	1,978
1952	320	999	790	2,109
1953	393	997	877	2,267
1954	463	1,012	967	2,442
1955	428	1,081	995	2,504

TABLE III

AGES OF OFFENDERS

Table showing the ages of persons found guilty of indictable homosexual offences during the five years ended 31st December, 1955

Year	No. of persons found guilty			Ages of persons found guilty								
	On indictment	Summarily (see Note (a))	Total	Under 14 years	14 and under 17	17 and under 21	21 and under 25	25 and under 30	30 and under 40	40 and under 50	50 and under 60	60 and over

(i) Buggery

1951	204	13	217	See Note (b)	15	42	23	27	62	30	12	6
1952	267	6	273		9	52	28	32	69	47	30	6
1953	306	12	318		23	54	40	42	74	58	20	7
1954	346	17	363		20	65	60	60	84	45	22	7
1955	392	25	417		38	65	58	58	81	78	27	12

(ii) Indecent Assault, &c. (see Note (c))

1951	232	648	880	36	67	83	74	89	212	171	99	49
1952	242	659	901	32	60	72	77	115	232	180	79	54
1953	293	637	930	35	69	73	66	119	217	169	108	74
1954	289	654	943	42	87	92	73	100	224	163	100	62
1955	274	710	984	34	83	80	80	124	263	164	107	49

(iii) Gross Indecency

Year												
1951	642	33	675	10	35	61	72	89	171	133	72	32
1952	654	45	699	8	56	69	70	76	161	128	86	45
1953	659	56	715	16	53	79	94	86	161	121	72	33
1954	838	52	890	13	63	101	103	110	217	160	76	47
1955	831	56	887	18	51	91	101	114	215	166	90	41

(iv) All Indictable Homosexual Offences (i.e., (i) + (ii) + (iii))

Year												
1951	1,078	694	1,772	46	117	186	169	205	445	334	183	87
1952	1,163	710	1,873	40	125	193	175	223	462	355	195	105
1953	1,258	705	1,963	51	145	206	200	247	452	348	200	114
1954	1,473	723	2,196	55	170	258	236	270	525	368	198	116
1955	1,497	791	2,288	52	172	236	239	296	559	408	224	102

NOTES: (a) Indecent assaults may be dealt with summarily—
  (i) Where the person alleged to have been assaulted is under sixteen, whatever the age of the offender; or
  (ii) Where the offender is under seventeen.
The other indictable homosexual offences can be dealt with summarily only where the offender is under seventeen.

(b) A child under fourteen is deemed in law to be incapable of committing this offence.

(c) This heading includes indecent assault on a male person, attempted buggery and assault with intent to commit buggery. Also included in the first column is a very small but not separately identifiable number of offenders convicted on indictment of importuning.

51824

TABLE IV

DISPOSAL OF OFFENDERS

Tables showing how the courts dealt with persons found guilty of indictable homosexual offences during the five years ended 31st December, 1955

TABLE IVA

COURTS OF ASSIZE AND QUARTER SESSIONS

(i) Buggery (see Note (b))

Year	Number of persons found guilty	Recognisance or conditional discharge	Fine	Probation	Borstal	Imprisonment (see Note (a)) 6 months or under	Over 6 months and up to 1 year	Over 1 year and up to 2 years	Over 2 years and up to 3 years	Over 3 years and up to 5 years	Over 5 years and up to 7 years	Over 7 years	Total	Otherwise dealt with
1951	204	14	4	36	7	7	18	30	22	31	14	4	126	17
1952	267	15	4	52	3	6	29	50	34	36	12	8	175	18
1953	306	17	13	52	18	7	30	43	30	36	14	8	168	38
1954	346	34	16	55	15	10	44	63	32	38	17	10	214	12
1955	392	45	15	84	10	9	41	59	37	42	16	10	214	24

134

(ii) Indecent Assault, &c. (see Note (c))

1951	232	25	18	47	4	10	33	42	2	23	17	5	132	6
1952	242	21	25	58	—	14	34	35	20	12	9	1	125	13
1953	293	27	22	58	1	15	42	58	24	21	4	5	169	16
1954	289	35	37	51	2	24	45	46	22	13	4	4	158	6
1955	274	18	32	53	2	22	44	44	25	23	2	4	164	5

(iii) Gross Indecency

1951	642	107	191	108	1	101	48	21	—	1	3	—	174	61
1952	654	92	218	100	4	70	60	28	4	5	1	1	169	71
1953	659	79	233	110	1	71	62	32	4	4	2	—	175	61
1954	838	182	290	144	8	96	56	31	3	2	1	—	189	25
1955	831	159	316	148	7	71	56	34	3	2	1	—	167	34

NOTES: (a) These figures include persons sentenced to corrective training or preventive detention. Where two or more sentences of imprisonment were awarded to run consecutively, they are shown added together in this table.

(b) This offence is not triable at quarter sessions.

(c) This heading includes indecent assault on a male person, attempted buggery, and assault with intent to commit buggery. Also included in these figures is a very small but not separately identifiable number of offenders convicted on indictment of importuning.

135

TABLE IV.—(continued)
Disposal of Offenders

TABLE IVb

MAGISTRATES' COURTS

(i) Buggery (see Note (a))

Year	Number of persons found guilty	Absolute discharge	Recognisances or conditional discharge	Fine	Probation	Attendance Centre	Detention Centre or Remand Home	Approved School	Care of fit person	Imprisonment: 14 days or under	Over 14 days and up to 1 month	Over 1 month and up to 2 months	Over 2 months and up to 3 months	Over 3 months and up to 6 months	Total	Otherwise dealt with
1951	13	—	—	—	12	—	—	1	—	—	—	—	—	—	—	—
1952	6	—	—	—	3	—	—	3	—	—	—	—	—	—	—	—
1953	12	—	1	—	10	—	1	1	—	—	—	—	—	—	—	—
1954	17	—	2	—	11	—	2	2	—	—	—	—	—	—	—	—
1955	25	1	1	—	15	—	—	5	—	—	—	—	—	—	—	3

136

(ii) Indecent Assault, &c. (see Note (b))

Year													
1951	648	11	57	159	197	—	—	5	3	2	9	16	43	102	172	44
1952	660	8	48	157	230	—	2	3	1	1	8	14	67	81	171	40
1953	637	7	58	173	193	1	1	11	1	—	4	8	42	101	155	37
1954	654	8	66	137	232	—	3	6	3	—	10	16	36	83	145	54
1955	710	8	55	178	263	1	6	10	1	—	2	13	47	82	144	44

(iii) Gross Indecency (see Note (c))

Year													
1951	33	5	2	—	26	—	—	—	—	—	—	—	—	—	—	—
1952	45	5	7	—	28	—	—	1	—	—	—	—	—	—	—	—
1953	56	1	14	2	35	—	—	3	—	—	—	—	—	—	3	—
1954	52	6	13	—	21	—	1	11	—	—	—	—	—	—	—	—
1955	56	2	13	—	32	2	1	6	—	—	—	—	—	—	—	—

NOTES: (a) Persons under fourteen are deemed in law to be incapable of this offence. Persons aged seventeen or over must be tried at assizes. These figures therefore relate to persons between fourteen and seventeen.

(b) This heading includes indecent assault on a male person, attempted buggery and assault with intent to commit buggery. Indecent assaults may be dealt with summarily.
  (i) Where the person alleged to have been assaulted is under sixteen, whatever the age of the offender;
  (ii) Where the offender is under seventeen.
The other offences can be dealt with summarily only where the offender is under seventeen.

(c) The offence is triable summarily only where the offender is under seventeen.

TABLE V

Importuning

Table showing how the courts dealt with the male persons convicted in 1954 and 1955([1]) of persistent soliciting or importuning for immoral purposes

	Number of persons found guilty	Absolute discharge	Recognisances or conditional discharge	Fine	Probation	\multicolumn{7}{c}{Imprisonment}	Otherwise dealt with
						1 month or under	Over 1 month up to 3 months	Over 3 months up to 6 months	Over 6 months up to 1 year	Over 1 year up to 2 years	Over 2 years([2])	Total	
1954—													
On indictment	22	—	1	8	2	—	—	4	2	4	1	11	—
On summary conviction	425	5	53	239	56	9	29	33	—	—	—	71	1
Total	447	5	54	247	58	9	29	37	2	4	1	82	1
1955—													
On indictment	17	—	1	—	5	—	—	2	5	3	1	11	—
On summary conviction	477	6	60	284	55	5	23	43	—	—	—	71	1
Total	494	6	61	284	60	5	23	45	5	3	1	82	1

([1]) As explained in paragraph 119 of the report, no corresponding figures are available for earlier years.

([2]) The maximum penalty for this offence is two years' imprisonment. The two men to whom the figures in this column relate were convicted at the same time of other offences.

TABLE VI

Table showing how the courts dealt with the 300 adult offenders convicted during the three years ended March 1956, of offences committed in private with consenting adults

How dealt with	Number of offenders	Buggery	Attempted buggery	Gross indecency
Absolute discharge	7	2	1	4
Bound over or conditional discharge	74	29	—	45
Probation	66	31	6	29
Fine	34	7	1	26
Imprisonment—				
6 months or less	21	5	2	14
Over 6 months and up to 12 months	43	34	3	6
Over 1 year and up to 2 years	44	36	5	3
Over 2 years and up to 3 years	6	6	—	—
4 years	1	1	—	—
5 years	3	3	—	—
Dealt with as a mental defective	1	1	—	—
Totals	300	155	18	127

TABLE VII

Table showing the disposal, otherwise than by way of imprisonment, of persons convicted of homosexual offences during 1955

	Buggery	Indecent assault, &c.	Gross indecency	Importuning	Total
Number of persons found guilty	417	984	887	494	2,782
Number of persons dealt with by way of—					
Absolute discharge	7	9	30	6	52
Conditional discharge	15	68	127	61	271
Binding over	31	5	45	—	81
Probation	99	316	180	60	655
Fine	15	210	316	284	825
Borstal	10	2	7	—	19
Detention Centre	—	6	1	—	7
Approved School	5	10	6	—	21
Care of fit person	—	1	—	—	1
Attendance Centre	—	1	2	—	3
Total number dealt with other than by way of imprisonment	182 (44%)	628 (64%)	714 (80%)	411 (85%)	1,935 (70%)

TABLE VIII

Previous Convictions

Table showing previous convictions of indictable offences recorded against persons over twenty-one found guilty of indictable offences during 1954

Offence of which convicted in 1954	Number of persons convicted	Persons with no previous convictions — Of an offence in the same category — No.	Per cent.	Of any indictable offence — No.	Per cent.	Persons with one, two or three previous convictions — Of an offence in the same category — No.	Per cent.	Of any indictable offence — No.	Per cent.	Persons with four or more previous convictions — Of an offence in the same category — No.	Per cent.	Of any indictable offence — No.	Per cent.
(a) Buggery	270	238	88	192	71	27	10·00	56	20·74	5	1·85	22	8·15
(b) Indecent assault, &c.([1])	700	517	74	406	58	139	19·86	195	27·86	44	6·29	99	14·14
(c) Gross indecency	704	617	88	549	78	77	10·94	118	16·76	10	1·42	37	5·26
(d) All homosexual offences (i.e., (a)+(b)+(c))	1,674	1,372	82	1,147	68	243	14·52	369	22·04	59	3·52	158	9·44
(e) Sexual offences other than homosexual offences	1,790	1,602	89	1,213	67	172	9·61	398	22·23	16	0·89	179	10·00
(f) All sexual offences (i.e., (d)+(e))	3,464	2,974	86	2,360	68	415	11·98	767	22·14	75	2·17	337	9·73
(g) Offences against the person other than sexual offences	3,283	2,914	89	2,006	61	349	10·63	766	23·33	20	0·61	511	15·56
(h) All offences against the person (i.e., (f)+(g))	6,747	5,888	87	4,366	65	764	11·32	1,533	22·72	95	1·41	848	12·57
(i) All indictable offences other than sexual offences	53,414	34,890	65	30,999	58	10,713	20·06	11,924	22·32	7,811	14·62	10,491	19·64
(j) All indictable offences (i.e., (f)+(i))	56,878	37,864	66	33,359	59	11,128	19·56	12,691	22·31	7,886	13·86	10,828	19·04

([1]) This heading includes indecent assault on a male person, attempted buggery, and assault with intent to commit buggery. Also included is a small but not separately identifiable number of offenders convicted on indictment of importuning.

(h) Scotland

NOTE: In Scotland, the criminal statistics do not distinguish, as regards indecent assaults and lewd and libidinous practices, between cases in which the offence was committed with a male and those in which the offence was committed with a female.

No statistics are available in respect of gross indecency prior to 1951.

It is not possible, therefore, to produce figures comparable with those in the foregoing tables relating to England and Wales, except as regards sodomy and gross indecency, and then only from 1951.

TABLE IX
DISPOSAL OF OFFENDERS

Table showing how the courts dealt with persons found guilty of recorded homosexual offences in the years 1951–56

Year	Total charges proved	Probation or absolute discharge without conviction	Caution with or without sureties	Fine	Probation	Borstal	Total sentenced to imprisonment, &c.	Imprisonment 6 months or under	Over 6 months and up to 1 year	Over 1 year and up to 2 years	Over 2 years and up to 3 years	Over 3 years and up to 7 years	Over 7 years	Admonished and otherwise disposed of

(a) Sodomy, including Attempts

1951	5	—	—	—	—	—	4	1	1	—	2	—	—	—
1952	6	—	—	—	—	1	5	—	1	1	2	1	—	—
1953	10	—	—	—	1	—	8	3	—	3	1	—	—	1
1954	13	—	—	—	2	—	10	3	—	5	—	2	—	1
1955	5	—	—	—	1	—	4	—	—	3	—	—	1	—
1956	7	4	—	—	1	—	2	—	1	—	1	—	—	—

(b) Gross Indecency between Males

1951	76	18	—	34	4	—	15	9	2	3	—	1	—	5
1952	117	7	—	92	—	—	14	11	2	1	—	—	—	4
1953	101	23	3	49	—	1	20	17	2	1	—	—	—	5
1954	75	10	—	38	1	1	21	16	1	4	—	—	—	4
1955	75	7	—	40	—	—	26	18	7	1	—	—	—	2
1956	64	14	—	37	—	—	10	8	2	—	—	—	—	3

TABLE X

Table showing the disposal, otherwise than by way of imprisonment, of persons convicted of homosexual offences during 1955

	Sodomy	Gross indecency between males	Total
Number of persons against whom charge proved	5	75	80
Without conviction—			
Probation or absolute discharge	—	7	7
With conviction or finding of guilt—			
Probation	1	—	1
Fine	—	40	40
Admonished and otherwise disposed of	—	2	2
Total number dealt with other than by way of imprisonment	1 (20%)	49 (65%)	50 (63%)

TABLE XI

Table showing how the courts dealt with the 7 adult offenders convicted during the three years ended March 1956, of offences committed in private with consenting adults

How dealt with	Number of offenders	Offence of which convicted — Sodomy	Offence of which convicted — Gross indecency
Fine	3	—	3
Imprisonment—			
30 days	1	—	1
2 months	1	—	1
12 months	2	1	1
Totals	7	1	6

APPENDIX II

STATISTICS RELATING TO PROSTITUTION OFFENCES

(a) England and Wales

TABLE XII

Street Offences

Table showing the number of prosecutions and convictions under:—
Section 54 (11) of the Metropolitan Police Act, 1839.
Section 35 (11) of the City of London Police Act, 1839.
Section 28 (16) of the Town Police Clauses Act, 1847.
Section 3 of the Vagrancy Act, 1824,
and similar provisions in local Acts, during the fifty years ended 31st December, 1955

Year	No. of prosecutions	No. of convictions	Year	No. of prosecutions	No. of convictions
1906	10,873	9,632	1931	1,303	1,163
1907	9,489	8,302	1932	1,412	1,383
1908	10,818	9,186	1933	1,748	1,678
1909	11,727	9,895	1934	2,152	2,054
1910	11,458	9,463	1935	3,303	3,176
1911	10,707	8,799	1936	3,542	3,343
1912	10,808	8,900	1937	3,110	3,021
1913	10,629	8,740	1938	3,280	3,192
1914	9,808	8,137	1939	2,031	1,977
1915	6,915	5,645	1940	1,809	1,761
1916	5,521	4,239	1941	1,661	1,621
1917	5,655	4,229	1942	2,155	2,122
1918	5,288	3,684	1943	2,394	2,371
1919	4,944	3,612	1944	1,643	1,630
1920	5,743	4,541	1945	2,117	2,096
1921	5,715	4,515	1946	4,423	4,393
1922	5,013	3,941	1947	5,079	5,041
1923	2,401	1,916	1948	5,696	5,647
1924	2,712	2,106	1949	5,794	5,766
1925	3,222	2,589	1950	6,868	6,843
1926	3,965	3,246	1951	7,906	7,872
1927	4,340	3,748	1952	10,319	10,291
1928	2,992	2,643	1953	10,269	10,229
1929	1,134	970	1954	11,562	11,518
1930	1,161	995	1955	11,916	11,878

TABLE XIII

LIVING ON THE EARNINGS OF PROSTITUTION

Table showing how the courts dealt with the persons convicted in 1954 and 1955([1]) of the offences set out in paragraph 298 of the report

Year	Number of persons found guilty M	Number of persons found guilty F	Conditional discharge M	Conditional discharge F	Fine M	Fine F	Probation M	Probation F	Imprisonment 1 month or under M	Imprisonment 1 month or under F	Over 1 month up to 3 months M	Over 1 month up to 3 months F	Over 3 months up to 6 months M	Over 3 months up to 6 months F	Over 6 months up to 1 year M	Over 6 months up to 1 year F	Over 1 year and up to 2 years M	Over 1 year and up to 2 years F	Total M	Total F
1954—																				
On indictment	8	1	—	—	1	1	—	—	—	—	—	—	1	—	1	—	5	—	7	—
On summary conviction	114	1	8	—	11	1	—	—	5	—	32	—	58	—	—	—	—	—	95	—
Total	122	2	8	—	12	2	—	—	5	—	32	—	59	—	1	—	5	—	102	—
1955—																				
On indictment	14	—	—	—	1	—	—	—	—	—	—	—	2	—	5	—	6	—	13	—
On summary conviction	113	4	2	—	7	—	3	—	1	—	33	1	67	3	—	—	—	—	101	4
Total	127	4	2	—	8	—	3	—	1	—	33	1	69	3	5	—	6	—	114	4

([1]) As explained in paragraph 300 of the report, no corresponding figures are available for earlier years.

TABLE XIV

BROTHEL KEEPING, &c.

Table showing the number of persons convicted, during the five years ended 31st December, 1955, of the offences set out in paragraph 308 of the report, and how the offenders were dealt with by the courts

Year	No. of persons found guilty M	No. of persons found guilty F	Absolute discharge M	Absolute discharge F	Conditional discharge M	Conditional discharge F	Fine M	Fine F	Probation M	Probation F	Imprisonment Over 14 days and up to 1 month M	Over 14 days and up to 1 month F	Over 1 month and up to 2 months M	Over 1 month and up to 2 months F	Over 2 months and up to 3 months M	Over 2 months and up to 3 months F	Over 3 months and up to 6 months M	Over 3 months and up to 6 months F	Total M	Total F	Otherwise dealt with M	Otherwise dealt with F
1951	67	158	—	—	—	2	56	124	—	3	1	1	2	11	7	13	1	3	11	28	—	1
1952	75	183	3	1	2	6	48	132	—	4	2	—	1	9	15	21	4	10	22	40	—	—
1953	79	152	—	—	4	3	55	113	—	9	2	2	2	6	10	19	6	—	20	27	—	—
1954	78	200	—	—	1	5	51	134	—	16	2	4	5	8	15	25	4	6	26	43	—	2
1955	88	145	—	2	1	7	50	88	—	5	1	8	6	8	21	22	9	5	37	43	—	—

TABLE XV

PROCURATION

Table showing how the courts dealt with the persons convicted in 1954 and 1955(¹) of the offences set out in paragraph 337 of the report

Year	No. of persons found guilty M	No. of persons found guilty F	Fine M	Fine F	Probation M	Probation F	6 months or under M	6 months or under F	Over 6 months and up to 1 year M	Over 6 months and up to 1 year F	Over 1 year and up to 2 years M	Over 1 year and up to 2 years F	Over 2 years and up to 3 years M	Over 2 years and up to 3 years F	Over 3 years and up to 5 years M	Over 3 years and up to 5 years F	Total M	Total F
1954	6	5	—	—	—	—	1	—	3	2	1	3	—	—	1	—	6	5
1955	6	5	1	—	1	2	—	1	3	2	1	—	—	—	—	—	4	3

(¹) As explained in paragraph 345 of the report, no corresponding figures are available for earlier years.

146

(b) Scotland

TABLE XVI

STREET OFFENCES

Table showing the number of prosecutions and convictions under section 381 (22) of the Burgh Police (Scotland) Act, 1892, and similar provisions in local Acts, during the fifty years ended 31st December, 1955

Year	No. proceeded against	No. of charges proved	Year	No. proceeded against	No. of charges proved
1906	2,757	2,544	1931	452	420
1907	2,997	2,790	1932	325	309
1908	3,192	2,989	1933	349	319
1909	2,969	2,750	1934	281	265
1910	2,870	2,496	1935	286	267
1911	2,485	2,219	1936	336	322
1912	2,487	2,147	1937	312	293
1913	1,884	1,642	1938	238	229
1914	1,696	1,481	1939	141	132
1915	1,328	1,141	1940	41	36
1916	956	812	1941	43	41
1917	580	470	1942	138	129
1918	460	389	1943	268	255
1919	635	515	1944	328	302
1920	803	641	1945	254	240
1921	686	589	1946	141	135
1922	648	585	1947	105	95
1923	837	807	1948	103	94
1924	608	558	1949	91	86
1925	425	387	1950	82	76
1926	544	476	1951	72	71
1927	472	413	1952	95	91
1928	480	438	1953	136	126
1929	439	402	1954	168	160
1930	394	362	1955	202	201

TABLE XVII

BROTHEL KEEPING, &C.

Table showing the number of persons against whom charges in respect of the offences set out in paragraphs 308 and 310 of the report were proved during the five years ended 31st December, 1955, and how the offenders were dealt with by the courts

Year	No. against whom charges proved M	No. against whom charges proved F	Probation M	Probation F	Fine M	Fine F	Imprisonment Up to 1 month M	Imprisonment Up to 1 month F	Imprisonment Over 1 month and up to 3 months M	Imprisonment Over 1 month and up to 3 months F	Imprisonment Over 3 months M	Imprisonment Over 3 months F	Total M	Total F
1951 ...	4	4	1	—	3	4	—	—	—	—	—	—	—	—
1952 ...	3	7	—	—	3	4	—	—	—	2	—	1	—	3
1953 ...	7	3	—	—	6	3	—	—	1	—	—	—	1	—
1954 ...	4	11	—	—	4	3	—	3	—	5	—	—	—	8
1955 ...	—	4	—	—	—	3	—	—	—	—	—	1	—	1

APPENDIX III

Homosexual Offences in European Countries

NOTE.—This is not intended to be an exhaustive or authoritative statement of the law in the countries mentioned; its purpose is to provide a conspectus of the principal homosexual offences recognised by the several criminal codes and the penalties attached to them. The penalties mentioned in each case are maximum penalties; as in Great Britain, other methods of treatment (*e.g.*, fines, probation) are available to, and used by, the courts in suitable cases.

Austria

All forms of "indecency against nature" committed with persons of the same sex (whether male or female) are punishable. The law does not distinguish between buggery and other homosexual acts, and "indecency against nature" has been defined by the courts as "any act which is designed and appropriate for seeking and finding sexual satisfaction from the body of a person of the same sex."

The offence is punishable with penal servitude up to a maximum of 5 years. If, however, the offence is committed by the application of "dangerous threats or actual physical violence or ruseful stupefaction of the other partner so as to render him unable to offer resistance", it is punishable with penal servitude up to a maximum of 10 years; and if one of the partners suffers, as a result of violence, serious injury to health, the sentence may be up to 20 years. If death results from the offence, the maximum penalty is life imprisonment.

In practice, first offenders do not, unless there are aggravating circumstances, receive more than 3 to 6 months' imprisonment, and probation is frequently used.

Minor acts of indecency not amounting to "indecency against nature" as defined by the courts are punishable by detention (*strenge Arrest*) for periods between 8 days and 6 months.

Belgium

Homosexual behaviour, as such, is not punishable, and a homosexual act is punishable only if it constitutes a general offence such as an indecent assault or an affront to public decency.

Consent is no defence to a charge of indecent assault if the victim is under 16. If the offender is one of the victim's parents, consent is no defence if the victim is under 21 unless he is married, in which case consent is a defence if he is over 16.

The maximum penalty for indecent assault is 15 years' imprisonment if the victim is under 16; 10 years' imprisonment if the victim is 16 or over but under 21; and 5 years' imprisonment in other cases.

The maximum penalty for outraging public decency is 1 year's imprisonment and a fine of 500 francs; or 3 years' imprisonment and a fine of 1,000 francs if a child under 16 is present.

Denmark

Homosexual acts committed with children under 15 are punishable with imprisonment up to a maximum of 6 years. Similarly punishable are homosexual acts procured by the use of force, fear, fraud or drugs, and offences against inmates of certain institutions (*e.g.*, orphanages and mental hospitals) when they are committed by persons employed in or supervising such institutions.

Homosexual acts committed with persons under 18 are punishable with imprisonment up to a maximum of 4 years. If the persons involved are of approximately the same age and development, the court may acquit them both.

Homosexual acts with a person under 21 are punishable if they are committed by abuse of superior age or experience. In this case, the maximum penalty is imprisonment for 3 years.

Indecent behaviour against any person of the same sex is an offence when the offender by his behaviour violates the other person's decency or gives public offence. The maximum penalty is 4 years' imprisonment.

The law does not distinguish between buggery and other homosexual acts.

(The effect of the foregoing provisions is that homosexual behaviour between consenting partners is not punishable unless it involves abuse of the young or dependent or an affront to public decency.)

France

A person who commits a homosexual act with a partner under 21 is liable to imprisonment up to a maximum of 3 years and a fine of 500,000 francs.

Where the victim is under 15, the offender is liable to imprisonment up to a maximum of 10 years. Where violence has been used, or where the offender is a parent or is otherwise in a position of authority over the victim, the prison sentence can be accompanied by hard labour. Where the offender is a parent of the victim, these higher penalties may also be awarded where the victim is under 21, unless he has been emancipated by marriage.

Offences against public decency are punishable with imprisonment up to a maximum of 2 years and a fine of 12,000 francs.

The law does not distinguish between buggery and other homosexual acts.

(The effect of the foregoing provisions is that homosexual behaviour between consenting partners over 21 is not punishable unless it offends against public decency.)

Germany (Federal Republic)

All homosexual acts between males are punishable. Homosexual acts between females are not punishable as such, and become so only if they constitute some other offence, *e.g.*, indecent assault.

Where the offence is committed with a boy under 14, or, if the offender is over 21, with a partner under 21, the offence is punishable with imprisonment up to a maximum of 10 years. The same maximum penalty is applicable where the act is accompanied by violence or threats of violence, or where the offender exploits a position of social dependence. Male prostitution or soliciting for the purposes of such prostitution is similarly punishable. In other cases, the maximum penalty is imprisonment for 5 years.

The law does not distinguish between buggery and other homosexual acts.

Greece

Unnatural sexual intercourse between males which has been perpetrated by abuse of a relationship of dependence arising from services of any kind, or by a person of full age by seduction of a person of less than 17 years of age, or for financial gain, is punishable by imprisonment up to a maximum of 5 years.

"Unnatural sexual intercourse" extends to all forms of indecency, and is not confined to buggery.

Italy

There are no provisions in the law for the punishment of homosexual behaviour as such.

Acts of sexual intercourse (*congunzione carnale*) brought about by the use of violence are punishable with imprisonment up to 10 years. Similar acts involving the abuse of authority are punishable with imprisonment up to 5 years, if violence is not used. These provisions apply to homosexual as well as heterosexual intercourse. If the act does not amount to *congunzione carnale*, the maximum punishment is reduced by one-third.

Anyone who commits an act of indecency with or in the presence of a child below the age of 16 is punishable with imprisonment up to a maximum of 3 years. Prosecution may be commenced only on the complaint of the victim or his parents or guardians.

Public indecency is similarly punishable.

Netherlands

Any person who commits an act of indecency with a child under 16 is punishable with imprisonment up to a maximum of 6 years. Similarly punishable are any acts of a sexual nature in which the offender abuses the temporary defencelessness of his victim, whatever his age. A person who, by violence or threats of violence, induces another person to commit or submit to an act of indecency, is punishable with imprisonment up to a maximum of 8 years. These provisions apply irrespective of the sex of the offender or the victim, so that they apply to homosexual as well as to heterosexual offences.

The law also provides for the punishment of persons over 21 who indulge in homosexual acts with minors between the ages of 16 and 21. The maximum penalty in this case is imprisonment for 4 years.

The law does not distinguish between buggery and other homosexual acts.

There are also special provisions for the punishment of indecent acts by parents, guardians or other persons in authority.

Acts of indecency committed in public are punishable with imprisonment up to a maximum of 2 years.

(The effect of the foregoing provisions is that homosexual acts which take place between mutually consenting partners both of whom are over 21, or both of whom are between 16 and 21, are not punishable unless public decency is affronted or there are certain other aggravating circumstances.)

Norway

Indecent intercourse between males is punishable by imprisonment up to a maximum of 1 year. The law provides, however, that an offender shall be prosecuted only if this is considered necessary in the public interest.

There are also special laws applicable to the sexual abuse of children, and these apply irrespective of the sex of the offender or the victim, so that they apply to homosexual offences committed with children. These laws distinguish between "indecent intercourse," which comprises coition and similar activities, and "indecent acts," which covers indecent practices not amounting to "indecent intercourse."

The maximum penalty for "indecent intercourse" with a child under 14 is 15 years' imprisonment, and if the victim suffers serious bodily harm, life imprisonment may be imposed. If the child is over 14 but under 16, the maximum is 5 years' imprisonment. Sixteen is the ordinary age limit, but if the young person is under the authority or charge of the offender the limit is 18 and the maximum penalty, if the victim is over 16, is imprisonment up to 1 year.

The maximum penalty for an "indecent act" with a child under 16 is 3 years' imprisonment.

Public indecency is punishable with imprisonment up to 3 months.

Spain

Homosexual acts are not punishable unless they amount to an indecent assault or cause public scandal or offend against public order.

Indecent assaults carry a maximum penalty of 6 years' imprisonment.

For offences "causing public scandal," the maximum penalty is 6 months' imprisonment and a fine of 5,000 pesetas (£170 approximate).

For offences "against public order," the maximum penalty is 30 days' imprisonment and a fine of 1,000 pesetas (£33 approximate).

The laws relating to rogues and vagabonds provide for "measures of security" for criminals whom the courts have declared to be "dangerous and anti-social," and persons who habitually indulge in homosexual behaviour may become liable to internment under these provisions.

Sweden

A person who commits a homosexual act with a child under 15 is liable to penal servitude up to a maximum of 4 years.

The law also prohibits:—

Homosexual acts committed with young persons under 18, if the offender had himself reached that age at the time of the offence;

Homosexual acts committed with persons under 21, if the offender is 18 or over and commits the act by abusing the other person's inexperience or dependence on him;

Homosexual acts committed with an insane or mentally defective person;

Homosexual acts committed with inmates of prisons, hospitals, almshouses, orphanages or similar institutions, if the offender is on the staff of the institution;

Homosexual acts committed with any person if the offender has committed the act by grave abuse of the other person's dependence on him.

The maximum penalty in each of these cases is 2 years' penal servitude. Imprisonment up to 6 years may, however, be imposed where the offender is a parent or guardian or other person in authority.

Public indecency is punishable by imprisonment up to a maximum of 2 years.

(The effect of the foregoing provisions is that homosexual acts between consenting parties over 18 are not punishable unless they affront public decency or there are other aggravating circumstances.)

APPENDIX IV

LIST OF WITNESSES

The following gave written and oral evidence:—

(i) Professional and public bodies

Association of Chief Officers of Police (England and Wales)
  Mr. C. Martin, C.B.E., Chief Constable of Liverpool.
  Mr. C. H. Watkins, Chief Constable of Glamorgan.

Association of Headmasters, Headmistresses and Matrons of Approved Schools
  Mr. Headley Chamberlain.   Mr. J. H. Clarke.
  Mr. J. H. Bennell.   Miss M. M. Brown.
             Mrs. M. M. Jackson

Association of Managers of Schools Approved by the Secretary of State
  Miss D. G. Anderson.   Mr. F. R. Groom.

Association for Social and Moral Hygiene
  Mrs. Corbett Ashby, LL.D.   Mrs. Elizabeth Abbott.
  Miss D. O. G. Peto, O.B.E.   Miss E. M. Steel, M.A.
       Miss M. Chave Collisson, M.A. (*General Secretary*).
Also in attendance:—
  Miss Florence A. Barry (St. Joan's Social and Political Alliance).
  Brigadier H. Langdon (Salvation Army).

Association of Municipal Corporations
  Mr. C. Barrett.   Councillor B. S. Langton.
  Miss D. L. Ridd.   Mr. E. L. Russell.
          Sir Harold Banwell (*Secretary*).
          Mr. K. P. Poole (*Assistant Secretary*).

Association of Sheriffs-Substitute (Scotland)
  Mr. F. Middleton.   Mr. A. M. Prain.

Boy Scouts Association
  Mr. D. Francis Morgan (Legal Adviser).

British Medical Association
  Dr. Dennis Carroll.   Dr. Ronald Gibson.
  Dr. T. C. N. Gibbens.   Dr. Ambrose King.
  Dr. Doris Odlum.   Dr. Leonard Simpson.
          Dr. E. E. Claxton (*Assistant Secretary*).

British Psychological Society
  Miss M. A. Davidson.   Dr. E. B. Strauss.
          Professor P. E. Vernon.

Central After-Care Association
  Mr. Frank C. Foster (Borstals and Young Prisoners Division).
  Miss H. L. Long (Women's and Girls' Division).
  Revd. Martin W. Pinker (Men's Division).

Church Commissioners
  Sir James R. Brown (Third Church Estates Commissioner).

Church of England Moral Welfare Council
  Revd. D. Sherwin Bailey, PH.D.
  Ven. E. N. Millard, M.A.
  Dr. F. G. Macdonald.

Davidson Clinic, Edinburgh
  Dr. W. P. Kreamer.   Dr. Winifred Rushforth.

General Council of the Bar
    Mr. N. R. Fox-Andrews, Q.C.   Mr. P. A. O. McGrath, M.C., T.D.
    Mr. R. Ormrod.   Mr. R. E. Seaton.

Glasgow Burgh Magistrates
    Mr. J. F. Langmuir, B.L. (Stipendiary Magistrate).
    Bailie T. B. Duncan.   Bailie J. J. Thomson.

Howard League for Penal Reform
    Mr. F. E. Baker.   Dr. T. C. N. Gibbens.
    Miss Mary Hamilton.   Mr. Hugh J. Klare (*Secretary*).

Institute of Psychiatry
    Dr. T. C. N. Gibbens.   Mr. Peter Scott.

Institute of Psycho-Analysis
    Dr. William H. Gillespie (*Chairman*).
    Dr. Wilfred Bion, D.S.O.   Dr. Elliott Jacques.

Institute for the Study and Treatment of Delinquency
    Mr. O. Cargill.   Dr. Dennis Carroll.
    Dr. Edward Glover.   Miss Eve Saville (*Deputy General Secretary*).

Law Society
    Mr. L. E. Barker.   Mr. W. O. Carter.
    Mr. A. F. Stapleton Cotton.   Mr. H. Horsfall-Turner.
    Mr. G. A. MacDonald.   Mr. G. R. Proudlove.

Magistrates' Association
    Sir Leonard Costello.   Mrs. M. S. Crewdson, J.P.
    Mr. J. P. Eddy, Q.C.   Mr. Claud Mullins.
    Miss Bartha de Blank, B. Com. (*General Secretary*).

Mayfair Association
    Mrs. M. Anderson.   The Earl Howe.
    Mr. W. R. Sloman.

Metropolitan Police
    Sir John Nott-Bower, K.C.V.O. (Commissioner).
    Mr. T. MacDonald Baker (Solicitor).
    Mr. A. Robertson, D.C.M. (Commander, A. Department).
    Mr. R. E. T. Birch (Prosecuting Solicitor, Solicitor's Department).

National Association of Mental Health and National Council of Social Service (Joint Group)
    Professor Norman Haycocks, M.A. (*Chairman*)
    Miss M. Appleby, O.B.E.   Mr. G. E. Haynes, C.B.E.
    Miss M. Lane.   Mr. E. J. Beattie (*Secretary*).

National Association of Probation Officers
    Mr. C. B. Trusler.   Miss Vera Williams.
    Mr. Frank Dawtry (*General Secretary*).

National Council of Women
    Mrs. M. F. Bligh.   Mrs. M. Lefroy, J.P.
    The Dowager Lady Nunburnholme.

Paddington Borough Council
    Councillor P. Dyas.   Alderman W. D. Goss, O.B.E.
    Mr. C. E. Jobson (*Deputy Town Clerk*).

Paddington Moral Reform Council
    Mr. Robert Allan, D.S.O., O.B.E., M.P.   Councillor Mrs. Eyre.
    Mr. M. P. Simpson.

Progressive League
    Mr. Alec Craig.   Mr. Robert Pollard, J.P.
                   Dr. Ernest Seeley.

Public Morality Council
    Revd. T. Holland, D.D.   Revd. D. Hubert Thomas, B.A., H.C.F.
            Mr. George Tomlinson (*General Secretary*).

Roman Catholic Advisory Committee on Prostitution and Homosexual Offences
            Very Revd. Monsignor G. A. Tomlinson, M.A.
    Revd. J. McDonald, L.C.L.   Mr. Richard Elwes, Q.C.

Royal Medico-Psychological Association
    Dr. Noel G. Harris.   Dr. J. D. W. Pearce.
    Dr. J. A. Hobson.   Dr. R. G. McInnes.

Society of Labour Lawyers
    Mr. Gerald Gardiner, Q.C.   Mr. C. R. Hewitt.
    Mr. Ben Hooberman.   Mr. P. R. Kimber.
                   Miss Jean Graham Hall.

Tavistock Clinic
    Dr. H. V. Dicks.   Dr. John Kelnar.

Westminster City Council
    Alderman Sir Arthur Howard, M.B.E., C.V.O., D.L., J.P.
    Alderman Charles P. Russell, C.V.O., J.P.
    Mr. W. Walsh (Messrs. Allen & Son, Solicitors to the Council).
    Mr. T. D. O'Brien, LL.B. (*Deputy Town Clerk*).

(ii) Government Departments

Admiralty
    Mr. G. C. B. Dodds, Head of Naval Law Branch.
    Capt. R. M. Freer, R.N., Deputy Director, Welfare and Service Conditions.

Air Ministry
    Air Commodore H. J. G. F. Proud, C.B.E., Director of Personal Services (Provost Marshal).
    Air Commodore J. B. Walmsley, C.B.E., D.F.C., Q.C., Director of Legal Services.
    Mr. E. W. Handley, C.B.E., Assistant Secretary.

Home Office
    Mr. Philip Allen, C.B., Assistant Under-Secretary of State.
    Mr. Francis Graham-Harrison, Assistant Secretary.

Prison Commission
    Sir Lionel W. Fox, C.B., M.C. (*Chairman*).
    Mr. R. L. Bradley, M.C., Director of Borstal Administration.
    Mr. R. Duncan Fairn, Director of Prison Administration.
    Dr. H. K. Snell, Director of Medical Services.
    Mr. A. Straker, Chief Psychologist.

Scottish Home Department
    Mr. J. Anderson, C.B., Assistant Under-Secretary of State.
    Mr. A. B. Hume, Assistant Secretary.
    Mr. K. M. Hancock, Director, Prison and Borstal Services.
    Dr. T. D. Inch, Medical Adviser, Prison and Borstal Services.

War Office
    Directorate of Personal Services—
        Brigadier R. B. F. K. Goldsmith, C.B., C.B.E.
        Lieut.-Col. R. A. Barron.
    Mr. C. M. Cahn, Assistant Judge Advocate-General.
    Brigadier R. Steel, Chief of Staff, London District.

(iii) Individual Witnesses

Dr. Clifford Allen.
Mr. Paul Bennett, v.c., Metropolitan Magistrate.
Dr. F. H. Brisby, Senior Medical Officer, Liverpool Prison.
Hon. Mr. Justice Cassels.
Dr. Eustace Chesser.
Hon. Mr. Justice Devlin.
Sir Laurence Dunne, m.c., Chief Metropolitan Magistrate.
Rt. Hon. Lord Goddard, Lord Chief Justice of England.
Rt. Hon. Viscount Hailsham, q.c.
Dr. R. Sessions Hodge.
Dr. J. J. Landers, o.b.e., Senior Medical Officer, Wormwood Scrubs Prison.
Miss Christina Mackenzie, j.p.
Dr. J. C. McI. Matheson, d.s.o., Senior Medical Officer, Brixton Prison.
Sir Theobald Mathew, k.b.e., m.c., Director of Public Prosecutions.
Mr. Frank J. Powell, Metropolitan Magistrate.
Mr. James Robertson, b.l., Procurator-Fiscal of Police, Glasgow.
Dr. W. F. Roper, Senior Medical Officer, Wakefield Prison.
Mr. Peter Wildeblood.
Mr. H. G. Wilkins.
Mrs. Rosalind Wilkinson.

The following gave oral evidence only:—

P.C. Anderson, Metropolitan Police.
Chief (Woman) Supt. Bather, Metropolitan Police.
P.C. Butcher, Metropolitan Police.
P.C. Darlington, Metropolitan Police.
Miss B. M. Denis de Vitre, Asst. Inspector of Constabulary, Home Office.
Mr. Lionel I. Gordon, o.b.e., Crown Agent, Scotland.
Mr. W. Hunter, Assistant Chief Constable, Edinburgh.
Mr. James A. Robertson, Assistant Chief Constable, Glasgow.
P.C. Scarborough, Metropolitan Police.
Woman P.S. Spalton, Metropolitan Police.
Woman P.C. White, Metropolitan Police.

The following submitted written memoranda:—

(i) Professional and Public Bodies and Government Departments

British Social Biology Council.
Counties of Cities Association (Scotland).
County Councils Association.
Ethical Union.
Faculty of Advocates.
Foundation International Committee for Sexual Equality.
Institute of Biology.
Metropolitan Boroughs Standing Joint Committee.
Ministry of Education.
Paddington Green Children's Hospital.
Royal College of Physicians.

(ii) Individual Witnesses

Dr. Reynold H. Boyd.
Miss Sybil Campbell and Mr. H. H. Maddocks, Metropolitan Magistrates (Joint Memorandum).
Professor C. D. Darlington, Sir Ronald Fisher and Dr. Julian Huxley (Joint Memorandum).
Mr. T. J. Faithfull, m.r.c.v.s.
Mrs. G. H. Forster.
Mr. H. A. Hammelmann.
Mrs. Katherine B. Hardwick.
Mr. John Scott Henderson, q.c., Recorder of Portsmouth.
Dr. F. J. G. Jefferiss, V.D. Department, St. Mary's Hospital.
Mr. David Linton.
Revd. Raphael Marshall-Keene, m.c.
Mr. Donald Mulcock.
Mr. Geoffrey Rose, Metropolitan Magistrate.
Mr. Harold Sturge, Metropolitan Magistrate.
Mr. Joseph Yahuda.